STRUCTURED COBOL:

AMERICAN NATIONAL STANDARD

WEST SERIES IN DATA PROCESSING
AND INFORMATION SYSTEMS

V. Thomas Dock, Consulting Editor

STRUCTURED COBOL;
AMERICAN NATIONAL STANDARD

V. Thomas Dock

School of Business Administration
University of Southern California

West Publishing Company
St. Paul   New York   Los Angeles   San Francisco

COPYRIGHT © 1979 By WEST PUBLISHING CO.
50 West Kellogg Boulevard
P.O. Box 3526
St. Paul, Minnesota 55165

Printed in the United States of America

Library of Congress Cataloging in Publication Data

Dock, V. Thomas.
  Structured COBOL, American National Standard.

  1. COBOL (computer program language)
2. Structured programming. I. Title. QA76.73.C25D623
001.6'424 78-13585 ISBN 0-8299-0181-7

To Mary and Steven, Jordanna, and Heather
my wife and children

*

PREFACE

Most digital computers in wide use today are capable of using several languages through which objectives can be successfully accomplished. COBOL is one of these languages. While there are several versions of COBOL, this textbook is concerned with full American National Standard (ANS) COBOL. This version is approved by the American National Standards Institute (ANSI). The current version of COBOL was adopted as the standard by the Institute in 1974.

The objective of this textbook is to provide the reader with a systematic explanation of the full American National Standard COBOL language. Those essential COBOL features that enable the reader to begin writing a program almost immediately are discussed in the first several chapters. The remaining chapters discuss those features that provide the reader with an indepth understanding of the potentiality of the COBOL language and versatility in writing a program.

The first eight chapters stress the use of punched cards as an input medium and the printer as an output medium. The last chapter stresses the use of magnetic disk and magnetic tape as either an input medium and/or output medium.

The author assumes that the reader has no prior knowledge of this language. Thus, the textbook begins—after several statements concerning the computer—with a fundamental discussion of COBOL. The potential applications of the language are presented through discussions of the various statements composing the language and examples of various uses of these statements to obtain one or more objectives. At the end of each chapter there are several questions and exercises which highlight the material discussed in that chapter and to varying degrees, reinforce the material discussed in previous chapters. The answers to these questions and exercises are provided at the end of the textbook so that the reader can immediately determine his correctness in answering them.

The theories of "top-down program design and structured programming" are used as the basis for presenting the material. The use of these two programming methods provides the means to reduce the costs of program development and maintenance.

The American National Standard COBOL language is available in three levels—low, middle, and high—of capability so that the language can be executed by computers with varying storage capacities. The low level version can be executed by a computer with 16,000 storage locations, the middle level version can be executed by a computer with 32,000 storage locations, and the high level version can be executed by a computer with

64,000 storage locations. The low level version, being a subset of the middle version, which in turn is a subset of the high level version, permits a computer to execute any level language lower than the maximum level it is capable of executing. The COBOL reserved words used by an ANS compiler vary depending on the level of the compiler and the extensions made to the standards by the computer manufacturer.

The author desires to express his indebtedness to Steve Teglovic of the University of Northern Colorado and Emerson Maxson of Boise State University for their suggestions concerning the manuscript.

V. Thomas Dock

ACKNOWLEDGMENT

The following extract is reproduced from COBOL Edition 1965, which was published by the Conference on Data Systems Languages (CODASYL) and printed by the U. S. Government Printing Office under Form Number 1965-0795689, and is presented for the information and guidance of the user:

"Any organization interested in reproducing the COBOL report and specifications in whole or in part, using ideas taken from this report as the basis for an instruction manual or for any other purpose is free to do so. However, all such organizations are requested to reproduce this section as a part of the introduction to the document. Those using a short passage, as in a book review, are requested to mention "COBOL" in acknowledgment of the source, but need not quote this entire section.

"COBOL is an industry language and is not the property of any company or group of companies, or of any organization or goup of organizations.

"No warranty, expressed or implied, is made by any contributor or by the COBOL Committee as to the accuracy and functioning of the programming system and language. Moreover, no responsibility is assumed by any contributor, or by the committee, in connection therewith.

"Procedures have been established for the maintenance of COBOL. Inquiries concerning the procedures for proposing changes should be directed to the Executive Committee of the Conference on Data Systems Languages.

"The authors and copyright holders of the copyrighted material used herein

   FLOW-MATIC (Trademark of Sperry Rand Corporation), Programming for the Univac I and II, Data Automation Systems copyrighted 1958, 1959, by Sperry Rand Corporation; IBM Commercial Translator Form No. F28-8013, copyrighted 1959 by IBM; FACT, DSI 27A5260-2760; copyrighted 1960 by Minneapolis-Honeywell

have specifically authorized the use of this material in whole or in part, in the COBOL specifications. Such authorization extends to the reproduction and use of COBOL specifications in programming manuals of similar publications."

CONTENTS

†

INTRODUCTION TO
THE COMPUTER AND COBOL

A discussion of COBOL assumes that the reader has a basic understanding of the computer and specifically, the type of computer that he will execute his COBOL program. Thus, the following is a brief discussion of the general implications of the term "computer" and the two main types of computers.

DEFINITION OF A COMPUTER

The term "computer," while validly applicable to any machine capable of arithmetical calculation, generally implies a machine possessing the following four characteristics:

1. *Electronic.* Achieves its results through the movement of electronic impulses rather than the physical movement of internal parts.

2. *Internal Storage.* Has the ability to simultaneously store program statements and data. This ability enables the computer to consecutively execute program statements at a high rate of speed.

3. *Stored program.* Executes a series of *statements* in its internal storage which instruct it in detail as to both the specific operations to perform and the order in which to perform them.

4. *Program-execution modification.* Can change the course of the execution of program statements (*branch*) because of a decision based on data in its internal storage and/or the results of one or more arithmetic or logical operations.

In summary, a computer is an electronic machine possessing internal storage capabilities, a stored program of instructions, and the capability for modification of the course of the execution of the set of instructions during the execution of the program.

THE TWO TYPES OF COMPUTERS

There are two main types of computers—digital and analog.

Digital Computers

A *digital computer* operates directly on numerical representation of either discrete data or symbols. It takes input and gives output in the form of numbers, letters, and special characters represented by holes in punched cards, magnitized fields on tapes, printing on paper, and so on. This is the type of computer most commonly thought of and referred to when the word *computer* is used either by itself or in context.

Digital computers are generally used for business and scientific data processing. Depending upon the particular characters of the digital computer and the precision of the data it is processing, the digital computer is capable of achieving varying degrees of accuracy in both intermediate and final values of data. Digital computers are the most widely used type of computers in business.

Analog Computers

The *analog computer,* in contrast to the digital computer, measures continuous electrical or physical magnitudes; it does not operate on digits. If digits are involved at all, they are obtained indirectly. Such physical quantities as pressure, temperature, shaft rotations, and voltage are directly measured as a continuous function. The output of an analog computer is often an adjustment to the control of a machine. For instance, an analog computer may adjust a valve to control the flow of fluid through a pipe, or it may adjust a temperature setting to control the temperature in an oven. For these reasons, analog computers are often used for controlling processes such as oil refining or baking. Digital computers can also be used for controlling processes. To do so, analog data must be converted to digital form, processed, and then the digital results must be converted to analog form. A digital computer possesses greater accuracy than an analog computer, but the analog computer can process data faster than a digital computer.

INTRODUCTION TO COBOL

The acronym COBOL is derived from the term COmmon Business Oriented Language. As implied by the term, COBOL is "common" to most computers manufactured in the United States and "business oriented," which means it is designed to solve business data processing problems. COBOL is also "file oriented," because it involves input and output organized in one or more files.

Most business data processing problems involve a large volume of input into the computer, few mathematical and/or logical operations, and a large volume of output from the computer. COBOL, being "business oriented" is specifically designed to effectively and efficiently process a problem of this nature.

As will quickly become evident, COBOL is also designed to facilitate documentation of a problem. This is due to the fact that COBOL is designed to make use of regular business data processing vocabulary to the greatest extent possible. Thus, many words in a COBOL program are either English words or combinations of letters that sound like the English translation. An additional aspect of documentation of this nature is that a program can be read and its objective understood with little difficulty by a person not familiar with the language.

THE CONVERSION OF A SOURCE
PROGRAM INTO AN OBJECT PROGRAM

The COBOL program written by a programmer consists of a set of program statements. This program is called a *source* program. However, the computer is only capable of executing only statements constructed in its language—machine language. Thus, as illustrated in Fig. 1-1, the COBOL statements composing the source program must be converted (compiled) into machine language prior to their execution by the computer.

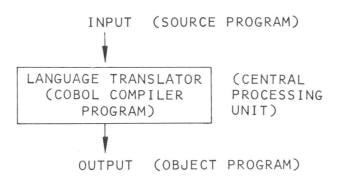

Figure 1-1: The Compilation of a COBOL Program

The translation process is called *compilation* and is accomplished through what is called a language translator program or, more specifically, a compiler program. This program also produces appropriate diagnostic error messages (see Appendix C) when it detects errors in the source program during compilation. The compiler program is located in the computer's central processing unit (CPU) during the process of compilation. The operating system of the computer controls the compiler program's operations.

The compiled program is called an *object* program; this is the same set of program statements composing the source program, except that they are in machine language form rather than in COBOL language form. As with the compiler program, the object program also operates under control of the operating system of the computer.

The object program can be immediately brought back into the CPU from either the system residence disk or tape if the statements composing it are to be executed, or stored for a period of time on an output device such as a disk, tape, or punch cards.

DATA CARDS

Data cards are distinct from program statement cards. Although it is possible for a COBOL program to generate and process its own data, in most instances this will not successfully accomplish the objective of the program. Thus, there are usually some source data that are acceptable to the computer. Today, the most common original source of data is the data card.

Data cards are *placed behind* the program statement cards when preparing a COBOL program for execution by the computer. The number and order of data cards are unique to each execution of both the same program and different programs. Data cards are not subject to the procedures and rules of program statement cards. Data may be punched in card columns 1 thorugh 80. Which specific punch card columns contain data is also unique to each execution of both the same program and different programs.

JOB CONTROL LANGUAGE CARDS

A third type of punched card (the first two types being program statement cards and data cards) that the reader will generally use to prepare his program for execution are Job Control Language cards (JCL cards).

The general purpose of these punched cards is to enable the computer to determine where the reader's program statements and data (if any) start, what factors are to be considered in the compilation and/or execution of the statements and data, and where the statements and data stop.

The number and content of these punched cards are unique to both each particular computer operating system and computer installation. For this and other reasons, these punched cards are not discussed any further in this textbook. Rather, the author suggests that the reader contact either his instructor or computer installation for additional information concerning the application of these punched cards.

THE CARD PUNCH

The use of punch cards, whether they be program, data, and/or JCL requires a basic knowledge of how to use the card punch. Whether or not the reader has this basic knowledge, he may desire to review Appendix B. This appendix contains a brief discussion of the IBM 29 Card Punch for either those readers who have already used it but wish to refresh themselves or those readers who have not had an opportunity to use it.

QUESTIONS

1. What are the characteristics of a computer?

2. Define a stored program.

3. Distinguish the basic differences between an analog computer and a digital computer.

4. What does the acronym COBOL represent?

5. What are the principle characteristics of "business oriented" data processing?

6. Discuss the basic benefits that can be gained by employing the COBOL language over other languages.

7. Define a source program.

8. Define an object program.

9. What distinguishes data cards from statement cards in a COBOL program?

2

COBOL STRUCTURE
AND DATA ORGANIZATION

Business data processing generally involves a large volume of input into the computer, few mathematical and/or logical operations, and a large volume of output from the computer. COBOL is designed to facilitate the processing of a problem of this nature. Two major implications of the previous statements are that the structure of the COBOL language and data organization are quite important. This chapter examines the nature of these implications.

THE COBOL CHARACTER SET

The COBOL Character Set is composed of the following three categories: alphabetic characters (A-Z and the space), numeric characters (0-9), and alphanumeric characters (any combination of alphabetic, numeric, and/or the special characters (Table 2-1)).

Table 2-1. COBOL Special Characters

Name	Character
Space	
Plus sign	+
Minus sign or hyphen	—
Multiplication sign or asterisk	*

Name	Character
Division sign or	
slash	/
Equal sign	=
Currency sign	$
Comma	,
Semicolon	;
Period or	
decimal point	.
Left parenthesis	(
Quotation mark	'
Right parenthesis	)
"Greater than" symbol	>
"Less than" symbol	<

These are the only special characters that can be used in a COBOL program.

All alphabetic characters are written in capital letter form. When writing characters, care must be taken to be sure they will not be confused with a similarly written character. Eight characters are especially subject to this problem. Thus, in an attempt to avoid this problem, the following characters should be *written* as shown:

Alphabetic Character	*Numeric Character*
$\emptyset$†	0
I	1
Z	2
S	5

THE COBOL CODING FORM

Although it is not absolutely necessary to use a COBOL Coding Form (see Fig. 2-1) in the process of writing (coding) the statements that compose a COBOL program, for accuracy and convenience, the author suggests that the reader should use this form. The basis for this statement will become clearer to the reader as the procedures and rules of COBOL are understood and when the reader writes his first program.

---

†Some computer centers and programmers reverse this convention and slash the numeric character rather than the alphabetic character $\emptyset$. The author suggests that the reader follow the above shown convention unless he is instructed otherwise by either his instructor or computer center.

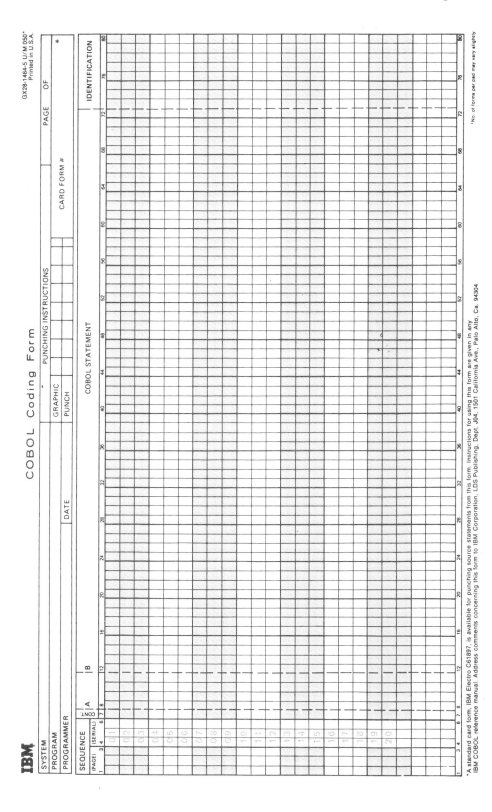

Figure 2-1: The COBOL Coding Form

The COBOL Coding Form may best be thought of as a convenient tool that may be used in the process of writing a program. Each 80-column line of the COBOL Coding Form represents the 80 columns on a punched card. After completion of the writing of the program, the statements composing it are correspondingly punched by column number on punch cards. When these statements are compiled, they are printed verbatim in the same print line sequence as punched card sequence and compose the source program listing.

EXPLANATION OF THE COBOL CODING FORM

The following is an explanation of the 80 columns composing each line of the COBOL Coding Form:

Punch Card Columns 1 through 3.

As indicated on the coding form, card columns 1 through 3 may contain the page number of a program statement. This page number usually is the same page number assigned the COBOL coding sheet on which the statement is written (refer to the upper right-hand corner of the coding form). The first coding sheet is generally numbered 001, the second coding sheet 002, etc.)

Punch Card Columns 4 through 6.

As also indicated on the coding form, card columns 4 through 6 may contain the serial number of a program statement. As indicated on the coding form, the first two of the three possible serial characters are preprinted. Thus, only the third character has to be inserted by the programmer and this is generally a zero. This results in the program statements being numbered by tens—010, 020, 030, etc.—so that at a later date the sequential insertion of between one and nine additional statements can be easily made. For example, if a program statement were accidentally omitted between the assigned serial numbers 010 and 020, it could be assigned serial number 011.

The primary function of sequence (page and serial) numbers is to assist the programmer in sequencing the program statements and, if necessary, resequencing the program statements. (Unfortunately, occasionally a program deck is inadvertently dropped.) If sequence numbers are assigned, they must be in ascending order.

Punch·Card Column 7.

As also indicated on the coding form, card column 7 is used for the continuation of a program statement. The continuation of a program statement is indicated by the punching of a hyphen.

The computer considers a space to exist between punch card column 72 and column 12 of the next card. Thus, a character may be punched in column 72 of a card and another character in column 12 of the next card, and the computer will consider the two characters to be part of two different words of the same statement.

If the character in column 72 and the character in column 12 should not be separated by a space, a hyphen must be placed in column 7 of the next punch card. For example, the word EMPLØYEES could have been spelled in columns 67 through 72, ending with the character Y in column 72. A hyphen would then have to be placed in column 7 and the character E would be placed in column 12 of the next card.†

If a nonnumeric literal (this term is discussed toward the end of this chapter) is continued to another line, the above procedure would be followed with one additional step. A quotation mark would be placed in column 12, and thus the next character would be placed in column 13.

A *second* function of colum 7 is to provide the means for comments by the programmer concerning either the overall COBOL program and/or a specific part of the program. Comment sentences are identified by an asterisk in column 7. The comment can be stated in columns 8 through 80. If a comment is continued on to additional cards, the asterisk must be punched in column 7 of each card.

The comment sentence is a nonexecutable sentence. That is, it is neither processed by the COBOL compiler (translated into machine language) nor affects the execution of the COBOL program. Rather, it is printed verbatim along with the COBOL statements on the source program listing in the same print line sequence as punched card sequence.

A *final* function of column 7 is to provide the means to eject the page on which the source program is being printed and print a comment sentence—and then the remainder of the source program listing—beginning at the top of the next page. This is accomplished by punching a slash in the column.

Punch Card Columns 8 through 72.

As indicated on the coding form, card columns 8 through 72 contain the program statements. As also indicated on the coding form, card columns 8 through 11 of a program statement are called area A, and card columns 12

---

†To avoid the possibility of making an error in the continuation of a word, the author recommends that whenever feasible a word not be continued to the next line. Rather. leave the one or more columns prior to column 73 blank and start the word on the next line.

through 72 are called area B. As will be appropriately indicated, certain program statements begin in area A, and other statements begin in area B. Program statements that begin in area A should start in card column 8, and program statements that begin in area B should start in card column 12. (The author suggests that for ease of reading and understanding, begin in either card column 8 or 12 or some multiple of 4 starting at card column 12.)

Punch Card Columns 73 through 80.

Finally, as indicated on the coding form, card columns 73 through 80 are not used for program statements. The reason for this is that only the first 72 punch card columns are significant to the COBOL compiler. Thus, card columns 73 through 80 cannot be used for program statements. These card columns may either be left blank or used for program identification, sequencing, or any other purpose by punching the desired code in one or more of these card columns. If, for example, the output device is the printer, the punched code would appear on the same print line as that on which the program statement located on that punched card appears.

The solid line beneath the twentieth line exists to remind the programmer that he should, if necessary, continue writing the program on another coding sheet. By doing so, he can use one or more of the four remaining lines to insert any program statements initially omitted on that coding sheet.

PROGRAM FLOWCHARTING

A simple yet quite helpful aid in preparing to write a program is the preparation of a flowchart. The more complicated a program, the greater assistance a flowchart can provide in writing the program. For these reasons, the author suggests that the reader refer to Appendix D for a discussion of program flowcharting prior to reading any further in this textbook.

A COBOL PROGRAM: AN OVERVIEW

A COBOL program is composed of four distinct *divisions*. These divisions are the following:

1. IDENTIFICATIØN DIVISIØN (001,01)†
2. ENVIRØNMENT DIVISIØN (001,03)
3. DATA DIVISIØN (001,11)
4. PRØCEDURE DIVISIØN (002,14)

---

†The following discussion will reference, where appropriate via page (the first three numbers) and serial number (the last two numbers) in parenthesis, Fig. 2-2. The reader should not become alarmed at this time if he does not fully understand the several concepts, procedures, and rules involved in the execution of this program.

The four divisions are always found in a program in the above order. The following is a summarization of the purpose of each division:

The Identification Division

The IDENTIFICATIØN DIVISIØN identifies a program by requiring that at a minimum it be assigned a name (001,02). Additional optional information may be provided to further identify the program, such as the author of the program, the installation in which it was written, the date it was written, the date it was compiled, and security requirements.

The Environment Division

The ENVIRØNMENT DIVISIØN has two primary functions. First, it describes the type of computer that will compile (001,05) and execute (001,06) the program. Second, it relates each file used in the program with the input device on which each file to be read is located (001,09) and the output device on which each file to be written is located (001,10).

The Data Division

The DATA DIVISIØN describes in great detail all of the data to be processed by the program. It also shows the relationship that exists between data (001, 13-18; 001,19-002,08; and 002,10-12).

The Procedure Division

The PRØCEDURE DIVISIØN contains the statements that instruct the computer in detail as to both the specific operations that it is to perform and the order in which it is to perform these operations (002,14 thru 004,09).

As the brief description of the four divisions composing a COBOL program indicates, COBOL is a highly structured language. Thus, an understanding of the structure of each division is important.

The first hierarchical element within a division may be a *section*. A section cannot be present in the IDENTIFICATIØN DIVISIØN and is rarely present in the PRØCEDURE DIVISIØN. However, the CØN-FIGURATIØN (001,04) and INPUT-ØUTPUT (001,07) SECTIØNS are always present in the ENVIRØNMENT DIVISIØN, and the FILE SEC-TIØN (001,12) is always present and the WØRKING-STØRAGE SECTIØN (002,09) is usually present in the DATA DIVISIØN.

The sections within each division, except the DATA DIVISIØN, are in turn composed of one or more *paragraphs*. In the IDENTIFICATIØN and ENVIRØNMENT DIVISIØNS, the paragraph names PRØGRAM-ID (001,02), SØURCE-CØMPUTER (001,05), ØBJECT-CØMPUTER (001,06),

IBM COBOL Coding Form

GX28-1464-5 U/M 050*
Printed in U.S.A.

SYSTEM	IBM-370-148	PUNCHING INSTRUCTIONS	PAGE 001 OF 004
PROGRAM	EMPLØYEES WAGES	GRAPHIC	CARD FORM # *
PROGRAMMER	V. THØMAS DØCK	DATE	PUNCH

```
SEQUENCE  |A   |B                                        COBOL STATEMENT                                IDENTIFICATION
(PAGE)(SERIAL)
       01  IDENTIFICATIØN DIVISIØN.
       02  PRØGRAM-ID. WAGES.
       03  ENVIRØNMENT DIVISIØN.
       04  CØNFIGURATIØN SECTIØN.
       05  SØURCE-CØMPUTER. IBM-370-148.
       06  ØBJECT-CØMPUTER. IBM-370-148.
       07  INPUT-ØUTPUT SECTIØN.
       08  FILE-CØNTRØL.
       09      SELECT EMPLØYEE-RECØRDS-FILE, ASSIGN TØ UR-2540R-S-CARDIN.
       10      SELECT EMPLØYEE-PAYRØLL-FILE, ASSIGN TØ UR-1403-S-PRØUT.
       11  DATA DIVISIØN.
       12  FILE SECTIØN.
       13  FD  EMPLØYEE-RECØRDS-FILE
       14      LABEL RECØRD IS ØMITTED.
       15  01  CARD-RECØRD.
       16      02 EMPLØYEE-NAME                PICTURE A(15).
       17      02 HØURS-WØRKED                 PICTURE 99.
       18      02 HØURLY-RATE                  PICTURE 9V99.
       19  FD  EMPLØYEE-PAYRØLL-FILE
       20      LABEL RECØRD IS ØMITTED.
```

*A standard card form, IBM Electro C61897, is available for punching source statements from this form. Instructions for using this form are given in any IBM COBOL reference manual. Address comments concerning this form to IBM Corporation, LDS Publishing, Dept. J04, 1501 California Ave., Palo Alto, Ca. 94304

*No. of forms per pad may vary slightly

Figure 2-2: A COBOL Program

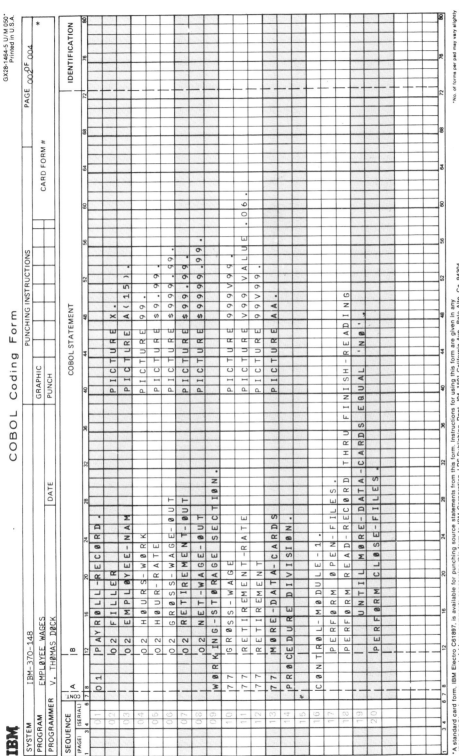

IBM

COBOL Coding Form

GX28-1464-5 U/M 050*
Printed in U.S.A.

SYSTEM	IBM-370-148			PUNCHING INSTRUCTIONS			PAGE 002 OF 004
PROGRAM	EMPLOYEE WAGES		GRAPHIC				
PROGRAMMER	V. THOMAS DOCK	DATE	PUNCH			CARD FORM #	*

COBOL STATEMENT

SEQUENCE		CONT		
01	01		PAYROLL-RECORD.	
02			02 FILLER	
03			02 EMPLOYEE-NAM	
04			02 HOURS-WORK	PICTURE 99.
05			02 HOUR-RATE	PICTURE 9.99.
06			02 GROSS-WAGE-OUT	PICTURE 999.99.
07			02 RETIREMENT-OUT	PICTURE $99.99.
08			02 NET-WAGE-OUT	PICTURE $999.99.
09		WORKING-STORAGE SECTION.		
10	77		GROSS-WAGE	PICTURE 999V99.
11	77		RETIREMENT-RATE	PICTURE V999 VALUE .06.
12	77		RETIREMENT	PICTURE 99V99.
13	77		MORE-DATA-CARDS	PICTURE AA.
14		PROCEDURE DIVISION.		
15	*			
16		CONTROL-MODULE-1.		
17			PERFORM OPEN-FILES.	
18			PERFORM READ-RECORD THRU FINISH-READING	
19			UNTIL MORE-DATA-CARDS EQUAL 'NO'.	
20			PERFORM CLOSE-FILES.	

PICTURE X.
PICTURE A(15).

IDENTIFICATION

*A standard card form, IBM Electro C61897, is available for punching source statements from this form. Instructions for using this form are given in any IBM COBOL reference manual. Address comments concerning this form to IBM Corporation, LDS Publishing, Dept. J04, 1501 California Ave., Palo Alto, Ca. 94304

*No. of forms per pad may vary slightly

IBM

COBOL Coding Form

GX28-1464-5 U/M 050*
Printed in U.S.A.

SYSTEM	IBM-370-148				PUNCHING INSTRUCTIONS			PAGE 003 OF 004
PROGRAM	EMPLOYEE WAGES			GRAPHIC				
PROGRAMMER	V. THOMAS DOCK		DATE	PUNCH			CARD FORM #	*

```
SEQUENCE   CONT
(PAGE)(SERIAL) A  B                          COBOL STATEMENT

01              STOP RUN.
02         *
03         OPEN-FILES.
04              OPEN INPUT EMPLOYEE-RECORDS-FILE
05                   OUTPUT EMPLOYEE-PAYROLL-FILE.
06         *
07         READ-RECORD.
08              MOVE SPACES TO PAYROLL-RECORD.
09              READ EMPLOYEE-RECORDS-FILE AT END
10                   MOVE 'NO' TO MORE-DATA-CARDS, GO TO FINISH-READING.
11         *
12         PROCESS-RECORD.
13              MOVE EMPLOYEE-NAME TO EMPLOYEE-NAM.
14              MOVE HOURS-WORKED TO HOURS-WORK.
15              MOVE HOURLY-RATE TO HOUR-RATE.
16              MULTIPLY HOURS-WORKED BY HOURLY-RATE GIVING GROSS-WAGE.
17              MULTIPLY RETIREMENT-RATE BY GROSS-WAGE GIVING RETIREMENT.
18              SUBTRACT RETIREMENT FROM GROSS-WAGE GIVING NET-WAGE-OUT.
19              MOVE GROSS-WAGE TO GROSS-WAGE-OUT.
20              MOVE RETIREMENT TO RETIREMENT-OUT.
```

IDENTIFICATION

*A standard card form, IBM Electro C61897, is available for punching source statements from this form. Instructions for using this form are given in any IBM COBOL reference manual. Address comments concerning this form to IBM Corporation, LDS Publishing, Dept. J04, 1501 California Ave., Palo Alto, Ca. 94304

*No. of forms per pad may vary slightly

IBM

COBOL Coding Form

GX28-1464-5 U/M 050*
Printed in U.S.A.

SYSTEM	IBM-370-148			PUNCHING INSTRUCTIONS		PAGE 004 OF 004
PROGRAM	EMPLOYEE WAGES		GRAPHIC			CARD FORM #
PROGRAMMER	V. THOMAS DUCK	DATE	PUNCH			*

COBOL STATEMENT

SEQUENCE (PAGE) (SERIAL)	CONT	A	B			IDENTIFICATION
01	*					
02		WRITE RECORD.				
03		WRITE PAYROLL-RECORD AFTER ADVANCING 2 LINES.				
04	*					
05		FINISH-READING.				
06		EXIT.				
07	*					
08		CLOSE-FILES.				
09		CLOSE-EMPLOYEE-RECORD-FILE, EMPLOYEE-PAYROLL-FILE.				
10						
11						
12						
13						
14						
15						
16						
17						
18						
19						
20						

*A standard card form. IBM Electro C61897, is available for punching source statements from this form. Instructions for using this form are given in any IBM COBOL reference manual. Address comments concerning this form to IBM Corporation, LDS Publishing, Dept. J04, 1501 California Ave., Palo Alto, Ca. 94304

*No. of forms per pad may vary slightly

and FILE-CØNTRØL (001,08) must be spelled as they are in the program. The one or more paragraph names in the PRØCEDURE DIVISIØN are formulated by the programmer according to the rules outlined in a later section of this chapter entitled "Programmer-supplied Names."

Each paragraph is, in turn, composed of one or more *sentences.* A sentence is one or more *statements.* A statement either provides information or instructs the computer to perform a specific operation, such as read or write.

Division and section names must begin in area A. They must be immediately followed by a period, and the remainder of the line must be left blank.

Paragraph names also begin in area A and must be immediately followed by a period and at least one space. However, the remainder of the line can contain one or more sentences.

One or more sentences can be written on a line beginning in area B. A sentence must adhere to the following punctuation rules:

1. There must be at least one space between two successive words and/or parenthetical expressions. If there is more than one space, the spaces are considered by the computer—except in nonnumeric literals—as being a single space. In a nonnumeric literal, each space is considered by the computer as a distinct space.

2. A period, semicolon, or comma following either a word or parenthetical expression should be located immediately after the last character of the word or expression. The period, semicolon, or comma *must* be followed by at least one space.

3. If a sentence contains more than one statement, each statement may be separated by a semicolon.

4. A sentence must be terminated by a period.

5. An arithmetic operator or an equal sign must be immediately preceeded and followed by at least one space.

6. A left parenthesis must not be followed immediately by a space; a right parenthesis must not be preceded immediately by a space.

7. If a series of operands are located within a statement, they must be separated by either a comma or the reserved word AND.

For ease of debugging and readability the author recommends that a paragraph name be on a line by itself. For similar reasons, it is recommended that a line contain only one sentence.

DATA ORGANIZATION

COBOL, being a business-oriented language, is designed to process the normally large amounts of data involved in business data processing. Just as the structure of the language is highly organized to accomplish this task, so also is the structure of the data highly organized. Thus, an understanding of the nature and organization of the data is also quite important.

All the data read and written by a program are logically organized into a hierarchical structure. Within this hierarchical structure, the broadest category of data is a *file*. A file is composed of one or more *records*. A record, in turn, is composed of one or more *group items* and/or *elementary items*.

Files. A file is an organized collection of a category of data. For example, Figure 2-2 contains two files, an EMPLØYEE-RECØRDS-FILE (001,09 and 13) and an EMPLØYEE-PAYRØLL-FILE (001,10 and 19).

In a business environment, such terms as payroll file, inventory file, accounts receivable file, etc. are used to reference all data of a specific nature.

In the COBOL data processing context, one or more files are read, processed, and written. While data may be read from, processed, and written into the same file, generally data are read from one or more files, processed, and written into one or more new files. For example, the EMPLØYEE-RECØRDS-FILE, which is a punched deck of cards containing data concerning each employee (001,15-18), will be read by the card reader and processed by this program. Also, the EMPLØYEE-PAYRØLL-FILE, which contains the results of processing the data concerning each employee (002,02-08), will be written by the printer.

Records. A file is composed of one or more types of records. Each record is an organized collection of data concerning a particular member of the file. For example, each CARD-RECØRD in the EMPLØYEE-RECØRDS-FILE contains data pertaining to each employee that are necessary to process his payroll check (001,16-18), and each PAYRØLL-RECØRD in the EMPLØYEE-PAYRØLL-FILE contains information pertaining to each employee's paycheck (002,03-08).

A file may contain records, each of which contain the same kind of data, such as a payroll file. A file may also contain records containing data that pertain to *two or more kinds* of data, such as an accounts receivable file that contains credit and debit records or an inventory file containing records on each of ten product lines.

Group Items and Elementary Items. A record is composed of one or more fields of data. A field is a specified area reserved for data of a specific nature. A field is classified as either a *group item* or an *elementary item*. A group item is a field of data that is logically subdivided into several elementary items, for example, a field containing an address that is subdivided into the name of the person or company, street address, city, state, and zip code, or a field containing a date that is subdivided into the month, day, and year.

An elementary item is a field of data that *is not* subdivided. In the previous example, the name of the person or company, street address, city, state, zip code, month, day, and year are all elementary items, as they are not subdivided.

Each CARD-RECØRD (001,15) contains the elementary item EMPLØYEE-NAME (001,16), HØURS-WØRKED (001,17), and HØURLY-RATE (001,18), because they are not subdivided. Each PAYRØLL-RECØRD (002,01) contains the elementary items EMPLØYEE-NAM (002,03), HØURS-WØRK (002,04), HØUR-RATE (002,05), GRØSS-WAGE-ØUT (002,06), RETIREMENT-ØUT (002,07), and NET-WAGE-ØUT (002,08), because they are not subdivided.

Independent Elementary Items

As previously stated, all data read and written by a program are part of a record and thus also part of a file. However, some elementary items processed by a program may not be part of a record and thus not located within a file. Elementary items of this nature are categorized as independent elementary items. For example, Fig. 2-2 contains the independent elementary items GRØSS-WAGE (002,10), RETIREMENT-RATE (002,11), and RETIREMENT (002,12), because they are not part of a record. In most instances, an independent elementary item is created by the programmer to store either an operand or intermediate result of an arithmetic calculation or a control total.

PROGRAMMER-SUPPLIED NAMES

Every file, record, group item, elementary item, and independent elementary item must be assigned a name by the programmer so that it can be appropriately used and referenced within the program. Each name must be assigned by the programmer so that it can be appropriately used and referenced within the program. Each name must be assigned according to the following rules:

1. It must not be a COBOL reserved word (refer to Appendix B), as each reserved word has a particular meaning to the COBOL compiler. A convenient way to avoid mistakingly using a reserved word is to use names containing a hyphen.

2. It can contain from 1 through 30 characters.

3. It can be composed of alphabetic and/or numeric characters and hyphens. The first

and last characters cannot be a hyphen; blanks within the name are not permitted.

4. If it is used either within the DATA DIVISIØN and/or within a paragraph located in the PRØCEDURE DIVISIØN, it must contain at least one alphabetic character. However, if it is a paragraph name within the PRØCEDURE DIVISIØN, it can be composed of only numeric characters.

5. It must be unique, or capable of becoming unique through qualification (the qualification of a name is discussed in Chapter 8).

6. For identification, a name should suggest the nature of the datum stored under it.

The following are the programmer-supplied names used in Fig. 2-2:

WAGES (001,02)	EMPLØYEE-NAM (002,03)
EMPLØYEE-RECØRDS-FILE (001,09 and 13)	HØURS-WØRK (002,04)
CARDIN (001,09)	HØUR-RATE (002,05)
EMPLØYEE-PAYRØLL-FILE (001,10 and 19)	GRØSS-WAGE-ØUT (002,06)
PRØUT (001,10)	RETIREMENT-ØUT (002,07)
CARD-RECØRD (001,15)	NET-WAGE-ØUT (002,08)
EMPLØYEE-NAME (001,16)	GRØSS-WAGE (002,10)
HØURS-WØRKED (001,17)	RETIREMENT-RATE (002,11)
PAYRØLL-RECØRD (002,01)	RETIREMENT (002,12)

TYPES OF DATA

Two types of data exist in COBOL. One type is called *variable* data, which is data stored under names whose values may change. The other type is called *constant* data, which is data that either may or may not be stored under names, but whose values will not change.

Variable Data

Most data are variable. This is due to the fact that each record within a file contains data concerning a particular member of the file. As such, the value of the data is likely to change each time a different record is read, processed, and written by the computer. For example, in Fig. 2-2 each time a record is read the elementary items EMPLØYEE-NAME (001,16), HØURS-WØRKED (001,17) and HØURLY-RATE (001,18) will have a different datum stored under them.

Constant Data

In certain instances, it is desirable to use data whose values will not change during execution of the program. There are two types of constant data—literals and figurative constants.

Literals. A datum is "literally" present in the program, rather than being read and stored under a name by the computer, is called a literal. There are two types of literals:

1. *Numeric Literals.* A numeric literal is a datum in either the DATA or PRØCEDURE DIVISIØNS that is used in one or more arithmetic calculations. In forming a numeric literal, the following rules must be observed:

a. It can be composed of from 1 to 18 numeric characters.

b. A decimal point can be located either to the left of the most significant numeric character or between two numeric characters. However, a decimal point cannot be located to the right of the least significant numeric character, except when to indicate the end of a sentence. If no decimal point is present, the computer assumes that the numeric literal is an integer (whole) number.

c. A plus or minus sign can be located to the immediate left of the leftmost character composing the numeric literal. If no sign is present, the computer assumes that the numeric literal is positive.

The following are examples of numeric literals:

$$1978$$
$$.33$$
$$+25.43$$
$$-150$$
$$-50.25$$
$$-.75$$

2. *Nonnumeric Literals.* A nonnumeric literal is a statement in either the DATA or PRØCEDURE DIVISIØNS. A nonnumeric literal may be used to provide a heading or title in an output record, communicate with a computer operator, and/or provide a name with a datum. In forming a nonnumeric literal, the following rules must be observed:

a. It can be composed of from 1 through 120 characters.
b. It is enclosed in quotation marks.
c. Any COBOL character can be used to form it.
d. To indicate possessiveness, two successive quotation marks are punched within the nonnumeric literal. However, only one quotation mark is printed.

The following are examples of nonnumeric literals:

```
'$1,000.00'
'5,325'
'150'
'50.25'
'JUNE 1,1978'
'THIS IS DOCK''S BOOK'
```

Figurative Constants. A figurative constant is a COBOL reserved work. It cannot be enclosed in quotation marks and the singular and plural form may be used interchangeably.

The following are four figurative constants and their meaning:

CONSTANT	REPRESENTS

1. ZERØ
   ZERØS
   ZERØES
	One or more zeros.

2. SPACE SPACES	One or more spaces (blanks).
3. QUØTE QUØTES	One or more occurrences of the quotation mark.
4. ALL literal	One or more occurrences of the string of characters composing the literal. The literal must be either a nonnumeric literal or a figurative constant other than the ALL literal. (When a figurative constant is used, the word ALL is redundant and is used for readibility only.)

A figurative constant can be used in place of a literal, unless the literal must be numeric, in which case only the figurative constant ZERØ, (ZERØES, ZERØS) can be used. The figurative constant QUØTE (QUØTES) cannot be used in place of a quotation mark to enclose a nonnumeric literal. Rather, the figurative constant should be used when it is desirable to store one or more quotation marks in a field.

The purpose and appropriate use of figurative constants will become clearer when the DATA and PRØCEDURE DIVISIØNS are discussed. Thus, they will not be more fully discussed until that time.

A PREVIEW OF THE REMAINING CHAPTERS

The first two chapters have provided the basis for the contents of Chapters 3, 4, 5, and 6. Specifically, this chapter presents the structure of the COBOL language and data organization. Chapters 3, 4, 5, and 6 use the concepts presented in this chapter in discussing the COBOL language.

A COBOL program is always composed of four divisions. Each of the following four chapters discusses the composition of one of these divisions. The divisions are presented in the order in which they are located in a COBOL program. The contents of each of the divisions in the COBOL program in Fig. 2-2 is discussed, and where appropriate expanded upon. Figure A-6 is the complete, expanded COBOL program.

Chapters 7, 8, and 9 present most of the advanced COBOL statements. Although one can write many COBOL programs using only the statement presented in the first six chapters, there are occasions when one or more of the statements presented in the last three chapters allow a program to be executed more efficiently and more sophisticated programs to be processed.

QUESTIONS

1. Of what use is the COBOL coding form to a programmer?

2. What information should be placed on the COBOL coding form in the following columns?

   a. Columns 1-3

   b. Columns 4-6

   c. Column 7

   d. Columns 8-72

   e. Columns 73-80

3. Discuss the function of the IDENTIFICATIØN DIVISIØN. The ENVIRØNMENT DIVISIØN. The DATA DIVISIØN. The PRØCEDURE DIVISIØN.

4. What is meant by the COBOL program hierarchy? What levels are included in the hierarchy?

5. What is meant by the COBOL hierarchical data structure? What levels are included in the hierarchy?

6. What are the two data types that can appear in a COBOL program? What is the difference between them?

EXERCISES

1. Which of the following COBOL programmer-supplied names are valid? Invalid? If invalid, why?

   a. CØST-ØF-PRØDUCT

   b. NET ASSETS

   c. $PRICE

   d. ZERØ

   e. HISTØRY-1865-TØ-PRESENT

   f. PRØDUCT.NAME

   g. GROSS-PROFIT

   h. PRICE-RANGE

2. Which of the following are numeric literals? Nonnumeric literals? Figurative constants? If none of the above, label as invalid.

   a. ZERØ   f. 300,000

   b. $1.95   g. SPACES

   c. 'QUØTES'   h. 3.1417

   d. +700

   e. 'ØVERFLØW ERRØR'

*

3

THE IDENTIFICATION DIVISION

The IDENTIFICATIØN DIVISIØN†(001,01) identifies a program by requiring that at a minimum it be assigned a name. This division is divided into the following paragraphs:

PRØGRAM-ID (001,02)
AUTHØR (001,03)
INSTALLATIØN (001,04)
DATE-WRITTEN (001,05)
DATE-CØMPILED (001,06)
SECURITY (001,07)

The only paragraph that is required is PRØGRAM-ID. The name of the program, which follows this paragraph name, is supplied by the programmer. The program name must be formed according to the following rules:

1. It can contain 1 through 30 characters (the first eight characters are used by the computer as the means of identifying the program and thus should be unique).
2. The characters can be either alphabetic, numeric, and/or hyphens.
3. The first character cannot be a hyphen and the name cannot contain spaces.

---

†The IDENTIFICATIØN DIVISIØN of the COBOL program "EMPLØYEE WAGES" (Fig. 2-2) will be expanded upon to present additional elements of this division.

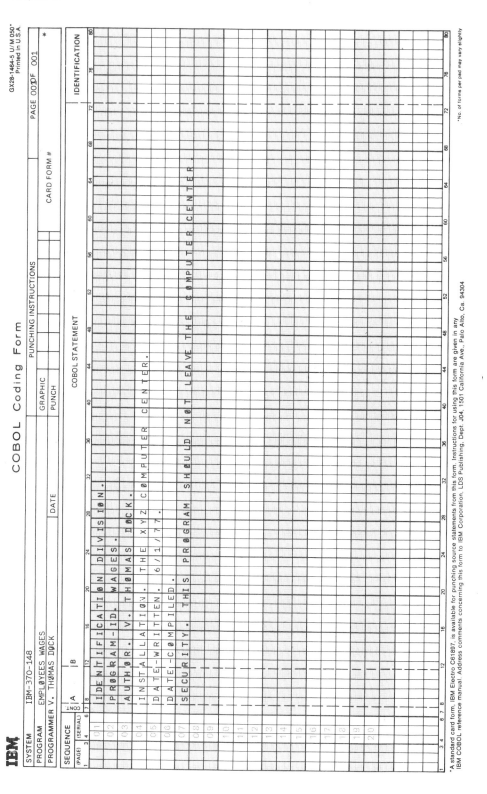

Figure 3-1: The IDENTIFICATIØN DIVISIØN

The remaining paragraphs provide additional information to further identify the program. Such information as the author of the program (AUTHØR), the installation in which it was written (INSTALLATIØN), the date it was written (DATE-WRITTEN), the date it was compiled (DATE-CØMPILED), and security requirements (SECURITY) are optional. However, if one or more of the paragraphs are used, they must be presented in the above order.

Note that the DATE-CØMPILED paragraph is blank. Whether or not the paragraph is left blank, the compiler will insert the actual date the program is compiled. This date will be printed on the source program listing. Generally, the paragraph is left blank.

Each optional paragraph name can be followed by one or more sentences. A sentence that cannot be completed on one line of the coding form can be continued to as many additional lines as are necessary to complete it.

QUESTIONS

1. What paragraph of the IDENTIFICATIØN DIVISIØN is mandatory for all COBOL programs?

2. What are the rules governing the PRØGRAM-ID name?

EXERCISE

Find the errors in the following IDENTIFICATIØN DIVISIØN and make the necessary corrections.

```
| A    |B
|_____|_____
|IDENTIFICATIØN-DIVISIØN.
|PRØGRAM ID.   TEST-PRØBLEM.
|ARTHUR.   STUDENT-NAME.
|INSTALLATIØN   UNIVERSITY CØMPUTER CENTER.
|DATE-WRITTEN.   MARCH 10, 1978.
|DATE CØMPILED.
|SECURITY.   NO REQUIREMENT SINCE THIS EXAMPLE IS FOR STUDENT USE
```

4

THE ENVIRONMENT DIVISION

The ENVIRØNMENT DIVISIØN provides information concerning the computer that is to compile the program, the computer that will execute the program, the input device on which each file to be read is located and the output device on which each file to be written is located. Thus, the sentences within this division are machine-dependent.

The ENVIRØNMENT DIVISIØN† (001,01) is composed of two sections: (1) the CØNFIGURATIØN SECTIØN (001,02) and (2) the INPUT-ØUTPUT SECTIØN (001,05).

CONFIGURATION SECTION

The CØNFIGURATIØN SECTIØN contains the required paragraphs SØURCE-CØMPUTER (001,03) and ØBJECT-CØMPUTER (001,04) and the optional paragraph SPECIAL-NAMES. The computer that will compile the program is referred to as the source computer. The computer that will execute the program is referred to as the object computer. The sentence within the SØURCE-CØMPUTER and the ØBJECT-CØMPUTER paragraphs contain two items: (1) the computer manufacturer, and (2) the computer system. If the computer has a model number assigned to it by the manufacturer, this can also be included for additional information purposes. For example, the "EMPLØYEE WAGES" program will be compiled and exe-

---

†The ENVIRØNMENT DIVISIØN of the COBOL program "EMPLØYEE WAGES" (Fig. 2-2) will be used to discuss this division.

31

IBM — COBOL Coding Form — GX28-1464-5 U/M 050* Printed in U.S.A.

SYSTEM	IBM-370-148	PUNCHING INSTRUCTIONS	PAGE 001 OF 001
PROGRAM	EMPLØYEE WAGES	GRAPHIC	CARD FORM # *
PROGRAMMER	V. THØMAS DØCK	DATE	PUNCH

SEQUENCE (PAGE) (SERIAL) | CONT. | A | B | COBOL STATEMENT | IDENTIFICATION

```
01 ENVIRØNMENT DIVISIØN.
02 CØNFIGURATIØN SECTIØN.
03 SØURCE-CØMPUTER. IBM-370-148.
04 ØBJECT-CØMPUTER. IBM-370-148.
05 INPUT-ØUTPUT SECTIØN.
06 FILE-CØNTRØL.
07     SELECT EMPLØYEE-RECØRDS-FILE ASSIGN TØ UR-2540R-S-CARDIN.
08     SELECT EMPLØYEE-PAYRØLL-FILE ASSIGN TØ UR-1403-S-PRØUT.
09
10
11
12
13
14
15
16
17
18
19
20
```

*A standard card form, IBM Electro C61897, is available for punching source statements from this form. Instructions for using this form are given in any IBM COBOL reference manual. Address comments concerning this form to IBM Corporation, LDS Publishing, Dept. J04, 1501 California Ave., Palo Alto, Ca. 94304

*No. of forms per pad may vary slightly

Figure 4-1: The ENVIRØNMENT DIVISIØN

cuted on a computer manufactured by IBM; the computer is a system/370; and it is model number 148.

This program is to be compiled and executed on the same computer. Generally, this will be the case, since compilation and execution are usually performed on the same computer. Sometimes, however, the program is to be compiled on one computer and executed on another computer. In these instances, the sentence in the SØURCE-CØMPUTER paragraph will be different from the sentence in the ØBJECT-CØMPUTER paragraph. For example,

```
A    B
ENVIRØNMENT DIVISIØN.
CØNFIGURATIØN SECTIØN.
SØURCE-CØMPUTER.   IBM-360-E30.
ØBJECT-CØMPUTER.   IBM-370-148.
```

In the above illustration, the program will be compiled on an IBM system/360, model 30 and executed on an IBM system/370, model 148.

INPUT-OUTPUT SECTION

The INPUT-ØUTPUT SECTIØN contains the required paragraph FILE-CØNTRØL. In the FILE-CØNTRØL paragraph, each file in the program is assigned to either the input device it is to read from or the output device it is to be written upon.

The FILE-CØNTRØL paragraph is composed of two or more clauses. The two required clauses are the SELECT and ASSIGN TØ clauses. These two clauses are generally located in the same sentence. The SELECT clause names a file used in the program, and the ASSIGN TØ clause assigns that file to either an input or output device.

The basic format of these two clauses is

SELECT file-name ASSIGN TØ system-name.

The file-name is the programmer-supplied name of the file assigned to the system-name. The system-name is divided into four fields, each of which is connected by a hyphen:

1. The device *class,* which is one of the following two-character fields: (1) UR (unit record)—card reader, card punch, and printer, (2) UT (utility)—magnetic tape, and (3) DA (mass storage)—magnetic disk and drum.

2. An input or output *device*, which is represented by a four- to six-digit field designated by the computer manufacturer. This field is optional.

3. A one-character field that specifies the file *organization*. One of the following three characters are to be used: (1) S (for standard sequential files), (2) D (for direct files), and (3) C (for ASCII files).

4. A *name*, which is a programmer-supplied one- through eight-character field that specifies the external-name by which the file is known to the computer system. This name is formed according to the rules for forming the name of the program. This name is the same as the one located on the JCL card for this file.

For example, in the ENVIRØNMENT DIVISIØN illustration the two programmer-supplied files named in the SELECT clauses are assigned to a card reader and a printer, respectively. The system-name UR-254OR-S-CARDIN indicates this to the computer via (1) UR (unit record device), (2) 254OR (computer manufacturer device name indicated on the machine itself), (3) S (a file on a unit record device is always sequentially organized), and (4) CARDIN (a programmer supplied name by which the file is known to the computer system. This is why the name is also punched on a JCL card.). The same analysis can be applied to the other ASSIGN TØ clause, which indicates a printer.

Every file used in the program *must* be named in a SELECT clause and assigned to either an input or output device in an ASSIGN TØ clause. The clauses can be separated by either a semicolon or comma and must be separated by at least one space. A period is placed *only* at the end of the sentence.

QUESTIONS

1. Is the ENVIRØNMENT DIVISIØN of a COBOL program compatible to all computers? If not, why not?

2. What are the two requirements of both the SØURCE-CØMPUTER and the ØBJECT-CØMPUTER paragraphs?

3. Discuss the function of the FILE-CØNTRØL paragraph.

4. What two clauses are required in the FILE-CØNTRØL paragraph, and what is the function of each?

5. What do the following device class abbreviations represent?

   a. DA

   b. UR

   c. UT

EXERCISE

1. Find the errors in the following ENVIRØNMENT DIVISIØN and make the necessary corrections.

```
A    B

ENVIRØMNENT DIVISIØN.
SØURCE-CØMPUTER.   IBM-370-148.
ØBJECT-CØMPUTER.   IBM.
INPUT ØUTPUT SECTIØN.
FILE-CØNTRØLS
     SELECT IN-FILE ASSIGN-TØ UR-2540-S-CARDS.
     SELECT ØUT-FILE.
```

2. Develop an ENVIRØNMENT DIVISIØN compatible with the computer system on which you will be executing COBOL.

❖

5

THE DATA DIVISION

The DATA DIVISIØN presents the characteristics of each field of data assigned a name that is to be stored in the computer's memory. That is, most fields of data used in a program are assigned a name, allocated storage space in the computer's memory, and described according to the type of data composing the field. The relationship of records, group items, and elementary items within each file is also established. Finally, any independent elementary items are described and defined.

The DATA DIVISIØN† (001,01) is composed of two sections: (1) the FILE SECTIØN (001,02) and (2) the WØRKING-STØRAGE SECTIØN (002,11).

The FILE SECTION

The FILE SECTIØN presents the characteristics of the input and output files in the program. An input file is a file that is to be transferred from an input device to the computer's memory, and an output file is a file that is to be transferred from the computer's memory to an output device. The file must have already been named in a SELECT clause within the ENVIRØNMENT DIVISIØN (Fig. 4-1: 001,07 and 08).

The description of a file begins with the entry FD (File Description) in area A (001,03,12) and is followed by the name of the file, which must begin in area B. This entry is followed by one or more clauses (001,04,13) in area B. (The clause(s) can begin on the same line as the name of the file and more than one clause can be on one line.)

---

†The DATA DIVISIØN of the COBOL program "EMPLØYEE WAGES" (Fig. 2-2) will be expanded upon to present additional elements of this division.

COBOL Coding Form

SYSTEM: IBM-370-148
PROGRAM: EMPLOYEE WAGES
PROGRAMMER: V. THOMAS DUCK

PAGE 001 OF 003

```
DATA DIVISION.
FILE SECTION.
FD EMPLOYEE-RECORDS-FILE
   LABEL RECORD IS OMITTED.
01 CARD-RECORD.
   02 EMPLOYEE-NAME            PICTURE A(15).
   02 FILLER                   PICTURE X(4).
   02 HOURS-WORKED             PICTURE 99.
   02 FILLER                   PICTURE XXX.
   02 HOURLY-RATE              PICTURE 9V99.
   02 FILLER                   PICTURE X(53).
FD EMPLOYEE-PAYROLL-FILE
   LABEL RECORD IS OMITTED.
01 PAYROLL-RECORD.
   02 FILLER                   PICTURE X.
   02 EMPLOYEE-NAM             PICTURE A(15).
   02 FILLER                   PICTURE X(6).
   02 HOURS-WORK               PICTURE 99.
   02 FILLER                   PICTURE X(8).
   02 HOUR-RATE                PICTURE $9.99.
   02 FILLER                   PICTURE X(8).
   02 GROSS-WAGE-OUT           PICTURE $$9.99.
   02 FILLER                   PICTURE X(11).
   02 FEDERAL-INCOME-TAX-OUT   PICTURE $$9.99.
```

Figure 5-1: The DATA DIVISION

IBM   COBOL Coding Form

GX28-1464-5 U/M 050*
Printed in U.S.A.

SYSTEM	IBM-370-148
PROGRAM	EMPLOYEE WAGES
PROGRAMMER	V. THOMAS DUCK

PAGE 0020F003

PUNCHING INSTRUCTIONS — GRAPHIC / PUNCH — CARD FORM # — IDENTIFICATION

```
01   02  FILLER                      PICTURE X(13).
02   02  STATE-INCOME-TAX-OUT        PICTURE $$9.99.
03   02  FILLER                      PICTURE X(12).
04   02  SOCIAL-SECURITY-TAX-OUT     PICTURE $$9.99.
05   02  FILLER                      PICTURE X(9).
06   02  RETIREMENT-OUT              PICTURE $$9.99.
07   02  FILLER                      PICTURE X(3).
08   02  NET-WAGE-OUT                PICTURE $$99.99.
09   02  FILLER                      PICTURE X(1).
10   01  PRINT-LINE                  PICTURE X(133).
11   WORKING-STORAGE SECTION.
12   77  GROSS-WAGE                  PICTURE 999V99.
13   77  OVERTIME-HOURS              PICTURE 99.99.
14   77  OVERTIME-RATE               PICTURE 99V99.
15   77  OVERTIME-WAGE               PICTURE 99V99.
16   77  FED-INCOME-TAX-RATE         PICTURE V99    VALUE .25.
17   77  FEDERAL-INCOME-TAX          PICTURE 99V99.
18   77  ST-INCOME-TAX-RATE          PICTURE V99    VALUE .06.
19   77  STATE-INCOME-TAX            PICTURE 99V99.
20   77  SOC-SECURITY-TAX-RATE       PICTURE V9999  VALUE .0605.
21   77  SOCIAL-SECURITY-TAX         PICTURE 99V99.
22   77  RETIREMENT-RATE             PICTURE V99    VALUE .06.
23   77  RETIREMENT                  PICTURE 99V99.
24   77  MORE-DATA-CARDS             PICTURE AAA    VALUE SPACES.
```

*A standard card form, IBM Electro C61897, is available for punching source statements from this form. Instructions for using this form are given in any IBM COBOL reference manual. Address comments concerning this form to IBM Corporation, LDS Publishing, Dept. J04, 1501 California Ave., Palo Alto, Ca. 94304

*No. of forms per pad may vary slightly

IBM

COBOL Coding Form

SYSTEM	IBM-370-148
PROGRAM	EMPLOYEE WAGES
PROGRAMMER	V. THOMAS DOCK
DATE	
PAGE	001 OF 003
CARD FORM #	

PUNCHING INSTRUCTIONS — GRAPHIC / PUNCH

GX28-1464-5 U/M 050·
Printed in U.S.A.

COBOL STATEMENT

```
SEQ
01   01  HEADING-1.
02       02  FILLER        PICTURE X      VALUE SPACE.
03       02  EMP-NAME      PICTURE A(13)  VALUE 'EMPLOYEE NAM
04  -                                    E'.
05       02  FILLER        PICTURE XXX    VALUE SPACES.
06       02  HRS-WRK       PICTURE A(12)  VALUE 'HOURS WORKED'.
07       02  FILLER        PICTURE X      VALUE SPACE.
08       02  HR-RAT        PICTURE A(11)  VALUE 'HOURLY RATE'.
09       02  FILLER        PICTURE X      VALUE SPACES.
10       02  GRS-WGS       PICTURE A(10)  VALUE 'GROSS WAGES'.
11       02  FILLER        PICTURE XXX    VALUE SPACES.
12       02  FED-INC-TAX   PICTURE A(18)  VALUE 'FEDERAL INCO
13  -                                    ME TAX'.
14       02  FILLER        PICTURE X      VALUE SPACE.
15       02  ST-INC-TAX    PICTURE A(16)  VALUE 'STATE INCOME
16  -                                    TAX'.
17       02  SOC-SEC-TAX   PICTURE A(19)  VALUE 'SOCIAL SECUR
18  -                                    ITY'.
19       02  FILLER        PICTURE X      VALUE SPACE.
20       02  RTRMT         PICTURE A(10)  VALUE 'RETIREMENT'.
21       02  FILLER        PICTURE X      VALUE SPACE.
22       02  FILLER        PICTURE X      VALUE SPACE.
23       02  NT-WGS        PICTURE A(9)   VALUE 'NET WAGES.'
```

IDENTIFICATION

*A standard card form, IBM Electro C61897, is available for punching source statements from this form. Instructions for using this form are given in any IBM COBOL reference manual. Address comments concerning this form to IBM Corporation, LDS Publishing, Dept. J04, 1501 California Ave., Palo Alto, Ca. 94304

*No. of forms per pad may vary slightly

The clause LABEL RECØRD IS ØMITTED (001,04,13) specifies that the first and last records of the file are not label records. Label records cannot be present in a file assigned to a unit-record device. There are other variations of this clause that are appropriately discussed later in this textbook. The LABEL RECØRD clause is *required* in every file description.

Record Description

After a file is described by the appropriate file description clause(s), each type of record within the file is described. Any further description, however, requires an understanding of the following two elements: (1) level numbers and (2) the PICTURE clause.

Level Numbers: Grouped Data

In COBOL, data are either associated or not associated with each other by means of level numbers. That is, level numbers show the relationship of data within a file. Specifically, they show the hierarchical structure of a file. The highest level indicator is FD, which indicates the most inclusive relationship of data—the file.

The next level of inclusiveness is the record. This is indicated by the fact that each type of record is always assigned the level number 01 (001,05,14). Similar to the FD level indicator, this record level number must be located in area A.

The organization of a record is reflected in the relationship of the group items and elementary items, as indicated by the level number assigned to each of them. The fact that a group item or an elementary item exists within a record is reflected by the assignment of one of the *subordinate* level numbers 02 through 49 to the item. Elementary items within a group item must be assigned a level number that is larger than the level number assigned to the group item. Elementary items independent of other elementary items within the record should be assigned the same level number. For example, the data composing the CARD-RECØRD (001,05) are all elementary items independent of each other. Thus, they are assigned the same level number, 02. If, however, the elementary item EM-PLØYEE-NAME (001,06) were a group item, level numbers could be assigned as follows:

```
|A  |B
|   |─────────────────────────
|   |02 EMPLØYEE-NAME
|   |   03 FIRST-NAME
|   |   03 MIDDLE-INITIAL
|   |   03 LAST-NAME
```

The level numbers 02 through 49 are usually located in area B. The level numbers need not be consecutive, although for clarity purposes the author recommends that they be consecutive. The only requirement is that a group item subordinate to another group item and an elementary item subordinate to a group item be assigned a level number that is greater than the level number assigned to the superior group item. Finally, a level number must be immediately followed by at least one space.

Level Numbers: Independent Elementary Items

Those elementary items that are not part of a record and thus not located within a file are assigned the level number 77. For example, the elementary items located on lines 002,12-23 are not part of either the EMPLØYEE-RECØRDS-FILE (001,03) or the EMPLØYEE-PAY-RØLL-FILE (001,02) and thus are assigned the level number 77.

Level Numbers: Condition-names

In certain instances, it is desirable to assign a value to each alternative of a particular condition. A condition name is then assigned to each alternative. To identify condition-names, they are assigned the level number 88. The use of condition-names is discussed in Chap. 8.

The PICTURE Clause

Within a record, each elementary item must be described in detail. This is the function of the PICTURE clause. The format of this clause is

$$\left\{ \begin{array}{l} \text{PICTURE} \\ \text{PIC} \end{array} \right\} \text{ IS description.}$$

A <u>PICTURE</u> clause specifies the *type* of data of which an *elementary item* is composed and the size of the field of data. A <u>PICTURE</u> clause cannot describe a group item.

Data Field Type. There are three types of data fields. A field of data must be classified as one of these three types. The particular type of data stored in the field is indicated by one of the following symbols:

Type of Data	Symbol
Alphabetic	A
Numeric	9
Alphanumeric	X

1. *Alphabetic.* A field classified as alphabetic can consist of only alphabetic characters and spaces.

2. *Numeric.* A field classified as numeric can be one of two subtypes: computational or report.

   Numeric *computational* data are used, as the name implies, in an arithmetic computation. It can consist of numeric characters, the alphabetic character S to represent a plus or minus sign, and the alphabetic character V to represent the decimal point.

   Numeric *report* data are used, as the name also implies, for printed output purposes. The field generally contains appropriate *editing* symbols, and as such *cannot* be used in arithmetic computations.

3. *Alphanumeric.* A field classified as alphanumeric can consist of any character in the COBOL character set. Whenever there is uncertainty concerning the type of data that may be stored in the field, the author recommends that the field be classified alphanumeric. However, a field classified as alphanumeric *cannot* be used in arithmetic computations, even though the field may be composed of numeric characters.

Data Field Size. The size of a field of data is indicated by the number of times its symbol is shown. For example, repeating the symbol A three times would indicate a three-character alphabetic field. If the field contains many characters, say five or more, it is inefficient to repeat the symbol that number of times. Rather, the author recommends that the symbol be written once and be immediately followed by a left parenthesis, a number indicating the character length of the field, and a right parenthesis. For example, a nine-character alphabetic field could be indicated by A(9).

1. *Alphabetic and Alphanumeric Data Fields.* The description of alphabetic and alphanumeric data fields is quite similar. The following are two examples of a description of each type of data field:

```
A    B
     02 EMPLØYEE-SEX        PICTURE A.
     02 EMPLØYEE-NAME       PICTURE A(20).
     02 EMPLØYEE-DEPARTMENT PICTURE XXX.
     02 EMPLØYEE-ADDRESS    PICTURE X(15).
```

The reserved word PICTURE may be located anywhere to the right of the name of the elementary item. However, there must be at least one space immediately preceding and following it.

2. *Numeric Data Fields.* As previously mentioned, a numeric data field may be either computation or report and may contain either implied or editing symbols, respectively. Thus, the field description of a numeric data field is somewhat more complicated than those for alphabetic or alphanumeric data fields.

Numeric Computational Data Fields. Numeric computational data fields are the *only* fields of data that can be used in arithmetic computations. This is due to the fact that only numeric characters, and an implied plus or minus sign and decimal point, can be located in the field.

(a) *The Implied Sign.* A data field used in an arithmetic computation cannot contain an actual plus or minus sign. Rather, the sign, if present, is "assumed" by the computer and thus does not actually occupy a storage position in its memory. The presence of an implied plus or minus sign is indicated by the alphabetic character S. This character, if present, must be the leftmost character in the field description. If the alphabetic character S is not present in the PICTURE clause, the data field is considered positive by the computer. For example, if the number $15\overline{0}$ is described by the statement

02 ITEM-1   PICTURE 999.

the number will be stored in the computer's memory as 150. That is, the number will be considered positive by the computer when it stores the number under the name ITEM-1. However, if the number $15\overline{0}$ is described by the statement

02 ITEM-1   PICTURE S999.

the number will be stored in the computer's memory as 150 (the field is only actually allocated three storage positions in the computer's memory), but the minus sign will be assumed by the computer when the number is used in arithmetic computations.

If the alphabetic character S is present in the PICTURE clause, its presence does not affect a positive number with respect to changing its sign. For example, if the number 150 is described by the statement

02 ITEM-1   PICTURE S999.

the number will be stored in the computer's memory as 150. Thus, if a number stored under a name either always will be negative or may be either positive or negative, the use of the alphabetic character S is appropriate.

A plus or minus sign is used with a numeric literal *on a punched card* by punching either a 12-row or an 11-row punch over the rightmost position of the data field. The plus sign is indicated by a 12-row punch and the minus sign is indicated by an 11-row punch. For example, the number $68\overset{+}{4}$ is indicated on the punched card by punching a 4 row punch and a 12-row punch in the rightmost position of the data field. Similarly, the number

$29.6\overline{7}$ is indicated on the punched card by punching a 7-row punch and a 11-row punch in the rightmost position of the data field.

(b) *The Implied Decimal Point.* A data field used in an arithmetic computation cannot contain an actual decimal point. Rather, the decimal point, if present, *must* be implied. The presence of an implied decimal point is indicated by the alphabetic character V. This character, if present, can be located either between two symbol 9's or to the immediate left of the left most symbol 9. For example, if the numbers 1.23 and .12 are to be stored in the computer's memory, the statements

02 NUMBER-1	PICTURE 9V99.
02 NUMBER-2	PICTURE V99.

will accomodate these numbers. The numbers will be stored as 123 and 12, but the location of the decimal point will be remembered by the computer in arithmetic computations.

The presence or absence of the decimal point in the input record is optional. If appropriate, however, the author recommends that the decimal point not be present in input data.

If the field contains many consecutive numeric characters, say five or more, it is inefficient to repeat the symbol that number of times. Rather, the author again recommends that the previously discussed method of describing the field be used. For example,

02 NUMBER-1	PICTURE 9(4)V99.
	(9999V99)
02 NUMBER-2	PICTURE 999V9(4).
	(999V9999)
02 NUMBER-3	PICTURE S9(4)V9(4).
	(S9999V9999)
02 NUMBER-4	PICTURE V9(4).
	(V9999)

(c) *The Storage of Numeric Literals in Numeric Computational Data Fields.* A numeric literal can be stored in a numeric computational data field. If there is a plus or minus sign and/or decimal point located in the numeric literal, they will be converted to implied characters by the computer when the numeric literal is stored in the numeric computational data field. Thus, the number can then be used in an arithmetic computation.

Numeric Report Data Fields. Since numeric computational data fields can contain only numeric characters, they are not capable of providing a written output that is easily readable and understandable. Thus, numeric report data fields are used for written output, as certain appropriate editing characters can also be included with the numeric characters which makes the written output resemble a standard business report. *An editing symbol cannot be used in an input data field, but only in an output data field.*

The following editing symbols can be incorporated in an output data field:

Editing Symbol	Meaning
B	Space
0	Zero
+	Plus†
—	Minus†
CR	Credit
DB	Debit
Z	Zero suppression
*	Check protection
$	Currency sign†
,	Comma
.	Period or Decimal Point

(a) *Space (B).* The character B is used to insert a space into a data field. Wherever the character B is located in the PICTURE clause, a space will be inserted in the written output. The character B can be used in combination with any other editing character.

(b) *Zero (0).* The character 0 is used to insert a zero into a data field. Wherever the character is located in the PICTURE clause, a zero will be inserted in the written output. The character 0 can be located anywhere in the PICTURE clause and can be used in combination with any other editing character.

(c) *Plus (+).* The plus sign is used to indicate the sign of a data field. It can be either the first or last character in the PICTURE clause. Use of the plus sign *forces* a plus or minus sign, depending upon the sign of the input data, to be written in a data field.

(d) *Minus (-).* The minus sign is used to indicate that a data field is negative. It can be either the first or last character in the PICTURE clause. Use of the minus sign will result in it being written if the data is negative; however, if the data is positive, no sign will be written.

---

† This editing symbol will "float" (move) to the position immediately to the left of the most significant (leftmost) numeric character in the data field.

(e) *Credit (CR) and Debit (DB)*. The credit and debit signs are used to indicate that a data field is, respectively, either negative or positive. The sign must be specified as the rightmost character in the PICTURE clause. The sign will be written if the data field is negative; however, if the data field is positive, spaces will replace the credit or debit sign positions.

(f) *Zero Suppression (Z)*. The zero suppression character is used to suppress a zero and replace it with a space. By placing the character in a numeric position of the data field, any zeros to the left of the most significant character will be suppressed. Any numeric character other than the 0, any embedded or trailing zeros, and any sign are not affected by the zero suppression character.

(g) *Check Protection (*)*. The check protection character is mainly used in the printing of checks to make sure that the amount of the check is not changed. One asterisk is used for each numeric character to the left of the decimal point. Any zeros and commas to the left of the most significant character are replaced by asterisks.

(h) *Currency Sign ($)*. The currency sign is used to cause a dollar sign to be written to the left of either the most significant nonzero character or the decimal point. Any zeros or commas to the left of either the most significant nonzero character or the decimal point are not written.

(i) *Comma (,)*. The comma is used to separate numeric characters. If no nonzero numeric character appears to the left of the comma, it is suppressed.

(j) *Period or Decimal Point (.)*. The period or decimal point may be located either to the left of or between two numeric characters, plus or minus sign, zero suppression, and currency sign.

The Determination of the Size of Data Fields

For readability and neatness, it is often desirable to determine the exact size of a field of data. The procedure used to accomplish this is dependent upon the type of data composing the field.

Alphabetic and Alphanumeric Data Fields. The determination of the size of either an alphabetic or alphanumeric data field is quite easy. The data field occupies one storage location in the computer's memory for each character composing the largest elementary item to be stored in that data field.

Numeric Data Fields. The determination of the size of a numeric data field is not quite as easy. The use of certain symbols must be considered, as they may or may not require a storage location in the computer's memory.

1. *Numeric Computation Data Fields*. In a numeric computational data field, only the number of numeric characters should be considered in determining its size. The implied plus or minus sign and decimal point must not be considered, as they are not actually stored in the computer's

memory. Rather, the computer only "assumes" their presence when using the elementary item in an arithmetic computation.

2. *Numeric Report Data Fields.* In a numeric report data field, each numeric character requires a storage location in the computer's memory. In addition, certain editing symbols require a storage location, while other editing symbols do not require a storage location.

Certain editing symbols are referred to as *insertion characters*. These editing symbols are inserted in the data field. The following are these editing symbols and the storage locations they require:

Table 5-1: Examples of the Use of Editing Symbols.

EDITING SYMBOL	SENDING FIELD		RECEIVING FIELD	
	DATA	PICTURE	PICTURE	EDITED RESULT
B	368469321	9(9)	999B99B9999	368 46 9321
	49215̄	9(5)	9(7)BCR	0049215 CR
0	693	999	999,00	693,00
	693	999	999.00	693.00
+	14321̄	S999V99	+999.99	+143.21
	88432̄	S9(5)	9(5)+	88432–
	632	999	++99	+632
–	14321	999V99	–999.99	143.21
	88432̄	S9(5)	9(6)–	088432
	632	999	––99	632
CR or DB	69134̄	S999V99	999.99CR	691.34CR
	869134	9(4)V99	9(4).99CR	8691.34
	69134̄	S999V99	999.99DB	691.34DB
	869134	9(4)V99	9(4).99DB	8691.34
Z	12345	999V99	ZZZ.99	123.45
	00123	999V99	ZZZ.99	1.23
	00123̄	S999V99	ZZZ.99	–1.23
*	345901	9(4)V99	$*,***.99	$3,459.01
	005901	9(4)V99	$*,***.99	$***59.01
	000001	9(4)V99	$*,***.99	$*****.01
	345901	9(4)V99	**,***.99	*3,459.01
$	964132	9(4)V99	$$,$$$.99	$9,641.32
	004132	9(4)V99	$$,$$$.99	$41.32
	4132	99V99	$$$.99	$41.32
	0032	99V99	$$.99	$.32

	SENDING FIELD		RECEIVING FIELD	
	764123	9(4)V99	$$,$$$.99	$7,641.23
	004123	9(6)	Z,ZZZZ9	4123
	000023	9(6)	Z,ZZZZ9	23
	61325	999V99	++++.+9	+613.25
	00325	999V99	ZZZ.Z9	3.25
	00025	999V99	$$$$.99	$.25

Editing Symbol	*Number of Storage Locations*
+	1 (if it is not floated)
-	1 (if it is not floated)
CR	2
DB	2
$	1 (if it is not floated)
,	1
.	1

Other editing symbols are referred to as *replacement characters*. These editing symbols are not inserted in the data field and thus do not require a storage location in the computer's memory. Rather, they replace a storage location allocation to a numeric character. The plus and minus signs and the currency sign, when floated, and zero suppression are replacement characters.

The Spacing of Input and Output Elementary Items

Although all input and output elementary items may be adjacent to each other, more often, for purpose of readability, it is desirable to have several spaces between them. This is accomplished through the reserved word FILLER.

When used in place of a programmer-supplied elementary item name, one or more spaces are considered an unused field of data. The number of spaces in the data field is dependent upon the number defined in its PICTURE clause. For example, in the input record CARD-RECØRD (001,05) the three elementary items are located, respectively, in punched card columns 1-15, 20-21, and 25-27. The reserved word FILLER is used to account for the four unused card columns between the first two elementary items, the three unused card columns between the second and third elementary items, and the remaining unused card columns. A similar logic, although different spacing, is involved in using FILLER in the output record PAYRØLL-RECØRD (001,14).

While the primary purpose of the reserved word FILLER is to "spread" elementary items, it should also be used to force a record to contain the proper number of characters. For example, all punch card records should contain 80 characters, and a print record, depending upon the type of printer, should contain 120, 132, or 144 characters, plus one character for carriage control. This use of FILLER is the basis for its use as the last entry in each input and output record (001,11; 002,09).

In Fig. 5-1 (001,03-24; 002,01-10), many of the aspects discussed in the previous several pages are presented. Specifically, notice the use of editing symbols only in the PAYRØLL-RECØRD (001,14). The function of the record PRINT-LINE is discussed in Chap. 6.

A Multi-record File

An input or output file can contain several types of records. In such a situation, the structure of each type of record would probably not be the same. Thus, each type of record must be described in the FILE SECTION.

Illustration. Assume the following statements:

```
A    B

DATA DIVISIØN.
FILE SECTIØN.
FD   RECØRD-FILE.
     LABEL RECØRD IS ØMITTED.
01   CARD-RECØRD-1.
     02 NAME          PICTURE A(20).
     02 ADDRESS       PICTURE X(20).
     02 CITY          PICTURE A(15).
     02 STATE         PICTURE A(15).
     02 FILLER        PICTURE X(10).
01   CARD-RECØRD-2.
     02 SØC-SEC-NUM    PICTURE X(11).
     02 AMØUNT-DUE     PICTURE 999V99.
     02 AMØUNT-PAID    PICTURE 999V99.
     02 FILLER         PICTURE X(59).
```

Two distinct input records, CARD-RECØRD-1 and CARD-RE-CØRD-2, are described. As illustrated, the two records do not have to agree in structure and in the number and size of data fields.

The description of several types of records belonging to the same input or output file in the FILE SECTION does not cause the computer to allocate storage areas for each type of record. Rather, a single input or output storage area is redefined in several ways.

The WORKING-STORAGE SECTION

The WØRKING-STØRAGE SECTIØN is the second major segment of the DATA DIVISIØN. As the name of the section implies, it is used to describe independent elementary and group items not contained in either an input or output file and thus not described in the FILE SECTIØN. These independent elementary and group items are needed to assist in the appropriate processing of the program. Two types of data are described in this section.

Independent Elementary Items

Often, elementary items not part of a file are required for inter-mediate results of arithmetic calculations and temporary storage. These items are called independent elementary items and are assigned the level 77. Independent elementary items can either precede—the author recommends this—or follow any group items in the WØRKING-STØRAGE SECTIØN.

If an independent elementary item is used as an intermediate result of an arithmetic calculation, it is important to remember that editing symbols cannot be used to describe the data field. Rather, the data field must be described as numeric computational. If, however, the elementary item is used as temporary storage, which at some later point in the program is to be transferred to the output record, editing symbols can be used to describe the field.

Group Items

It is generally desirable to design group items that are not contained in a file. Such group items as an output heading and an array are often used by a program.

A group item may be assigned any level number 01 through 49. The level number 01 can only be assigned to the name of the group item.

The VALUE Clause

The PICTURE clause is the most important clause used in the DATA DIVISIØN. Another clause, however, the VALUE clause, is also quite important.

The VALUE clause, like the PICTURE clause, can be used only to

define an *elementary item.* The clause assigns an *initial* value to the storage
position of the elementary item in whose statement it is present. It must
agree with both the type of data stored under the name of the elementary
item and the size of the data field. The clause follows the data field description and must be immediately preceded and followed by at least one space.

The following is an illustration of a VALUE clause used with an
alphabetic, numeric, and alphanumeric data field:

1. 02 NAME   PICTURE A(13) VALUE 'V THØMAS DØCK'.
2. 02 NUMBER   PICTURE 999V99 VALUE 150.00.
3. 02 ADDRESS   PICTURE X(15) VALUE '6937 JAY STREET'.

In the first example, the nonnumeric literal is enclosed in quotation
marks, as required. The literal contains exactly the number of characters
specified in the PICTURE clause.

In the second example, the numeric literal has a decimal point as, by
definition, it must. Remember, however, that a numeric literal can be
stored in a numeric computational data field. The decimal point in the
numeric literal is then "assumed" by the computer in the numeric computational data field.

In the third example, the nonnumeric literal is enclosed in quotation
marks, as required. In contrast to the nonnumeric literal in the first example, which has an alphabetic data field designation, this literal can contain any character in the COBOL character set, as it has an alphanumeric
data field designation.

The VALUE clause is used primarily in the WØRKING-STØRAGE
SECTIØN. *It can only be used in the FILE SECTIØN to define a condition-
name.*

An Example of a WORKING-STORAGE SECTION

In Fig. 5-1 (002,11-23;003,01-23), many of the aspects discussed in
the previous several pages are presented. Specifically, notice that the independent elementary items precede the group item and that the group
item, in this instance, is an output heading. Also notice the use of the
VALUE clause.

QUESTIONS

1. What is the function of the FILE SECTIØN?

2. What is the only clause required in the file description (FD) paragraph when the input device is the card reader?

3. How are record names, group data names, and elementary item names differentiated in the FILE SECTIØN?

4. How is an elementary item differentiated from an independent elementary item in the DATA DIVISIØN? By use?

5. In a PICTURE clause, what would an A, an X, and a 9 represent? What types of data can be stored in each?

6. What is the function of the reserved word FILLER in the FILE SECTIØN?

7. What is a VALUE clause, and under what circumstances does it appear in the DATA DIVISIØN?

EXERCISES

1. In each of the following, determine the contents of the resultant fields (where appropriate, use the character b to represent a blank):

	Sending Field		Receiving Field	
	PICTURE	Contents	PICTURE	Contents
a.	9(5)	12345	9(6)	_____
b.	99V99	12^34	9(3)V9(3)	_____
c.	9V99	7^89	9V9	_____
d.	999V9	678^9	99V99	_____
e.	99	56	XX	_____
f.	99	56	XXX	_____
g.	XX	AB	XXX	_____
h.	X(4)	CODE	XXX	_____
i.	XXX	124	999	_____
j.	AAA	ABC	XXX	_____
k.	AAA	ABC	A(5)	_____

2. Given the number 293.65, determine the output from the following edited output PICTURE clauses.

a. 9999.99

b. $$$$.99

c. ZZZZZ.Z9

d. $9999.99

e. 9B99.99

f. $****.*9

g. $$.$9

h. 999.999

i. *****9

3. Determine the errors in the following FILE SECTIØN (assuming a card reader as the input device).

```
A       B
FILE-SECTIØN.
    RECØRD-FILE.
01 RECØRD-1 .
    02 ITEM-1              PICTURE 99.
    02 ITEM-2              PICTURE 9 VALUE ZERØ
    02 GRØUP-1.
        01 SUB-ITEM-1      PICTURE XX .
        03 SUB-ITEM-2      PICTURE A(20)
        03 FILLER          PICTURE 9(65).
```

4. Find the errors in the following WØRKING-STØRAGE SECTIØN (assuming a printer as the output device).

```
A    B
WØRKING-STØRAGE SECTIØN.
77  INTERMEDIATE-RESULT    PICTURE 99V99.
77  FIRST-PRØDUCT          PICTURE 99V999 VALUE SPACES.
77  SECØND-PRØDUCT         PICTUER 9999 VALUE ZERØS.
01  HEADER-LINE.
    02 FILLERS             PICTURE X(5) VALUE SPACES.
    02 CØLUMN-1-HEADING.   PICTURE A(19) VALUE 'INTERMEDIAT
E RESULT'.
    02 FILLER              PICTUER X(5) VALUE SPACES.
    02 CØLUMN-2-HEADING    PICTURE X(9) VALUE '1ST PRØDUCT'.
    02 FILLER              PICTURE X(5) VALUE SPACES
    02 CØLUMN-3-HEADING    PICTURE A(11) VALUE 'THE VALUE Ø
'F PRØDUCT TWØ'.
    02 FILLER              PICTURE X(77) VALUE SPACES.
```

6

THE PROCEDURE DIVISION

The PRØCEDURE DIVISIØN is the last division of a COBOL program. It contains the statements that instruct the computer during execution of the program. That is, it is the PRØCEDURE DIVISIØN that causes the data to be read and processed, and the resultant information to be written.

ORGANIZATION OF THE PROCEDURE DIVISION

This division has greater flexibility with respect to organization than the other three divisions. This flexibility is necessary to accomodate the possible structure and combination of statements necessary successfully to execute the program.

The PRØCEDURE DIVISIØN† (001,01), while it can be divided into sections, usually is not in short programs. If one or more sections are established, each section name is supplied by the programmer. The name must be followed by the word SECTIØN, as are the section names in the previous two divisions. Generally, however, the PRØCEDURE DIVISIØN is divided into paragraphs. The division must contain at least one paragraph.

---

†The PRØCEDURE DIVISIØN of the COBOL program "EMPLØYEE WAGES" (Fig. 2-2) will be expanded upon to present additional elements of this division.

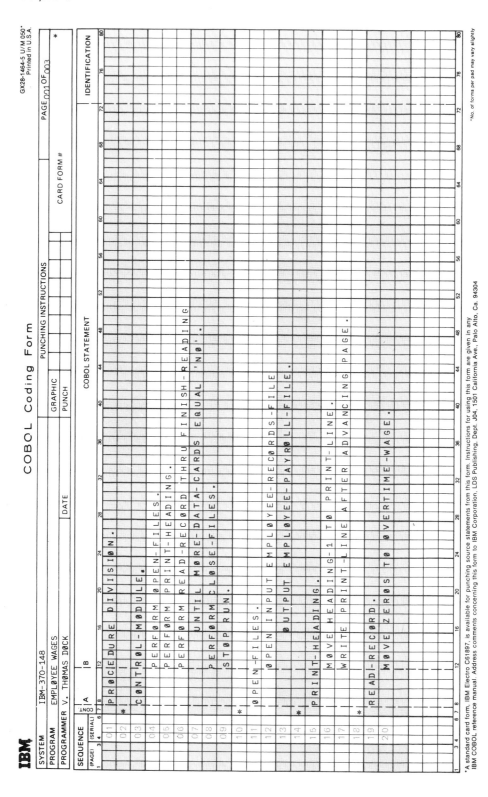

Figure 6-1: The PRØCEDURE DIVISIØN

IBM COBOL Coding Form

SYSTEM	IBM-370-148
PROGRAM	EMPLOYEE WAGES
PROGRAMMER	V. THOMAS DOCK
DATE	
PAGE	002OF003

PUNCHING INSTRUCTIONS — GRAPHIC / PUNCH — CARD FORM #

```
SEQUENCE
(PAGE)(SERIAL)  CONT  A      B                          COBOL STATEMENT
 01            MOVE SPACES TO PAYROLL-RECORD.
 02            READ EMPLOYEE-RECORDS-FILE AT END
 03            MOVE 'NO' TO MORE-DATA-CARDS, GO TO FINISH-READING.
 04
 05        PROCESS-RECORD.
 06            MOVE EMPLOYEE-NAME TO EMPLOYEE-NAM.
 07            MOVE HOURS-WORKED TO HOUR-WORK.
 08            MOVE HOURLY-RATE TO HOUR-RATE.
 09            IF HOURS-WORKED LESS THAN 41 GO TO NO-OVERTIME.
 10  *
 11        OVERTIME.
 12            SUBTRACT 40 FROM HOURS-WORKED GIVING OVERTIME-HOURS.
 13            MULTIPLY HOURLY-RATE BY 1.5 GIVING OVERTIME-RATE.
 14            MULTIPLY OVERTIME-HOURS BY OVERTIME-RATE GIVING
 15            OVERTIME-WAGE.
 16            MOVE 40 TO HOURS-WORKED.
 17  *
 18        NO-OVERTIME.
 19            MULTIPLY HOURS-WORKED BY HOURLY-RATE GIVING GROSS-WAGE.
 20            ADD OVERTIME-WAGE TO GROSS-WAGE.
```

GX28-1464-5 U/M 050
Printed in U.S.A.

*A standard card form, IBM Electro C61897, is available for punching source statements from this form. Instructions for using this form are given in any IBM COBOL reference manual. Address comments concerning this form to IBM Corporation, LDS Publishing, Dept. J04, 1501 California Ave., Palo Alto, Ca. 94304

*No. of forms per pad may vary slightly

COBOL Coding Form

GX28-1464-5 U/M 050*
Printed in U.S.A.

SYSTEM	IBM-370-148
PROGRAM	EMPLOYEE WAGES
PROGRAMMER	V. THOMAS DOCK

PAGE 003 OF 003

PUNCHING INSTRUCTIONS — GRAPHIC / PUNCH — CARD FORM # — DATE

```
COBOL STATEMENT

01   MULTIPLY FED-INCOME-TAX-RATE BY GROSS-WAGE GIVING
02   FEDERAL-INCOME-TAX.
03   MULTIPLY ST-INCOME-TAX-RATE BY GROSS-WAGE GIVING
04   STATE-INCOME-TAX.
05   MULTIPLY SOC-SECURITY-TAX-RATE BY GROSS-WAGE GIVING
06   SOCIAL-SECURITY-TAX.
07   MULTIPLY RETIREMENT-RATE BY GROSS-WAGE GIVING RETIREMENT.
08   SUBTRACT FEDERAL-INCOME-TAX, STATE-INCOME-TAX, SOCIAL-SECURIT
09   Y-TAX, RETIREMENT FROM GROSS-WAGE GIVING NET-WAGE-OUT.
10   MOVE GROSS-WAGE TO GROSS-WAGE-OUT.
11   MOVE FEDERAL-INCOME-TAX TO FEDERAL-INCOME-TAX-OUT.
12   MOVE STATE-INCOME-TAX TO STATE-INCOME-TAX-OUT.
13   MOVE SOCIAL-SECURITY-TAX TO SOCIAL-SECURITY-TAX-OUT.
14   MOVE RETIREMENT TO RETIREMENT-OUT.
15 *
16   WRITE-RECORD.
17   WRITE PAYROLL-RECORD AFTER ADVANCING 2 LINES.
18 *
19   FINIISH-READING.
20   EXIT.
21 *
22   CLOSE-FILES.
23   CLOSE EMPLOYEE-RECORDS-FILE, EMPLOYEE-PAYROLL-FILE.
```

*A standard card form, IBM Electro C61897, is available for punching source statements from this form. Instructions for using this form are given in any IBM COBOL reference manual. Address comments concerning this form to IBM Corporation, LDS Publishing, Dept. J04, 1501 California Ave., Palo Alto, Ca. 94304

*No. of forms per pad may vary slightly

IBM

COBOL STATEMENTS

A COBOL statement in the PRØCEDURE DIVISIØN is one of four types: (1) input or output, (2) data manipulation, (3) arithmetic, or (4) control. In discussing the basic statements within each type, certain writing conventions are used to present the reserved word(s), option phrase(s), etc. of each statement. These conventions are

1. A capitalized word is a COBOL reserved word. As such, it must be spelled exactly as illustrated.
2. A reserved word that is underlined is required each time the statement is used. A reserved word not underlined is optional and can be included for readability.
3. A word written in small letters represents a datum that is programmer-supplied.
4. Items and/or phrases enclosed in braces { } indicate that the programmer must select one of them to use in the statement.
5. A phrase enclosed in square brackets [ ] is optional. If it is used in the statement, it must be employed as shown.
6. Three dots (...) indicate that the previous phrase may be used several times.

THE INPUT STATEMENT

For data to be processed by a computer, they must be transferred into the computers's memory. The transferring of data into the computer's memory is caused by the execution of an input statement.

The Opening of Files

Before data can be transferred either from or into a file, however, the file must be "opened." The opening of a file establishes whether the file is to either provide data or receive data; that is, whether it is an input or output file. A file is opened through execution of the following statement:

ØPEN [*INPUT*   file-name ...]   [*ØUTPUT*   file-name ...]

Each file used in the program must be opened before one attempts to either read from or write into it. A file should only be opened once in a program. As illustrated in Figure 6-1, the input file, EMPLØYEE-RE-CØRDS-FILE (001,12), and the output file, EMPLØYEE-PAYRØLL-FILE (001,13) can be opened in a single statement.

The READ Statement

After a file has been opened, its contents can be read by the READ statement. This statement causes the computer to read the next data record located on a particular input device into the computer's memory. Frequently, the data are stored on punched cards, magnetic disk, or magnetic tape. The general format of this statement is

READ file-name RECØRD   AT *END*   imperative-statement

It should be noted that while the statement cites the name of the file, a *record* within that file is actually read. Each time the READ statement is executed, the contents of the record being read that are properly described in the DATA DIVISIØN are transferred into the computer's memory.

The READ statement is destructive. That is, each time it is executed, the contents of the record just read *replaces* in the computer's memory the contents of the immediately preceding record read from that file. If it is the first record of the file to be read, it *establishes* the contents stored in the computer's memory.

It is generally desirable to execute a particular statement when there are no more records to be read. To facilitate this desire, the AT END phrase is *always* used in a READ statement. The AT END phrase causes the computer to execute whatever statement appears after it if there are no more records to be read. Otherwise, the next statement is executed. Thus, the AT END phrase is a "conditional," as the *false* branch is executed if there is another record to be read and the *true* branch is executed if there is not another record to be read. The statement appearing after the AT END phrase may be any imperative COBOL statement.

In Figure 6-1, each time the READ statement (002,02) is executed, the next data record of the EMPLØYEE-RECØRDS-FILE is read, and its contents are transferred to the computer's memory. When the READ statement is executed and there are no more data records in the file to read, the computer will execute the statement(s) following the AT END phrase. In this instance, the program will execute a MØVE statement and then branch to and begin executing the statement in the paragraph FINISH-READING (003,17).

THE DATA MANIPULATION STATEMENT

The processing of data involves the movement of data within the computer's memory. The MØVE statement causes the computer to transfer data in one storage area to one or more storage areas within the computer's memory. The general format of this statement is

$$\underline{M\emptyset VE} \quad \left\{ \begin{array}{l} \text{name-1} \\ \text{literal-1} \end{array} \right\} \underline{T\emptyset} \ \text{name-2} \quad [\text{name-3}] \ \ldots$$

The MØVE statement instigates a duplicating operation by causing data stored in one area to be duplicated in one or more other areas of the computer's memory. Thus, the same data exist in two or more areas of the computer's memory. If there are any data stored at the area to which the data is being transferred, however, that data are destroyed.

Illustration. Assume that the following statement is executed:

MØVE SØURCE-1 TØ DESTINATIØN-1.

Contents of SØURCE-1 and DESTINATIØN-1 before execution of the statement:

SØURCE-1	DESTINATIØN-1
123	12345

Contents of SØURCE-1 and DESTINATIØN-1 after execution of the statement:

SØURCE-1	DESTINATIØN-1
123	00123

As illustrated above, the contents of an area named SØURCE-1 is being transferred to an area named DESTINATIØN-1. The contents of DESTINATIØN-1 before execution of the statement is 12345. However, its contents after execution of the statement are 00123; its original contents have been destroyed.

It should be noted that even though the number stored at SØURCE-1 has fewer characters than the number stored at DESTINATIØN-1, the MØVE statement completely destroys the original contents and a zero is stored in each unused storage position. (if the field had been described as either alphabetic or alphanumeric, a space would have been stored in each unused storage position.)

The Transferring of Elementary Items, Group Items, and Records

The MØVE statement is generally used to transfer elementary items, as just illustrated and as also illustrated in Figure 6-1 (001,16 and 20; 002,01,06-08,14; 003,08-12). In the latter illustration, any contents of the elementary items ∅VERTIME-WAGE (001,20) and PAYR∅LL-REC∅RD (002,01) are replaced with zeros and spaces, respectively. Thus, only the data specifically transferred to these elementary items will be written. In the remaining M∅VE statements, the contents of the three elementary items located in the input record, CARD-REC∅RD (002,06-08) and the contents of the five independent elementary items (003,08-12) are transferred to the output record, PAYROLL-REC∅RD. An elementary item assigned a level number 88 cannot be transferred.

Occasionally, it is desirable to transfer the contents of either a group item or a record. For example, in Figure 6-1 a M∅VE statement (001,16) is used to transfer the entire heading (HEADING-1) to the output record PRINT-LINE in Figure 5-1 (002,10).

The type of data field to which a datum can be transferred is dependent upon the type of the datum being transferred. Table 6-1 indicates which type of field(s) a particular type of data can be transferred to:

Table 6-1: A Summary of the Characteristics of the M∅VE Statement

Type of Source Datum	Type of Receiving Data Field			
Data Field	Alphabetic	Alphanumeric	Numeric Computational	Numeric Report
Alphabetic	YES[b]	YES[b]	NO	NO
Alphanumeric	YES[a&b]	YES[b]	NO	NO
Numeric Computational	NO	Numeric Characters Only[b]	YES[c]	YES[c]
Numeric Report	NO	YES[b]	NO	NO

[a]Alphabetic characters and spaces only.

[b]The source data are positioned in the receiving data field from left to right. Any unused positions to the right are filled with spaces. If the source datum contains more characters than positions available in the receiving data field, the excess right-most characters of the source are truncated.

[c]The source datum is aligned by the decimal point in the receiving data field. Any unfilled positions on either end of the data field are filled with either spaces or zeros. If the source datum contains more characters than positions available in the receiving field on either side of the decimal point, the excess characters of the source data field are truncated.

THE OUTPUT STATEMENT

After the data have been processed, they must be transferred from the computer's memory into an output file located on an output device.

This is accomplished by a WRITE statement. The general format of this statement is

The WRITE Statement

WRITE record-name [FRØM name-1]

$$\left[\begin{Bmatrix} \underline{BEFØRE} \\ \underline{AFTER} \end{Bmatrix} \text{ ADVANCING } \begin{Bmatrix} \begin{Bmatrix} \text{name-2} \\ \text{integer} \end{Bmatrix} \begin{bmatrix} \underline{LINE} \\ \underline{LINES} \end{bmatrix} \\ \begin{Bmatrix} \text{mnemonic-name} \\ \underline{PAGE} \end{Bmatrix} \end{Bmatrix}\right]$$

Each time a WRITE statement is executed, the contents of the named record are transferred from the computer's memory and written into the appropriate output file.

The WRITE statement differs fundamentally from the READ statement in two respects. First, it does not destroy the contents of the record being written in the computer's memory. Rather, the contents being transferred are a duplicate of the contents of the record stored in the computer's memory. The record contents in the memory are not destroyed until new data are transferred to the record. Second, the WRITE statement references the name of an output *record,* whereas the READ statement references the name of input *file.*

Since data read into the computer's memory is generally processed before being written out, the contents of an input data record are different from the contents of an output data record. Thus, the computer memory area for the input record is different from the computer memory area for the output record.

Normally, the data to be written are stored under the record named in the WRITE statement. However, use of the FRØM option causes the statement to process the data similarly to both a MØVE and WRITE statement. That is, the data would first be moved from the storage area represented by name-1 to the regular output area represented by record-name; then, the data is written on the appropriate output device. The storage area represented by name-1 may be described in either an input or output area of the FILE SECTIØN or the WØRKING-STØRAGE SECTIØN.

Illustration. Assume that the following statement is executed:

    WRITE ØUTPUT-RECØRD FRØM HEADING-1 AFTER
    ADVANCING 2 LINES.

The computer will first move the data from the storage area reserved for HEADING-1 to the storage area reserved for ØUTPUT-RECØRD. Then the data will be written on the printer after advancing 2 lines.

If the BEFØRE ADVANCING option is used, the record is written *prior* to the printer page being advanced. If the AFTER ADVANCING option is used, however, the record is written *after* the printer page is advanced. In either case, the number of lines on a page advanced by the printer is determined by the use of one of the following two options:

1. If "name-2 LINE OR LINES" is used (where name is a programmer-supplied name of an elementary item), the printer will advance the number of lines specified by the value of the integer number stored under it. The number must be positive and have a value of less than 100.
2. If "integer LINE or LINES" is used, the printer will advance the number of lines specified by the value of the integer number. The number must be positive and have a value of less than 100.

The SPECIAL-NAMES paragraph (CØNFIGURATION SECTIØN) provides a means of relating function-names to programmer-supplied mnemonic-names. (A more detailed discussion of the SPECIAL-NAMES paragraph and the use of mnemonic names within the paragraph is presented in Chapter 8. However, it is not necessary for the reader to refer to the paragraph at this time.) To advance the printer to the first line of the next printer page, the function-name CO1 must be used. This function must be assigned a mnemonic-name, such as TØP-ØF-PAGE, in the SPECIAL-NAMES paragraph. For example, in the following illustration.

```
|A    |B
|SPECIAL-NAMES.
|     |C01 IS TØP-ØF-PAGE.
```

the function-name CO1 is assigned the mnemonic-name TØP-ØF-PAGE.

A second and more convenient alternative to advance the printer to the first line of the next printer page is to use the reserved word PAGE.

In Figure 6-1, two WRITE statements are used. The first one (001,17) causes the heading (HEADING-1) described in the DATA DIVISIØN (Figure 5-1: 003,01) to be written on the first print line of the next printer page. The second WRITE statement (003,15) causes the PAYRØLL-RECØRD in the DATA DIVISIØN (Figure 5-1; 001,14) to be written after skipping two print lines.

ARITHMETIC STATEMENTS

A computer is capable of performing arithmetic calculations. COBOL offers two types of arithmetic statements. One type of statements, called *simple* arithmetic statements, is capable of performing a single arithmetic computation. The other type of statements, called *compound* arithmetic statements, is capable of performing several arithmetic computations. Each type of statements will be discussed separately.

The Components of an Arithmetic Statement

Before we discuss each type of arithmetic statements, however, a discussion of the components of an arithmetic statement is appropriate. An arithmetic statement is composed of two types of components—*operands* and arithmetic *operators*. An operand is a name or literal involved in a computation. It must be of numeric computational mode. An arithmetic operator is an arithmetic operational word or symbol that represents one of the computer's basic arithmetic capabilities.

The area in the computer's memory in which the result of an arithmetic computation is stored is called the *receiving area*. A receiving area must be either a numeric computational or numeric report data field.

In the following example,

ADD ITEM-1, ITEM-2 GIVING ITEM-3.

ADD is the operator, ITEM-1 and ITEM-2 are the operands, and ITEM-3 is the receiving area.

Simple Arithmetic Statements

The four basic arithmetic operations are addition, subtraction, multiplication, and division. A simple arithmetic statement is provided for each of these operations. Where appropriate within each statement, the connectives *comma* or AND may be used.

The Simple Addition Statement. Simple addition involves the summation of one or more names and/or literals. The general format of this statement is

$$\underline{\text{ADD}} \quad \begin{Bmatrix} \text{name-1} \\ \text{literal-1} \end{Bmatrix} \begin{bmatrix} , & \begin{Bmatrix} \text{name-2} \\ \text{literal-2} \end{Bmatrix} & \dots \end{bmatrix} \quad \underline{\text{T\O}} \text{ name-n}$$

Each name must be an elementary item, and the contents of a name and any literal data must be numeric computational. The contents of the names and/or literals are summed and stored at the area name-n. Name-n functions as both an operand and the receiving area. Thus, only a name can be located after the reserved word T∅, as a literal cannot function as a receiving area.

To illustrate the simple addition statement, assume that two areas in the computer's memory, AREA-1 and AREA-2, each contain the following number:

AREA-1	AREA-2
5	10

If the statement "ADD AREA-1 TØ AREA-2" is executed, the following will result:

AREA-1	AREA-2
5	15

The contents of AREA-1 are not changed. Its contents have been added to the contents of AREA-2, and the sum has been stored at AREA-2.

To further illustrate the simple addition statement, assume that three areas in the computer's memory, AREA-1, AREA-2, and AREA-3, each contain the following number:

AREA-1	AREA-2	AREA-3
5	10	15

If the statement "ADD AREA-1, 150 AND AREA-2 TØ AREA-3" is executed, the following will result:

AREA-1	AREA-2	AREA-3
5	10	180

The contents of AREA-1 and AREA-2 are not changed. Their contents and the number 150 have been added to the contents of AREA-3 and the sum stored has been stored at AREA-3. While the two optional connectives, the comma and AND, are used in the statement, either one or both could have been omitted. Their only function is to improve readability.

The simple addition statement develops the *algebraic sum* of the operands. Thus, the statement "ADD -80 TØ AREA-3" would result in the sum 100 being stored at AREA-3, assuming its previous contents had been 180. If the statement had been "ADD -200 TØ AREA-3," the sum -20 would have been stored at AREA-3.

The GIVING Option. In certain instances, it is desirable to store the sum in an area not involved in the summation process and thus avoid destroying the contents of one of the elementary items being summed. This can be accomplished by using the GIVING option in the simple addition statement. The general format of this statement is

$$\underline{\text{ADD}} \quad \begin{Bmatrix} \text{name-1} \\ \text{literal-1} \end{Bmatrix} \quad \left[\begin{Bmatrix} \text{name-2} \\ \text{literal-2} \end{Bmatrix} \; \dots \right] \quad \underline{\text{GIVING}} \; \text{name-n}$$

To illustrate this version of the addition statement, assume that the following four computer storage areas each contain the following number:

AREA-1	AREA-2	AREA-3	AREA-4
5	10	15	20

If the statement "ADD AREA-1, AREA-2 AND AREA-3 GIVING AREA-4" is executed, the following results:

AREA-1	AREA-2	AREA-3	AREA-4
5	10	15	30

The contents of AREA-1, AREA-2, and AREA-3 are not changed. The sum of their contents has been stored in AREA-4. The previous contents of AREA-4, 20, were destroyed.

There are two basic differences between the two kinds of simple addition statements:

1. When the GIVING option is used, the contents of name-n are *not* summed with the contents of the operands prior to name-n being destroyed.
2. Whe the GIVING option is used, name-n does *not* function as both an operand and a receiving area. Rather, it functions only as a receiving area.

It should also be noted that *either* the reserved word TØ or GIVING is used, depending upon the kind of simple addition statement. The substitution of the second reserved word in the statement occurs only in the addition statement. In the statements used to execute the other three arithmetic operations, the reserved word GIVING is the third reserved word of the statement, the first two reserved words being the arithmetic operator and TØ.

The Simple Subtraction Statement. Simple subtraction, like simple addition can be performed by one of two kinds of statements:

$$\underline{\text{SUBTRACT}} \quad \begin{Bmatrix} \text{name-1} \\ \text{literal-1} \end{Bmatrix} \quad \left[\begin{array}{c} \begin{Bmatrix} \text{name-2} \\ \text{literal-2} \end{Bmatrix} & \dots \end{array} \right] \quad \underline{\text{FRØM}} \text{ name-n}$$

$$\underline{\text{SUBTRACT}} \quad \begin{Bmatrix} \text{name-1} \\ \text{literal-1} \end{Bmatrix} \quad \left[\begin{array}{c} \begin{Bmatrix} \text{name-2} \\ \text{literal-2} \end{Bmatrix} & \dots \end{array} \right] \quad \underline{\text{FRØM}} \quad \begin{array}{c} \text{name-3} \\ \text{literal-3} \end{array} \quad \underline{\text{GIVING}} \text{ name-n}$$

In the first kind, the remainder is stored at the area name-n, which functions as *both* an operand and a receiving area. In the second kind, the remainder is stored at the area name-n, which functions as *only* a receiving area. Thus, the contents of name-n is not involved in the subtraction process prior to its destruction. The simple subtraction statement, like the addition statement, develops the *algebraic remainder*.

To illustrate the two kinds of statements, assume that the following four computer storage areas each contain the indicated number:

AREA-1	AREA-2	AREA-3	AREA-4
5	10	−15	20

If the statement "SUBTRACT AREA-1 AND AREA-2 FRØM AREA-3" is executed, the following will result:

AREA-1	AREA-2	AREA-3	AREA-4
5	10	−30	20

The contents of AREA-1, AREA-2, and AREA-4 are not changed. The contents of AREA-1 and AREA-2 are first summed and then subtracted from the contents of AREA-3 and stored in AREA-3.

If the statement "SUBTRACT AREA-4 AND AREA-2 FRØM AREA-1 GIVING AREA-3" is executed, the following will result:

AREA-1	AREA-2	AREA-3	AREA-4
5	10	−25	20

The contents of AREA-1, AREA-2, and AREA-4 are not changed. The contents of AREA-4 and AREA-2 are first summed and then subtracted from the contents of AREA-1 and stored in AREA-3.

The Simple Multiplication Statement. Simple multiplication can also be performed by one of two kinds of statements:

MULTIPLY $\begin{Bmatrix} \text{name-1} \\ \text{literal-1} \end{Bmatrix}$ BY   name-2

or

MULTIPLY $\begin{Bmatrix} \text{name-1} \\ \text{literal-1} \end{Bmatrix}$ BY $\begin{Bmatrix} \text{name-2} \\ \text{literal-2} \end{Bmatrix}$ GIVING name-n

In the first kind, the product is stored at the area name-2, which functions as *both* an operand and a receiving area. In the second kind, the product is stored at the area name-n, which functions as *only* a receiving area. Thus, the contents of name-n are not involved in the multiplication process prior to its destruction.

To illustrate the two kinds of statements, assume the following three computer storage areas, each containing the indicated number:

AREA-1	AREA-2
−5	10

If the statement "MULTIPLY AREA-1 BY AREA-2" is executed, the following will result:

AREA-1	AREA-2
−5	−50

The contents of AREA-1 are not changed. Its contents are multiplied by the contents of AREA-2, and the product is stored at AREA-2. Since standard sign rules are followed, a -50 is stored at AREA-2.

The contents of an area may be multiplied by itself to obtain its square. If the statement "MULTIPLY AREA-1 BY AREA-1 GIVING AREA-2" is executed, the following will result:

AREA-1	AREA-2
−5	25

The contents of AREA-1 are not changed. Its contents are squared and the *positive* product is stored in AREA-2. While other powers can be obtained in a similar fashion, the compound arithmetic statement can obtain the results more efficiently.

The Simple Division Statement. Similar to the other three simple arithmetic statements, simple division can be performed by one of two kinds of statements:

$$\underline{\text{DIVIDE}} \quad \left\{ \begin{array}{l} \text{name-1} \\ \text{literal-1} \end{array} \right\} \quad \underline{\text{INT}\emptyset} \quad \text{name-2}$$

$$\underline{\text{DIVIDE}} \quad \left\{ \begin{array}{l} \text{name-1} \\ \text{literal-1} \end{array} \right\} \quad \underline{\text{INT}\emptyset} \quad \left\{ \begin{array}{l} \text{name-2} \\ \text{literal-2} \end{array} \right\} \quad \underline{\text{GIVING}} \ \text{name-n}$$

In the first kind, the quotient is stored at the area name-2, which functions as *both* an operand and a receiving area. In the second kind, the quotient is stored at the area name-n, which functions as *only* a receiving area. Thus, the contents of name-n are not involved in the division process prior to its destruction.

To illustrate the two kinds of statements, assume that the following three computer storage areas each contain the indicated number:

AREA-1	AREA-2	AREA-3
–5	10	15

If the statement "DIVIDE AREA-1 INTØ AREA-3" is executed, the following will result:

AREA-1	AREA-2
–5	–3

The contents of AREA-1 are not changed. Its contents are divided into the contents of AREA-3, and the quotient is stored at AREA-3. Since standard sign rules are followed, a –3 is stored in AREA-3.

If the statement "DIVIDE AREA-1 INTØ AREA-3 GIVING AREA-2" is executed, the following will result:

AREA-1	AREA-2	AREA-3
–5	–3	15

The contents of AREA-1 and AREA-3 are not changed. AREA-1 is divided into AREA-3, and the quotient is stored at AREA-2.

A Summary of the Simple Arithmetic Statements

The simple arithmetic statements have several common characteristics. The following are the most important of these characteristics:

1. Except for the ability to sum the subtrahend in a subtraction statement, each statement can execute only one type of arithmetic operation.
2. Arithmetic symbols *cannot* be used. Rather, the reserved words ADD, SUBTRACT, MULTIPLY, and DIVIDE must be used.
3. The sign of an operand is used in appropriate algebraic fashion.
4. A decimal point is appropriately aligned.

The ROUNDED Option

If the result of an arithmetic statement contains more decimal positions (characters to the right of the decimal point) than allocated for in the PICTURE clause describing the receiving area, the excess rightmost decimal positions are truncated. By placing the reserved word RØUNDED *immediately after the name of a receiving area*, however, the result will be rounded in the least significant (rightmost) decimal position allocated for in the PICTURE clause if the most significant (leftmost) truncated decimal position is a value of 5 or greater.

To illustrate this option, assume that the following two computer storage areas each contain the indicated contents:

CONTENTS

AREA-1	PICTURE 99V999	29627
AREA-2	PICTURE 99V99	6383

The statement "ADD AREA-1 TØ AREA-2 RØUNDED" is executed. Since AREA-2, the receiving area, is allocated only two decimal positions, the third decimal position in AREA-1 is truncated. However, use of the RØUNDED option causes the least significant decimal position allocated for in the PICTURE clause to be rounded. Thus, the results 9346 rather than 9345 are stored in the receiving area.

The SIZE ERROR Option

As mentioned during the discussion of the PICTURE clause in Chapter 5, the maximum number of numeric characters the computer can store in a particular data field is determined by the number of numeric character positions allocated in the clause. It is possible, however, that the result of an arithmetic computation may contain more numeric characters than have been allocated for in the PICTURE clause. For example, assume that the following two computer storage areas each contain the indicated contents:

CONTENTS

AREA-1	PICTURE 99V999	7462
AREA-2	PICTURE 99V99	6534

The statement "ADD AREA-1 TØ AREA-2" is executed. The result of the execution is an attempt by the computer to store the sum 13996 in AREA-2, the receiving area. However. this is impossible, as only two positions to the left of the decimal point have been allocated for in the PICTURE clause. Thus, the sum *overflows* the receiving area, and the incorrect result 3996 is stored in the data field.

This programming error can be averted by the use of the SIZE ERRØR option in the arithmetic statement. This option is always the last part of the statement, and thus if the RØUNDED option is also used, the

SIZE ERRØR option would follow it. It should be used whenever over-flow of the result is possible. The general format of this option is

ØN *SIZE ERRØR* imperative-statement

If the result of the arithmetic statement overflows the receiving area, the computer will execute the statement following the reserved word ERROR rather than the next statement. In such an instance, the result of the arithmetic statement is not stored in the receiving area; thus, the contents of the receiving field are *not* changed.

To illustrate this option, assume that the addition statement in the previous example was "ADD AREA-1 TØ AREA-2 ØN SIZE ERRØR MØVE 'SUM ØF AREA-1 AND AREA-2 CAUSED ØVERFLOW' TØ PRINT-AREA." Now, instead of storing the incorrect result 3996 in AREA-2, the computer will, upon determining that the receiving field is too small, execute the MØVE statement. The contents of AREA-2 will remain what they were prior to execution of the arithmetic statement, 6534.

The Compound Arithmetic Statement

In certain instances, it is desirable to perform more than one type of arithmetic operation in a single arithmetic statement. As previously indicated, this is not possible with a simple arithmetic statement. Thus, the compound arithmetic statement is available, which allows the combination of almost any combination of arithmetic operations. The general format of this statement is

CØMPUTE name-1 [RØUNDED] =   arithmetic expression   [ØN SIZE ERRØR

imperative statement]

The result is stored under the name to the left of the equal sign. That is, the name on the left side of the equal sign is the *receiving area*. On the right side of the equal sign, there can be a combination of elementary items and/or numeric literals, each of which must be separated by an arithmetic operator. The RØUNDED and ØN SIZE ERRØR options function as they do in the simple arithmetic statements.

Arithmetic Operators. The compound arithmetic statement, in contrast with the simple arithmetic statement, uses the standard arithmetic operators rather than the arithmetic words to designate arithmetic operations. Thus, the reserved words ADD, SUBTRACT, MULTIPLY, and

DIVIDE cannot be used in the CØMPUTE statement. The arithmetic operators that can be used and their respective operational meanings are

Arithmetic Operator	Operation
**	Exponentiation
*	Multiplication
/	Division
+	Addition
−	Subtraction

An arithmetic operator *must* be immediately preceded and followed by at least one space. Also, parentheses must be used to separate two successive operators.

The evaluation of the various operands composing an arithmetic expression is from left to right. However, the left-to-right evaluation sequence may be broken by either the use of parentheses and/or the hierarchy of arithmetic operations.

One or more sets of parentheses may be used in an arithmetic expression. The programmer has the option of enclosing in parentheses any combination of operands composing the arithmetic expression. When a set of parentheses is used, the operands enclosed in the parentheses are evaluated prior to evaluating those operands not enclosed in parentheses. If more than one set of parentheses is used in an arithmetic expression, the computer will evaluate from left to right the operands within each set of parentheses. If one or more sets of parentheses are enclosed within another set of parentheses, the computer will evaluate the operands within each set of parentheses from the innermost set of parentheses to the outermost set of parentheses.

The hierarchy of evaluation of operands, both within and outside a set of parentheses is

1. All exponentiations (**) are performed.
2. All multiplications (*) and divisions (/) are performed.
3. All additions (+) and subtractions (-) are performed.

Although the CØMPUTE statement may compute several intermediate results during the process of evaluation of an arithmetic expression, *only the final answer is derived from the statement.* Thus, if it is desirable to derive one or more of the intermediate results, another statement must be used to obtain each desired intermediate result. (The computation of several intermediate results during the process of evaluation of an arithmetic expression may cause a final answer to be inaccurate. This possible inaccuracy can be avoided by increasing the field size description on both the left and the right of the decimal point by one or more positions beyond the determined size.)

The following illustrations demonstrate some of the uses and capability of the CØMPUTE statement:

Illustration 1. The following elementary items are available to the computer in a payroll problem.

REG-HØURS   represents the number of regular hours worked by an employee.

ØVERTIME-HØURS   represents the number of overtime hours worked by an employee.

RATE   represents the hourly wage of the employee.

Problem: Compute the employee total salary (TØTAL-PAY) of each employee, which is the sum of regular pay plus overtime pay; overtime is paid at two times the regular rate.

Solution: The net pay of the employee may be calculated as follows:

CØMPUTE TØTAL-PAY RØUNDED = (RATE * REG-HØURS)
+ (2 * RATE * ØVERTIME-HØURS).

The two sets of parentheses are used to increase readability. In this instance, the operands within each set of parentheses are executed from left to right. The sum will be stored under TØTAL-PAY.

Illustration 2. The following elementary items are available to the computer in a cost problem:

UNITS represents the number of purchases inventory items.

UNIT-CØST represents the cost per item.

DISCØUNT represents the discount rate.

Problem: Compute the net cost (NET-CØST) of the items.

Solution: The net cost of the items can be calculated as follows:

CØMPUTE NET-CØST = (UNITS * UNIT-CØST) −
(DISCØUNT * (UNITS * UNIT-CØST − 5.00)).

In this instance, the use of a set of parentheses enclosed within another set of parentheses is necessary to obtain the proper sequence of execution of operands. (If the set of parentheses enclosing the operands UNITS,

UNIT-CØST, and 5.00 were not present, the discount would be computed on a total unit cost that would be five dollars higher than it is supposed to be.)

CONTROL STATEMENTS

The computer normally executes statements in their order within a program. However, it is often desirable to "break" that order of execution; that is, to branch to a statement located either prior to or after it in the program.

Control statements provide the means by which a transfer to a statement other than the next statement can be made. There are two types of control statements. One type is an unconditional transfer, and the other type is a conditional transfer.

The Unconditional Transfer

The unconditional transfer statement causes the computer to branch to a particular paragraph. It is called an "unconditional" transfer, because there is no particular condition necessary for the transfer to be made. The computer will always branch to the paragraph identified in the statement. The general format of this statement is

GØ TØ procedure-name

Procedure-name is the name of a particular paragraph in the PRØCEDURE DIVISIØN. For example, when there are no more records to read from the file, the GØ TØ statement in the AT END phrase (002,02) will be executed, and the program will transfer to the paragraph FINISH-READING (003,17).

The General Conditional Statements

While the unconditional GØ TØ statement always transfers "unconditionally" to the same specified statement, in certain instances it is desirable to transfer to one of several possible statements, depending upon a certain "condition." This can be accomplished by means of one of several types of conditional statements.

The IF Statement

The IF statement is the basic conditional statement. The reserved word IF is followed by a condition. If the condition is met, the program branches to a particular statement. If the condition is not met, the program branches to another statement. The branch followed if the condition is met is called the *true* branch; the branch followed if the condition is not met is called the *false* branch. The condition following the reserved word IF can be either simple or compound (these two conditions are discussed later in this chapter). The general format of the IF statement is

$$\underline{IF} \text{ condition} \left\{ \begin{array}{l} \text{statement-1} \\ \underline{NEXT\ SENTENCE} \end{array} \right\} \left[\underline{ELSE} \left\{ \begin{array}{l} \text{statement-2} \\ \underline{NEXT\ SENTENCE} \end{array} \right\} \right]$$

Figure 6-2: Flowchart of the IF Statement

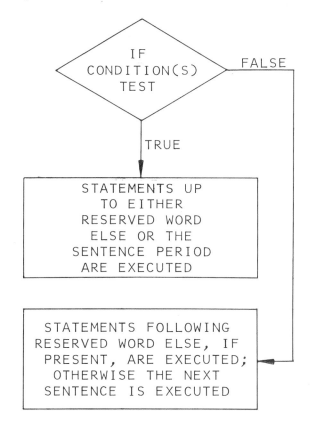

If the condition is true and a statement represented by statement-1 (which can be one or more imperative-statements) immediately follows the condition, that statement is executed. However, if the condition is true and the reserved words NEXT SENTENCE immediately follow the condition, the next sentence is executed. Unless it is desired to always have the computer execute the statement designated the *false* branch, an unconditional transfer statement should always be the last statement of the *true*

branch. This is due to the fact that after the computer has executed the last statement of the *true* branch, it proceeds to the next sentence and executes it.

If the condition is false and the ELSE option is used, either the statement represented by statement-2 (which can be one or more imperative-statements) or the NEXT SENTENCE is executed, depending upon which of the two elements are present. If the condition is false and the ELSE option is not used, the next sentence is executed.

Simple Conditional Statements. In a simple conditional statement, the computer branches to either the *true* branch or the *false* branch based upon a test of *one* condition. There are three types of simple conditional tests:

A. The Class Test. The class test is used to determine whether or not the contents of a data field are either numeric or alphabetic. The general format of this statement is

$$\underline{\text{IF}} \text{ name IS } [\underline{N\emptyset T}] \left\{ \frac{NUMERIC}{ALPHABETIC} \right\} \text{ imperative-statement}$$

The data field represented by the name can be described as alphabetic, alphanumeric, or numeric edited. A name described as either alphabetic or alphanumeric can be tested to determine if its contents are alphabetic. A name described as either alphanumeric or numeric edited can be tested to determine if its contents are numeric. If the PICTURE clause describing the data field represented by the name does not contain an operational sign, the name is determined to be numeric only if its contents are numeric and there is *no* operational sign.

Table 6-2: Valid Forms of Class Tests

Name	Valid Forms of the Class Test	
Alphabetic	ALPHABETIC	NOT ALPHABETIC
Alphanumeric	ALPHABETIC NUMERIC	NOT ALPHABETIC NOT NUMERIC
Numeric Edited	NUMERIC	NOT NUMERIC

If the test is true, the statement following the reserved word NUMERIC or ALPHABETIC is executed; otherwise, the next sentence is executed. If the reserved word NØT is used, the test is true if the contents of the name are not what is being tested (either numeric or alphabetic).

Illustration: Assume that it is desirable to determine if a field of data called ITEM-1 is numeric. The following statement could be used:

IF ITEM-1 IS NUMERIC GØ TØ PARA-1

If the contents of ITEM-1 are numeric, the computer will branch to PARA-1. However, if the contents are not numeric, the next sentence will be executed.

B. The Relation Test. The relation test is used to determine the relative magnitude of two values. The general format of the test is

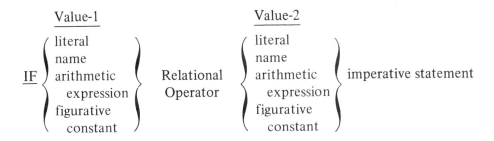

Literal may be either numeric or nonnumeric and name may be an elementary item with either a numeric or nonnumeric datum stored under it. Any one of the four types of value-1 can be tested against any one of the four types of value-2; for example, a literal can be tested against a name. However, value-1 and value-2 must be of the same mode.

Relational Operators. The following six relation operators can be used:

1. GREATER THAN (symbolized by >, which may be used in place of the reserved words). If value-1 is algebraically larger than value-2, the test is TRUE; otherwise, the test if FALSE.
2. NØT GREATER. If value-1 is either algebraically equal to or less than value-2, the test is TRUE; otherwise, the test is FALSE.
3. EQUAL TØ (symbolized by =, which may be used in place of the reserved word(s). If value-1 is algebraically equal to value-2, the test if TRUE; otherwise, the test is FALSE.
4. NØT EQUAL TØ. If value-1 is either algebraically greater than or less than value-2, the test is TRUE; otherwise, the test is FALSE.
5. LESS THAN (symbolized by <, which may be used in place of the reserved words).

If value-1 is algebraically less than value-2, the test if TRUE; otherwise, the test is FALSE.

6. <u>NØT</u> <u>LESS</u>. If value-1 is either algebraically greater than or equal to value-2, the test is TRUE; otherwise, the test is FALSE.

Relational Test Illustrations. For the illustrations, assume that the following five computer storage areas each contain the indicated contents:

Name	Contents
AREA-1	5
AREA-2	10
AREA-3	15
AREA-4	20
AREA-5	

1. The Comparison of a Literal and Name. Assume that the following statement is executed:

    IF 10 LESS THAN AREA-3 GØ TØ PARA-1.

Since 10 is less than the contents of AREA-3, the test is true. Thus, the GØ TØ statement is executed.

2. Two Successive Comparisons. Assume that the following statements are executed:

    IF AREA-4 EQUAL AREA-1 CØMPUTE SUM RØUNDED = 3 * AREA-1 + 100
    IF 2 * AREA-2 GREATER THAN AREA-1 GØ TØ PART-3.

In the first statement, since the contents of AREA-4 and AREA-3 are not equal, the test is false. Thus, the computer will not execute the CØMPUTE statement, but rather the next statement. In the second statement, since the result of the arithmetic expression is greater than the contents of AREA-4, the test is true. Thus, the computer will execute the GØ TØ statement.

3. The Comparison of a Nonnumeric Literal and a Figurative Constant. Assume that the following statement is executed:

    IF AREA-5 EQUAL SPACES MØVE 'NØ NUMBER' TØ AREA-5.

Since AREA-5 is blank, the test is true. Thus, the MØVE statement is executed.

C. The Sign Test. The IF statement can also be used to test either the algebraic sign or zero condition of a number. The general format of the statement is

$$\underline{\text{IF}} \left\{ \begin{array}{l} \text{name-1} \\ \text{arithmetic-expression} \end{array} \right\} \quad [\underline{\text{NØT}}] \quad \left\{ \begin{array}{l} \text{PØSITIVE} \\ \underline{\text{ZERØ}} \\ \underline{\text{NEGATIVE}} \end{array} \right\} \text{imperative-statement}$$

If the sign of the name or the result of the arithmetic expression agrees with the condition being tested, the test is true; otherwise, the test is false.

The sign test is a subdivision of the relational test. Using PØSITIVE is the same as using GREATER THAN ZERØ; using ZERØ is the same as using EQUAL ZERØ; and using NEGATIVE is the same as using LESS THAN ZERØ. However, a sign test can generally be written faster than its relational counterpart.

Sign Test Illustrations. For the illustrations, assume that the following three computer storage areas each contain the indicated contents:

Name	Contents
AREA-1	50
AREA-2	00
AREA-3	−10

1. A POSITIVE Test. Assume that the following statement is executed:

    IF AREA-1 PØSITIVE GØ TØ PARA-1.

Since the contents of AREA-1 are positive, the GØ TØ statement is executed.

2. A ZERO Test. Assume that the following statement is executed:

    IF AREA-2 ZERØ GØ TØ PARA-2.

Since the contents of AREA-2 are zero, the GØ TØ statement is executed.

3. A NEGATIVE Test. Assume that the following statement is executed:

    IF AREA-3 NEGATIVE GØ TØ PARA-3.

Since the contents of AREA-3 are negative, the GØ TØ statement is executed.

Compound Conditional Statements. In a compound conditional statement, the computer branches to either the TRUE branch or the FALSE branch, depending upon a test of *several* conditions. The relational and/or sign tests are the basis of evaluation.

The Use of Connectives. A compound conditional statement must contain either the connective AND and/or the connective ØR. Use of the connective AND means that both the test immediately preceding and following it must be true for that portion of the condition to be true. Use of the connective ØR means that either the test immediately preceding or

The Procedure Division 81

following it or both tests must be true for that portion of the condition to be true.

The Evaluation Process. If the connectives AND and ØR are both present in a statement, evaluation of the statement occurs in the following order:

1. All compound conditionals within parentheses (if applicable, from the innermost to the outermost set).
2. All conditionals connected by AND.
3. All conditionals connected by ØR.
4. Left to right through the statement.

The Writing of a Compound Conditional. The normal formation of a conditional can be modified if certain conditions are present. For example, if several relational conditionals are written in sequence, the subject of each conditional after the first one need not be written if it is the same as the subject of the first conditional. Thus, the compound conditional statement

IF PARM EQUAL SUM-1 ØR PARM EQUAL SUM-2 GØ TØ BEGIN.

may also be written

IF PARM EQUAL SUM-1 ØR EQUAL SUM-2 GØ TØ BEGIN.

In the second conditional statement, the subject of the second conditional is "implied."

If a subject of a conditional is implied *and* the relational operator is the same as the relational operator of the first conditional, it may also be "implied." Thus, the above second conditional statement may also be written as follows:

IF PARM EQUAL SUM-1 ØR SUM-2 GØ TØ BEGIN.

Since the second relational operator is the same as the first, it is omitted.

The use of either an implied subject or implied relational operator must follow certain rules. These are

1. They can be implied *only* in a relational conditional.
2. The relational conditionals of which they are a part must be adjacent to each other.
3. The subject can be implied only as long as it does not change.
4. The relational operator can be implied only if the subject is implied and as long as it does not change.

Illustration 1. Assume that the following compound *relational* conditional statement is executed:

IF RATE GREATER THAN .01 AND LESS THAN 1.00 GØ TØ PARA-2

If the contents of RATE is greater than .01 and less than 1.00, the test is true; otherwise, the test is false. Note that because the subject of the second conditional, RATE, is the same as the subject of the first conditional, it is omitted in the second conditional.

Illustration 2. Assume that the following compound *relational* and *sign* conditional statement is executed:

IF SUM LESS THAN 25.00 ØR TAX ZERØ MØVE ZERØ TØ RETIREMENT.

If the contents of SUM is either less than 25.00 and/or the contents of TAX is zero, the test is true; otherwise, the test is false.

A Summary of Simple and Compound Conditionals. Table 6-3 summarizes all simple and compound conditionals and the circumstance(s) under which the test is either true or false.

Table 6-3: A Summary of Simple and Compound Conditionals

If the conditional specifies:	TRUE For the TRUE branch to be executed, the test must be:	FALSE For the FALSE branch to be executed, the test must be:
GREATER	GREATER	LESS or EQUAL
NØT GREATER	EQUAL or LESS	GREATER
EQUAL	EQUAL	GREATER or LESS
NØT EQUAL	GREATER or LESS	EQUAL
LESS	LESS	EQUAL or GREATER
NØT LESS	EQUAL or GREATER	LESS
PØSITIVE	PØSITIVE	ZERØ or NEGATIVE
NØT PØSITIVE	ZERØ or NEGATIVE	PØSITIVE
ZERØ	ZERØ	PØSITIVE or NEGATIVE
NØT ZERØ	PØSITIVE or NEGATIVE	ZERØ
NEGATIVE	NEGATIVE	ZERØ or PØSITIVE

NØT NEGATIVE	PØSITIVE or ƵERØ	NEGATIVE
Condition-A AND Condition-B	Both Conditional-A and Condition-B TRUE	Either Conditional-A or Condition-B or both FALSE
Condition-A ØR Condition-B	Either Condition-A or Condition B, or both TRUE	Both Conditional-A and Condition-B FALSE

TERMINAL STATEMENTS

Two types of statements are used to terminate a program. One type closes all of the files opened in the ØPEN statement. The other type terminates execution of the program.

The CLOSE Statement

Every file "opened" in the ØPEN statement must be "closed" prior to termination of execution of the program. This is the function of the CLØSE statement. The general format of this statement is

CLØSE file-name [, file-name-2] . . .

In Figure 6-1, the two files EMPLØYEE-RECØRDS-FILE AND EMPLØYEE-PAYRØLL-FILE are closed (003,21). The files may be listed in any order. Whether they are an input or output file is neither mentioned in the statement nor important with respect to their listing in the statement. When a file is closed, it must be reopened by repeating the ØPEN statement before a READ or WRITE statement can access the file.

The STOP RUN Statement

When the logical termination point in a program is reached by the computer, it must have some means of terminating execution of the program. This is the function of the STØP RUN statement. The general format of this statement is

STØP RUN

The STØP RUN statement (001,09) can be located at one or more places within the program, depending upon how many logical termination points are present in the program. Thus, it may not be the last physical statement of the program.

QUESTIONS

1. Discuss the function of the PRØCEDURE DIVISIØN.

2. What is the purpose of the ØPEN statement? The CLØSE statement?

3. Discuss the function of the READ statement. What is meant by destructive reading?

4. What are the components of the ADVANCING option, and what is its purpose?

5. Discuss the function of the MØVE statement. What types of receiving fields can be used with an alphabetic sending field? An alphanumeric sending field? A numeric computational sending field? A numeric report sending field?

6. Define an arithmetic operator and an arithmetic operand.

7. What rules govern a receiving area in COBOL arithmetic statements?

8. Distinguish the difference in COBOL ADD or SUBTRACT statements with and without the GIVING option.

9. How does the CØMPUTE statement differ from other arithmetic statements?

10. What are the relational operators that can be used in a relational IF statement?

11. Discuss the different types of IF statements and the distinguishing characteristics of each.

12. What determines the evaluation process of compound conditional statements?

EXERCISES

1. When the computer encounters a READ or WRITE command in the PRØCEDURE DIVISIØN, how does it know which input or output device to activate?

2. Given: A = 50; B = -10; C = 20; D = Ƶ; and E = blank, what will be the result of the following statements (and, if applicable, what will be the result in associated storage positions)? Assume the initial conditions for each statement.

   a.   ADD A TØ B.

   b.   SUBTRACT A FRØM B GIVING C.

   c.   MULTIPLY A BY 1.50 GIVING B.

   d.   DIVIDE B INTØ A.

   e.   CØMPUTE F = A * C / B ** 2.

   f.   IF D NUMERIC GØ TØ FINISH-RUN.

   g.   IF A LESS THAN 30 ADD 5 TØ B.

   h.   IF A - (2 * C) NØT ƵERØ GØ TØ FINISH-RUN.

3. Given:

Name	Picture Size	Contents
NAME-1	999V99	23456
NAME-2	9999	7890
NAME-3	99V999	65432

Determine the results of the following examples and the related storage areas (assume the initial conditions for each).

a. CØMPUTE NAME-2 = NAME-2 + 2500.

b. CØMPUTE NAME-2 RØUNDED = NAME-1 + 1000.

c. CØMPUTE NAME-1 RØUNDED = NAME-1 + 500.

d. CØMPUTE NAME-1 RØUNDED = NAME-3 * 10.

e. CØMPUTE NAME-1 = NAME-2 + NAME-3 ØN SIZE ERRØR GØ TØ ER-RØR-RØUTINE.

f. CØMPUTE NAME-3 = 1.234 + 79.75 ØN SIZE ERRØR GØ TØ END-RUN.

g. CØMPUTE NAME-1 RØUNDED = NAME-3 + 500 ØN SIZE ERRØR ADD 500 TØ NAME-2.

4. In each of the following cases, what will be the contents of the data field, FIELDA, after the MOVE operation:

a. MØVE 'ABC' TO FIELDA.

b. MØVE ABC TO FIELDA.

c. MØVE 100.00 TO FIELDA.

d. MØVE 'SPACES' TO FIELDA.

e. MØVE SPACES TO FIELDA.

5. Use the following statement to complete the questions:

MØVE TAX TO TØTAL

	TAX		TOTAL	TOTAL Contents (at end of operation)
	PICTURE	CONTENTS	PICTURE	
a.	99V99	10ᴧ35	999V999	_____
b.	99V9	37ᴧ2	999	_____
c.	9(4)	1234	999	_____
d.	V99	ᴧ12	V9	_____
e.	99V99	02ᴧ34	9V9	_____
f.	9V9	1ᴧ2	_____	ᴧ20

6. Use the following statement to complete the questions:

MØVE 12.35 TO AREA-1

AREA-1

	PICTURE	Contents
a.	999V99	_____
b.	999V9	_____
c.	999V999	_____
d.	9V9	_____
e.	V999	_____
f.	_____	012ᴧ3

7. Use the following statement to complete the questions (where appropriate, use the character b to represent a blank):

MØVE FLD1 TO FLD2

	PICTURE	Contents	PICTURE	Contents
a.	X(4)	AB12	X(6)	_____
b.	X(4)	AB12	X(3)	_____
c.	XXX	ABC	_____	AB

TOP-DOWN PROGRAM DESIGN
AND STRUCTURED PROGRAMMING

In recent years, data processing personnel have been searching for ways to improve program design techniques to reduce the costs of program development and maintenance. Using traditional methods of program design, programming costs have continued to rise in relation to computer hardware and software costs. Many programmers consider programs to be a personal creation. Programmers with this viewpoint often write programs that are complex and obscure. These programs are hard for other programmers to understand. Even the original programmer may find it difficult to understand months later. Such programs are also difficult to maintain, especially if they become the responsibility of another programmer. One new approach to program design and coding that is receiving widespread attention is called top-down program design. It can provide the following benefits:

1. Program standardization is improved because program design is emphasized.
2. Programmers are more productive; they write more program instructions per day and make fewer errors.
3. Program complexity is reduced; as a result programs are easier to read, write, debug, and maintain.

TOP-DOWN PROGRAM DESIGN

Top-down program design differs from traditional methods of program design. Instead of being concerned about details through flowcharting, top-down design attempts to primarily focus on the major functional modules of a program. After these modules have been planned, the programmer can decide on the next level of modules, and so on. When this method of program design is used, many details of the solution plan can be put off until the lowest-level modules are designed.

When top-down design is used, the program flowchart is preceded by a *structure chart.* This chart, unlike a program flowchart, is designed to show the program modules and the relative importance of each of these modules. The result is that the program is shown by means of a chart as being (1) viewed as a clear and simple, straight (top-down) flow of logic, and (2) composed of a series of interconnected modules, each module being simple and clear as to its purpose. For instance, Figure A-1 shows a structure chart with one level of processing modules. This structure chart is based on the update, order-writing, and invoicing portion of a system flowchart for a tape update program.

Figure A-1. Structure chart for update, order-writing, and invoicing program.

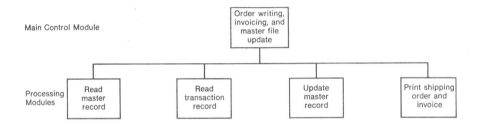

The main module controls the execution of each processing module directly below in the hierarchy. Thus, after the execution of each processing module ("Read master record" through "Print shipping order and invoice"), control returns to the main module before the next module is executed.

There can be as many levels of processing as needed in a program. Two more levels of processing modules have been added to the update, order-writing, and invoicing program in Figure A-2.

Notice that the "Update master record" module is now both a processing module and a control module; it causes the execution of the "Write new master record" module. The "Write new master record" module is also a processing and control module; it controls two processing modules directly below it. As this example suggests, a structure chart can be an effective alternative to a system flowchart when top-down program design is used.

One of the principles of top-down program design is to keep all modules *functional.* Each module should represent one program function. One way to make sure that each module does one function is to describe it by a single imperative sentence, such as, "update the records in the master file." On the structure chart itself, the programmer can describe each module

Figure A-2. Structure chart for update, order-writing, and invoicing program with three levels of processing modules

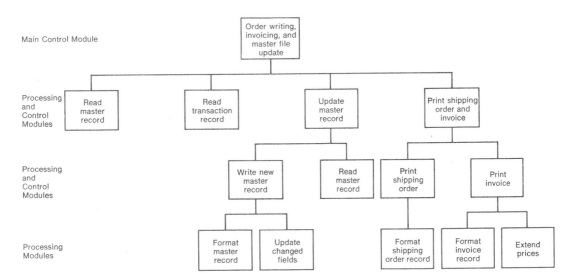

by one imperative verb, one adjective, and one noun like "update master records." In contrast to top-down program design, modules created through flowcharting techniques are often *procedural* rather than functional; that is, they are related because they are part of the same procedure.

Another principle of top-down program design is that each module should be *independent* of all modules except the one directly above it. The module should communicate only with the module above it and it should begin execution only when control is passed to it from that module. In contrast, flowcharting, with its emphasis on procedures, tends to develop modules that are not independent.

An important technique of good program design is to divide a problem into modules of manageable size. Thus, top-down program design has rules for determining module size. In general, the program designer tries to plan modules that will be no longer than 50 program statements, the number that can be printed on a single computer printout page. Experience has shwon that programs that consist of modules ranging from 30 to 50 statements can be tested and debugged more efficiently than programs made up of smaller or larger modules.

Two notions associated with top-down program design are *top-down coding* and *top-down testing*. Each module should be coded and tested independently of the rest, starting with the highest-level modules and working down. In other words, the update-master-file module (the control module) in Figure A-1 should be coded and tested first. This can be done by creating *dummy modules* for each of the four modules it controls. The dummy modules can be programmed so that they simply receive control from the control module, perhaps print a message that they have received control, and return to the control module. In the case of an input module, the dummy module might pass some dummy data back to the control module. After the control module has been tested, coding and testing can proceed by combining one of the level 1 modules with the control module.

One advantage of top-down coding and testing is that testing proceeds in an orderly fashion. Modules are added to the control module one at a time. If a bug is detected during testing, it is easy to isolate the erroneous module. In contrast, the traditional method of testing a program in its entirety gives few or no clues to the location of a bug. When a large program, perhaps containing hundreds of bugs, must be tested, the programmer faces the inefficient process of analyzing the entire program to determine the cause of each bug.

HIPO DIAGRAMS

Traditionally, the program flowchart has been one of the primary pieces of program documentation. When top-down program design is used, however, there is a movement away from program flowcharting. Why? Because it has been found in many cases that flowcharting has not proved to be effective for program coding and documentation. Therefore, many programmers do not see the value of flowcharting a program completely before they begin coding it. As a result, the program is written and debugged before the final flowcharts are prepared. Also, once the program is complete, the programmer is often in a rush to start the next programming assignment. Thus, flowcharts are likely to be done hastily. This can result in flowcharts that are inaccurate for documentation purposes.

When top-down program design is used, the structure chart is the overall guide to design and documentation. After the structure chart is prepared, each of the identified modules must be further documented before coding begins. Although a program flowchart can be used for this purpose, several other documentation techniques are being tried.

One of these documentation techniques is illustrated in Figure A-3. It is a HIPO (Hierarchy plus Input-Process-Output) diagram for the update-master-records module in Figure A-2. A HIPO diagram can be used as both a program design aid and the documentation for a completed program. A complete HIPO package includes diagrams that graphically describe each program module, from the general to the detail level. The number of levels of HIPO diagrams that must be prepared for an application depends on its complexity. When HIPO is used together with a structure chart, the structure chart is called a *visual table of contents*. An *overview* diagram like the one in Figure A-3 is prepared for each module shown in the visual table of contents.

Figure A-3. HIPO diagram for "Update master record" module

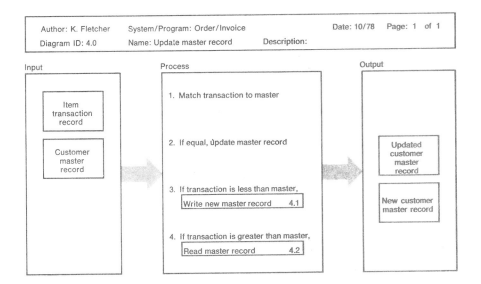

The diagram shows the inputs, outputs, and processing for a module. If the module passes control to a lower level during its processing, so that it can perform a certain processing step (function), that step is boxed in the "Process" portion of the diagram. (See steps 3 and 4 in Figure A-3. Note that the referenced modules are identified as lower-level modules to this module in Figure A-2.) *Detail diagrams* are prepared as necessary to further describe the modules shown in the visual table of contents. The complete HIPO package is the basis for coding the program and is also the final documentation of the program.

Thus, HIPO documentation can serve the manager who needs an overview of a program, other designers and programmers who are responsible for related programs, and programmers who must locate specific functions in the program so they can be changed.

STRUCTURED PROGRAMMING

Another programming method that is being widely discussed is called structured programming. This approach (1) facilitates program development, (2) improves program clarity—the ease with which a person unfamiliar with the program, including possibly the original programmer, can read the code and determine what is occurring, and (3) simplifies t] rpgram debugging.

A structured program is written using only three basic control structures (logical modules (sections or paragraphs) of code, each module being composed of a maximum of 50 program statements): (1) sequence, (2)

selection, and (3) iteration. A characteristic of each of these structures is *single* entry and exit points. *This is accomplished by having each section or paragraph executed via the PERFØRM statement.* This characteristic results in a program being simple because there is no branching (forward or backward) to other modules of code—control flows from top to bottom.

Sequence Structure

The *sequence structure* is simply the idea that program statements are executed in the order in which they are written. In flowchart form, the sequence structure is represented as follows:

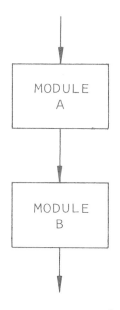

The sequence structure (DO)

As indicated in the flowchart, there is no branching in sequence structuring. One of the objectives of structured programming is to minimize the use of the GØ TØ statement. The reason for this objective is that branching may cause the programmer difficulty when debugging or revising the program. The sequence structure is represented by one or more READ, WRITE, MØVE, ADD, SUBTRACT, MULTIPLY, DIVIDE or CØMPUTE statements.

Selection Structure

The *selection structure* is a choice between two program paths based on a true or false condition. In flowchart form, the selection structure is represented as follows:

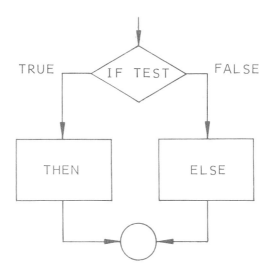

The selection structure (IF-THEN-ELSE)

This structure is often referred to as the IF-THEN-ELSE structure. The selection structure is represented in COBOL by the IF statement.

Iteration Structure

The *iteration structure* provides for performing a module *until* a condition is true. When the condition is true, the program continues with the next structure. In flowchart form, the iteration structure is represented as follows:

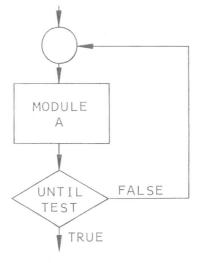

The iteration structure (DO-UNTIL)

The iteration structure is often referred to as the DO-UNTIL structure and is represented in COBOL by the PERFØRM UNTIL statement.

CASE Structure

The IF-THEN-ELSE structure is convenient when there are only two alternatives to test. When there are three or more alternatives to test, a *variation* of the IF-THEN-ELSE structure, the CASE structure, should be used. In flowchart form, the structure is represented as follows:

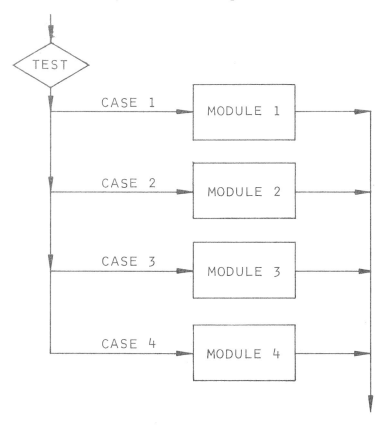

The CASE structure is represented in COBOL by the nested IF statement.

SUMMARY

A disciplined approach to programming has been discussed in this module. As already illustrated in Figures 2-2 and A-6, this text uses the structured programming method. When writing the PRØCEDURE DIVISIØN, the program design and coding rules followed are

1. A program is divided into modules. Each module consists of a paragraph (or section of paragraphs) which performs a single function in the program.

2.   There is a hierarchy of modules. The first level is the control module, which directs the execution of second-level modules. Second-level modules invoke third-level modules, etc.

3.   Each module (paragraph or section) has one entry point and one exit point.

4.   There is very restricted use of the GØ TØ statement.

5.   Rules for indentation and comments are followed to aid in clarity of documentation:

   (a)   Each new sentence begins on a new line. Unless other indentation applies, a sentence begins at the B margin (column 12).

   (b)   Sentences are broken up into statements, each placed on a separate line to enhance the clarity of the code. All lines belonging to a sentence (after the first) are indented. Therefore, if the first line of a sentence starts at the B margin, the second line would start at column 16.

   (c)   Statements within the range of an IF statement are indented beyond the indentation of the word IF.

   (d)   Comments (an asterisk or slash in column 7) are used to document the purpose and relationship of program sections and paragraphs. For example, a blank comment card (asterisk in column 7 and rest of card blank) can be used before each paragraph to highlight the new module visually in the program listing. Another comment line might explain the purpose of the paragraph if it is not evident from the code.

A COMPLETE COBOL PROGRAM

The four divisions of the program in Figure A-6 have served as the basis for many of the illustrations of each of the divisions discussed in Chapters 3,4,5, and 6. The author recommends that the reader execute this program and use it as a basis for writing additional COBOL programs.

The PERFØRM statement is used in the program. The reader must understand the use of this statement before the sequence of execution of the statements can be understood. Thus, please read the discussion of this statement at this time.

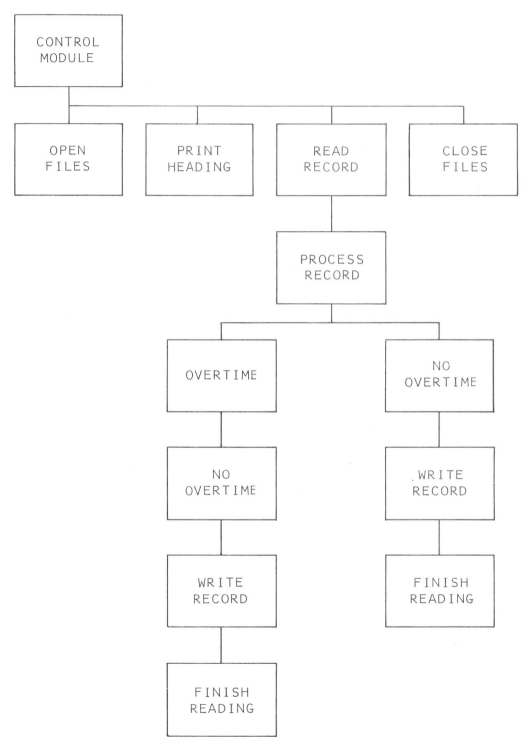

Figure A-4: Structure chart for the following COBOL program.

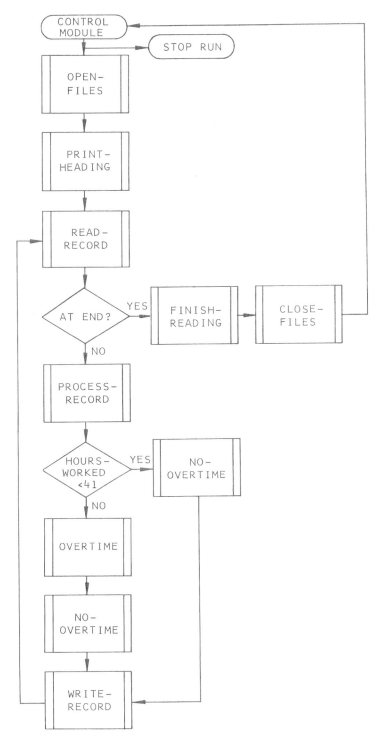

Figure A-5: Modular and detailed program flowcharts for each of the modules in the following cobol program.

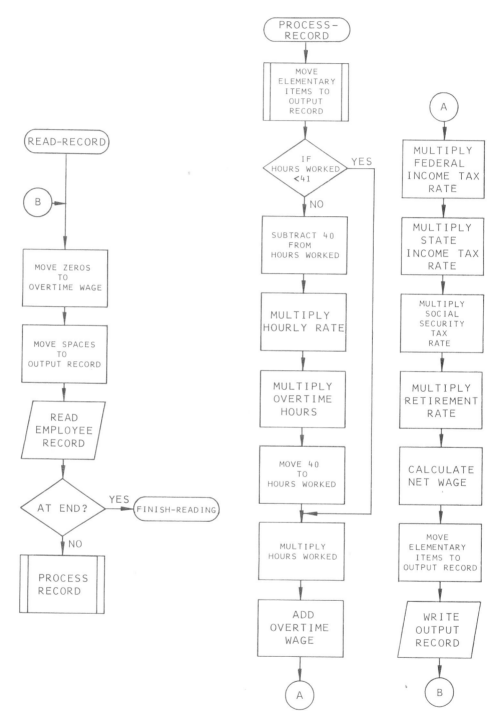

Figure A-5: Detailed program flowcharts for each of the modules in the following
COBOL program (continued)

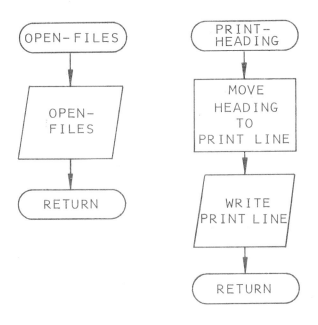

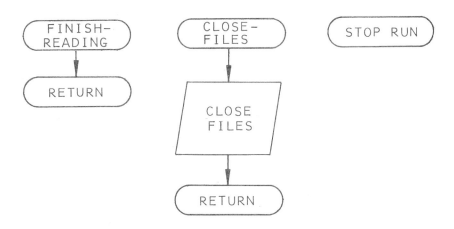

Figure A-5: Detailed program flowcharts for each of the modules in the following COBOL program (continued)

COBOL Coding Form

IBM

GX28-1464-5 U/M 050*
Printed in U.S.A.

SYSTEM	IBM-370-148			PAGE 001 OF 001
PROGRAM	EMPLOYEE WAGES	PUNCHING INSTRUCTIONS		
PROGRAMMER	V. THOMAS DOCK	GRAPHIC		CARD FORM #
	DATE	PUNCH		

```
SEQUENCE  CONT  A   B                    COBOL STATEMENT

01        IDENTIFICATION DIVISION.
02        PROGRAM-ID. WAGES.
03        AUTHOR. V. THOMAS DOCK.
04        INSTALLATION. THE XYZ COMPUTER CENTER.
05        DATE-WRITTEN. 6/1/77.
06        DATE-COMPILED.
07        SECURITY. THIS PROGRAM SHOULD NOT LEAVE THE COMPUTER CENTER.
08     *  THIS PROGRAM CALCULATES THE WEEKLY WAGES OF THE EMPLOYEES OF
09     *  XYZ COMPANY.
10        ENVIRONMENT DIVISION.
11        CONFIGURATION SECTION.
12        SOURCE-COMPUTER. IBM-370-148.
13        OBJECT-COMPUTER. IBM-370-148.
14        INPUT-OUTPUT SECTION.
15        FILE-CONTROL.
16        SELECT EMPLOYEE-RECORDS-FILE ASSIGN TO UR-2540R-S-CARDIN.
17        SELECT EMPLOYEE-PAYROLL-FILE ASSIGN TO UR-1403-S-PROUT.
18
19
20
```

IDENTIFICATION

*A standard card form, IBM Electro C61897, is available for punching source statements from this form. Instructions for using this form are given in any IBM COBOL reference manual. Address comments concerning this form to IBM Corporation, LDS Publishing, Dept. J04, 1501 California Ave., Palo Alto, Ca. 94304

*No. of forms per pad may vary slightly

Figure A-6: A COBOL Program

IBM

COBOL Coding Form

GX28-1464-5 U/M 050*
Printed in U.S.A.

SYSTEM	IBM-370-148
PROGRAM	EMPLOYEE WAGES
PROGRAMMER	V. THOMAS DOCK	DATE

PUNCHING INSTRUCTIONS

| GRAPHIC | | PUNCH | |

PAGE 0020F0C7

CARD FORM #

*

SEQUENCE			COBOL STATEMENT	IDENTIFICATION

```
01  DATA DIVISION.
02  FILE SECTION.
03  FD  EMPLOYEE-RECORDS-FILE
04      LABEL RECORD IS OMITTED.
05  01  CARD-RECORD.
06      02  EMPLOYEE-NAME         PICTURE A(15).
07      02  FILLER                PICTURE X(4).
08      02  HOURS-WORKED          PICTURE 99.
09      02  FILLER                PICTURE XXXX.
10      02  HOURLY-RATE           PICTURE 9V99.
11      02  FILLER                PICTURE X(53).
12  FD  EMPLOYEE-PAYROLL-FILE
13      LABEL RECORD IS OMITTED.
14  01  PAYROLL-RECORD.
15      02  FILLER                PICTURE X.
16      02  EMPLOYEE-NAME         PICTURE A(15).
17      02  FILLER                PICTURE X(6).
18      02  HOURS-WORK            PICTURE 99.
19      02  FILLER                PICTURE X(8).
20      02  GROSS-WAGE-OUT        PICTURE $9.99.
21      02  HOUR-RATE             PICTURE X(8).
22      02  GROSS-WAGE-OUT        PICTURE $$9.99.
23      02  FILLER                PICTURE X(11).
24      02  FEDERAL-INCOME-TAX-OUT PICTURE $$9.99.
```

*A standard card form, IBM Electro C61897, is available for punching source statements from this form. Instructions for using this form are given in any IBM COBOL reference manual. Address comments concerning this form to IBM Corporation, LDS Publishing, Dept. J04, 1501 California Ave., Palo Alto, Ca. 94304

*No. of forms per pad may vary slightly

COBOL Coding Form

GX28-1464-5 U/M 050*
Printed in U.S.A.

SYSTEM	IBM-370-148			PUNCHING INSTRUCTIONS	PAGE 003 0F 007
PROGRAM	EMPLOYEE WAGES			GRAPHIC	CARD FORM # *
PROGRAMMER	V. THOMAS DUCK	DATE		PUNCH	

IDENTIFICATION

```
01   02 FILLER                    PICTURE X(13).
02   02 STATE-INCOME-TAX-OUT      PICTURE $$9.99.
03   02 FILLER                    PICTURE X(12).
04   02 SOCIAL-SECURITY-TAX-OUT   PICTURE $$9.99.
05   02 FILLER                    PICTURE X(9).
06   02 RETIREMENT-OUT            PICTURE $9.99.
07   02 FILLER                    PICTURE X(3).
08   02 NET-WAGE-OUT              PICTURE $$99.99.
09   02 FILLER                    PICTURE X(13).
10 01 PRINT-LINE
11    WORKING-STORAGE SECTION.
12 77 GROSS-WAGE                  PICTURE 999.99.
13 77 OVERTIME-HOURS             PICTURE 99.
14 77 OVERTIME-RATE              PICTURE 999V99.
15 77 OVERTIME-WAGE              PICTURE 999V99.
16 77 FED-INCOME-TAX-RATE        PICTURE V999   VALUE .25.
17 77 FEDERAL-INCOME-TAX         PICTURE 99V99.
18 77 ST-INCOME-TAX-RATE         PICTURE V999   VALUE .06.
19 77 STATE-INCOME-TAX           PICTURE 99V99.
20 77 SOC-SECURITY-TAX-RATE      PICTURE V9999  VALUE .0585.
21 77 SOCIAL-SECURITY-TAX        PICTURE 99V99.
22 77 RETIREMENT-RATE            PICTURE V99    VALUE .06.
23 77 RETIREMENT                 PICTURE 99V99.
24 77 MORE-DATA-CARDS            PICTURE AA     VALUE SPACES.
```

*A standard card form, IBM Electro C61897, is available for punching source statements from this form. Instructions for using this form are given in any IBM COBOL reference manual. Address comments concerning this form to IBM Corporation, LDS Publishing, Dept. J04, 1501 California Ave., Palo Alto, Ca. 94304

*No. of forms per pad may vary slightly

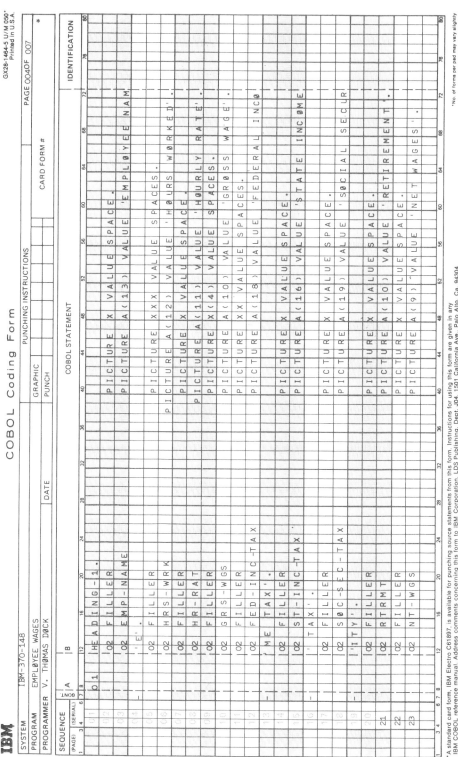

COBOL Coding Form

SYSTEM: IBM-370-148
PROGRAM: EMPLOYEE WAGES
PROGRAMMER: V. THOMAS DOCK
PAGE 0040F 007

```
01  HEADING-1.
    02  FILLER        PICTURE X     VALUE SPACE.
    02  EMP-NAME      PICTURE A(13) VALUE 'EMPLOYEE NAM
E'.
    02  FILLER        PICTURE XXX   VALUE SPACES.
    02  HRS-WRK       PICTURE A(12) VALUE 'HOURS WORKED'.
    02  FILLER        PICTURE X     VALUE SPACE.
    02  HR-RAT        PICTURE A(11) VALUE 'HOURLY RATE'.
    02  FILLER        PICTURE X(4)  VALUE SPACES.
    02  GRS-WGS       PICTURE A(10) VALUE 'GROSS WAGE'.
    02  FILLER        PICTURE XXX   VALUE SPACES.
    02  FED-INC-TAX   PICTURE A(18) VALUE 'FEDERAL INCO
ME'.
    02  FILLER        PICTURE X     VALUE SPACE.
    02  ST-INC-TAX    PICTURE A(16) VALUE 'STATE INCOME'.
    02  FILLER        PICTURE X     VALUE SPACE.
    02  SOC-SEC-TAX   PICTURE A(19) VALUE 'SOCIAL SECUR
ITY'.
    02  FILLER        PICTURE X     VALUE SPACE.
    02  RTRMT         PICTURE A(10) VALUE 'RETIREMENT'.
    02  FILLER        PICTURE X     VALUE SPACE.
    02  NT-WGS        PICTURE A(9)  VALUE 'NET WAGES'.
```

GX28-1464-5 U/M 050*
Printed in U.S.A.

*A standard card form, IBM Electro C61897, is available for punching source statements from this form. Instructions for using this form are given in any IBM COBOL reference manual. Address comments concerning this form to IBM Corporation, LDS Publishing, Dept. J04, 1501 California Ave., Palo Alto, Ca. 94304

*No. of forms per pad may vary slightly

COBOL Coding Form

GX28-1464-5 U/M 050*
Printed in U.S.A.

SYSTEM	IBM-370-148				PAGE 005 OF 007
PROGRAM	EMPLOYEE WAGES	PUNCHING INSTRUCTIONS			
PROGRAMMER	V. THOMAS DOCK	GRAPHIC		CARD FORM #	*
	DATE	PUNCH			

SEQUENCE (PAGE) (SERIAL)	CONT	A	B	COBOL STATEMENT	IDENTIFICATION
01		PROCEDURE DIVISION.			
02	*				
03		CONTROL-MODULE.			
04		PERFORM OPEN-FILES.			
05		PERFORM PRINT-HEADING.			
06		PERFORM READ-RECORD THRU FINISH-READING			
07		UNTIL MORE-DATA-CARDS EQUAL 'NO'.			
08		PERFORM CLOSE-FILES.			
09		STOP RUN.			
10	*				
11		OPEN-FILES.			
12		OPEN INPUT EMPLOYEE-RECORDS-FILE			
13		OUTPUT EMPLOYEE-PAYROLL-FILE.			
14	*				
15		PRINT-HEADING.			
16		MOVE HEADING-1 TO PRINT-LINE.			
17		WRITE PRINT-LINE AFTER ADVANCING PAGE.			
18	*				
19		READ-RECORD.			
20		MOVE ZEROS TO OVERTIME-WAGE.			

*A standard card form, IBM Electro C61897, is available for punching source statements from this form. Instructions for using this form are given in any IBM COBOL reference manual. Address comments concerning this form to IBM Corporation, LDS Publishing, Dept. J04, 1501 California Ave., Palo Alto, Ca. 94304

*No. of forms per pad may vary slightly

COBOL Coding Form

GX28-1464-5 U/M 050*
Printed in U.S.A.

SYSTEM	IBM-370-148
PROGRAM	EMPLOYEE WAGES
PROGRAMMER	V. THOMAS DOCK

PUNCHING INSTRUCTIONS — GRAPHIC / PUNCH — CARD FORM #

PAGE 006 OF 007 *

IDENTIFICATION

```
01        MOVE SPACES TO PAYROLL-RECORD.
02        READ EMPLOYEE-RECORDS-FILE AT END
03          MOVE 'NO' TO MORE-DATA-CARDS, GO TO FINISH-READING.
04  *
05    PROCESS-RECORD.
06        MOVE EMPLOYEE-NAME TO EMPLOYEE-NAM.
07        MOVE HOURS-WORKED TO HOURS-WORK.
08        MOVE HOURLY-RATE TO HOUR-RATE.
09        IF HOURS-WORKED LESS THAN 41 GO TO NO-OVERTIME.
10  * OVERTIME.
11        SUBTRACT 40 FROM HOURS-WORKED GIVING OVERTIME-HOURS.
12        MULTIPLY HOURLY-RATE BY 1.5 GIVING OVERTIME-HOURS.
13        MULTIPLY OVERTIME-HOURS BY OVERTIME-RATE GIVING
14          OVERTIME-WAGE.
15
16        MOVE 40 TO HOURS-WORKED.
17  * NO-OVERTIME.
18        MULTIPLY HOURS-WORKED BY HOURLY-RATE GIVING GROSS-WAGE.
19        ADD OVERTIME-WAGE TO GROSS-WAGE.
20
```

*A standard card form, IBM Electro C61897, is available for punching source statements from this form. Instructions for using this form are given in any IBM COBOL reference manual. Address comments concerning this form to IBM Corporation, LDS Publishing, Dept. J04, 1501 California Ave., Palo Alto, Ca. 94304

*No. of forms per pad may vary slightly

COBOL Coding Form

SYSTEM	IBM-370-148
PROGRAM	EMPLOYEE WAGES
PROGRAMMER	V. THOMAS DUCK

PUNCHING INSTRUCTIONS — GRAPHIC / PUNCH — DATE

PAGE 007 OF 007   CARD FORM #

GX28-1464-5 U/M 050*
Printed in U.S.A.

```
01   MULTIPLY FED-INCOME-TAX-RATE BY GROSS-WAGE GIVING
02       FEDERAL-INCOME-TAX.
03   MULTIPLY STATE-INCOME-TAX-RATE BY GROSS-WAGE GIVING
04       STATE-INCOME-TAX.
05   MULTIPLY SOC-SECURITY-TAX-RATE BY GROSS-WAGE GIVING
06       SOCIAL-SECURITY-TAX.
07   MULTIPLY RETIREMENT-RATE BY GROSS-WAGE GIVING RETIREMENT.
08 - SUBTRACT FEDERAL-INCOME-TAX, STATE-INCOME-TAX, SOCIAL-SECURIT
09   Y-TAX, RETIREMENT FROM GROSS-WAGE GIVING NET-WAGE-OUT.
10   MOVE GROSS-WAGE TO GROSS-WAGE-OUT.
11   MOVE FEDERAL-INCOME-TAX TO FEDERAL-INCOME-TAX-OUT.
12   MOVE STATE-INCOME-TAX TO STATE-INCOME-TAX-OUT.
13   MOVE SOCIAL-SECURITY-TAX TO SOCIAL-SECURITY-TAX-OUT.
14   MOVE RETIREMENT TO RETIREMENT-OUT.
15
16 * WRITE-RECORD.
17   WRITE PAYROLL-RECORD AFTER ADVANCING 2 LINES.
18 * FINISH-READING.
19   EXIT.
20 * CLOSE-FILES.
21   CLOSE EMPLOYEE-RECORDS-FILE, EMPLOYEE-PAYROLL-FILE.
22
23
```

7

AN ADVANCED CONTROL STATEMENT
AND TABLE HANDLING

The control statements generally used in a program were discussed in the previous chapter. In certain situations, however, it is desirable to control the execution of the program in a manner not capable via the fundamental control statements already discussed. An advanced control statement, the PERFØRM statement, is capable of more complicated branching and control of the execution of the program.

In certain instances, it is necessary to similarly process by means of the computer several related numbers. In such situations, it is desirable both to reflect in a program the fact that these numbers are related and to retain each number's identity for processing purposes. In COBOL, a table is the means through which this can be accomplished. The PERFØRM statement is frequently used to process a table, and it is for this reason that these two topics are presented in the same chapter.

THE PERFORM STATEMENT

The PERFØRM statement is used to branch to a series of statements in order to execute them either a specified number of times or until a predetermined condition is satisfied. After the statement or statements are executed, the program always branches back to the statement immediately following the PERFØRM statement.

There are four basic versions of the PERFØRM statement. In each of the versions, the program branches to the section or paragraph name desig-

107

nated in the statement, which may be located in the program either prior to or after the PERFØRM statement. The statements composing that section or paragraph through the statements composing the second section or paragraph, if designated, are executed. The computer then returns to the statement immediately following the PERFØRM statement. The following is a discussion of each of these versions:

Version 1: The Basic PERFORM Statement

The general format of the fundamental version of the PERFØRM statement is

$$\underline{PERF\text{Ø}RM} \quad \begin{Bmatrix} \text{section-name-1} \\ \text{paragraph-name-1} \end{Bmatrix} \quad \begin{bmatrix} \underline{THRU} & \begin{Bmatrix} \text{section-name-2} \\ \text{paragraph-name-2} \end{Bmatrix} \end{bmatrix}$$

When the PERFØRM statement is executed, the computer branches to the section or paragraph name representing either section-name-1 or paragraph-name-1, respectively. The computer then executes the statements in the section or paragraph. If the THRU option is designated, the computer will execute from either section-name-1 or paragraph-name-1 through either section-name-2 or paragraph-name-2. There can be one or more sections or paragraphs located between the two sections and/or paragraph names designated in the PERFØRM statement.

The "range" of a PERFØRM statement is the statements in the section or paragraph name and, if present, through the second section or paragraph name designated in the statement. The computer will execute the statements once and then return to the statement immediately following the PERFØRM statement.

Illustration 1. If the following PERFØRM statement were executed,

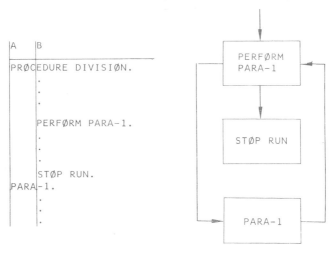

the computer would branch to PARA-1 and execute the statements composing it one time. It would then return to the statement immediately following the PERFØRM statement. The range of this PERFØRM statement is the statements composing PARA-1.

Illustration 2. If the following PERFØRM statement were executed,

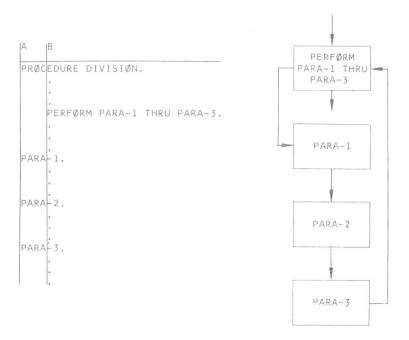

the computer would branch to PARA-1 and execute the statements composing it through the statements composing PARA-3 one time. It would then return to the statement immediately following the PERFØRM statement. The range of this PERFØRM statement is the statements composing PARA-1 through the statements composing PARA-3.

This version of the PERFØRM statement is quite useful when one or more relatively small program subdivisions must be written, but the programmer does not want to place them at the logical execution point in the program. As with all four versions of the PERFØRM statement, the statement serves as the "bridge" between the location in the program where they should be logically located and where they are actually located in the program.

Version 2: The PERFORM n TIMES Statement

This version of the PERFØRM statement differs from the first version in that the statements executed as a result of a branch from the PERFØRM statement are executed several times, while in the first version they are executed only once. The general form of this version of the PERFØRM statement is

$$\underline{PERFØRM} \quad \begin{Bmatrix} \text{section-name-1} \\ \text{paragraph-name-1} \end{Bmatrix} \quad \begin{bmatrix} \underline{THRU} & \begin{Bmatrix} \text{section-name-2} \\ \text{paragraph-name-2} \end{Bmatrix} \end{bmatrix}$$

$$\begin{Bmatrix} \text{integer-1} \\ \text{name-1} \end{Bmatrix} \quad \underline{TIMES}$$

If a name is used, it must be described in either the FILE SECTIØN or WØRKING-STØRAGE SECTIØN of the DATA DIVISIØN. Also, it must represent an unsigned integer. If a literal is specified, it too must be an unsigned integer. In either instance, the computer will execute the statements the specified number of times prior to returning to the statement immediately following the PERFØRM statement.

Illustration 1. If the following PERFØRM statement were executed,

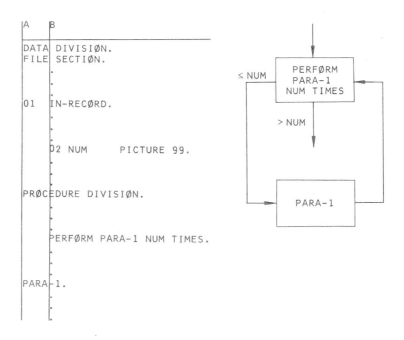

the computer will execute the statements in PARA-1 the number of times designated by the value stored under the name NUM.

Illustration 2. If the following PERF∅RM statement were executed,

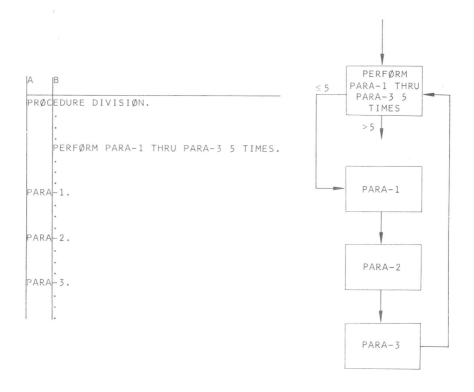

the computer would execute the statements in PARA-1 through the statements composing PARA-3 five times.

Version 3: The PERFORM UNTIL Statement

The general format of the third version of the PERF∅RM statement is

$$\underline{PERF\text{∅}RM} \quad \begin{Bmatrix} \text{section-name-1} \\ \text{paragraph-name-1} \end{Bmatrix} \begin{bmatrix} \underline{THRU} & \begin{Bmatrix} \text{section-name-2} \\ \text{paragraph-name-2} \end{Bmatrix} \end{bmatrix}$$
$$\underline{UNTIL} \quad \text{condition-1}$$

This version permits the programmer to specify a condition, chosen from among the "General Conditional Statements" discussed in Chapter 6, to be fulfilled. The PERF∅RM statement tests the specified conditional and, if it is false, causes the computer to branch to the designated section or paragraph name. After the statements have been executed once, the PERF∅RM statement again tests the specified conditional. If the conditional is still false, the statements are executed another time. This process continues until the test is true, at which time the computer branches to the statement immediately following the PERFØRM statement instead of the statements in the PERFØRM's range. Thus, the range of the PER-FØRM statement is, in this version of the statement, the *false* branch of the conditional, whereas the true branch is the main program

The fact that the condition is tested *prior* to the computer's executing the statements and the range of this version of the PERFØRM is the false branch enhances the need for the programmer to check to be sure that the desired number of iterations through the range are made. To illustrate this need, assume that the following PERFØRM statement is used to control one iteration of the statements in its range:

```
MØVE 1 TØ CØUNTER.
PERFØRM PARA-1 UNTIL CØUNTER EQUAL 1.
```

Since CØUNTER has the value 1 stored under it and the test to determine if the condition is true or false is made prior to the statements in the PERFØRM's range are executed, the statements will not be executed at all. Rather, the test will be true, and the computer will execute the statement immediately following the PERFØRM statement. For the statements in the PERFØRM's range to be executed, either zero must be moved to CØUNTER or the PERFØRM statement must be written as follows (assuming that a value of 1 is added to CØUNTER during each iteration of PARA-1):

```
PERFØRM PARA-1 UNTIL CØUNTER GREATER THAN 1.
```

If either change is made, the statements in the PERFØRM's range will be executed one time.

Illustration 1. If the following **PERFØRM** statement were executed,

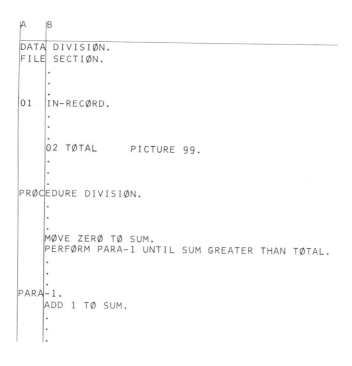

```
A    B
DATA DIVISIØN.
FILE SECTIØN.
     .
     .
     .
01   IN-RECØRD.
     .
     .
     02 TØTAL     PICTURE 99.
     .
     .
PRØCEDURE DIVISIØN.
     .
     .
     .
     MØVE ZERØ TØ SUM.
     PERFØRM PARA-1 UNTIL SUM GREATER THAN TØTAL.
     .
     .
     .
PARA-1.
     ADD 1 TØ SUM.
     .
     .
```

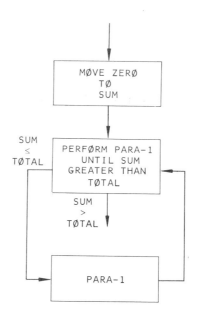

the computer would execute the statements in PARA-1 until the contents of SUM are greater than the contents of TØTAL.

Illustration 2. If the following PERFØRM statement were executed,

```
A  |B
DATA DIVISIØN.
FILE SECTIØN.
     .
     .
     .
01   IN-RECØRD.
     .
     .
     02 NUMBER      PICTURE 99.
     .
     .
PRØCEDURE DIVISIØN.
     .
     .
     .
     MØVE ZERØ TØ CØUNTER.
     PERFØRM PARA-1 THRU PARA-3 UNTIL CØUNTER EQUAL NUMBER.
     .
     .
PARA-1.
     .
     .
PARA-2.
     .
     .
PARA-3.
     ADD 1 TØ CØUNTER.
     .
     .
```

the computer would execute the statements in PARA-1 through the statements in PARA-3 until the contents of CØUNTER equaled the contents of NUMBER.

If desired, version 3 of the PERFØRM statement can be used in place of version 2. In such a situation, condition-1 would, in effect, be a counter that would be incremented until the desired number of iterations of execution of the statements has been achieved. For example, the statement in Illustration 2 above could have been written:

PERFØRM PARA-1 THRU PARA-3 UNTIL CØUNTER EQUAL 10.

The computer will cyclically execute the statements until the contents of CØUNTER equal 10. Generally, however, it is easier to use version 2 when the statements within the range of the PERFØRM statement are to be executed a predetermined number of times. Version 3 should be used primarily when the number of iterations necessary to satisfy a condition cannot be predetermined.

Version 4: The PERFORM VARYING Statement

The last and most powerful version of the PERFØRM statement incorporates the ability to vary the value of a name with the testing abilities of version 3. The general format of the statement is

$$\underline{PERF\emptyset RM} \quad \begin{Bmatrix} \text{section-name-1} \\ \text{paragraph-name-1} \end{Bmatrix} \quad \begin{bmatrix} \underline{THRU} & \begin{Bmatrix} \text{section-name-2} \\ \text{paragraph-name-2} \end{Bmatrix} \end{bmatrix} \quad \underline{VARYING} \text{ name-1}$$

$$\underline{FR\emptyset M} \quad \begin{Bmatrix} \text{numeric-} \\ \text{literal-1} \\ \text{name-2} \end{Bmatrix} \quad \underline{BY} \quad \begin{Bmatrix} \text{numeric-} \\ \text{literal-2} \\ \text{name-3} \end{Bmatrix} \quad \underline{UNTIL} \text{ condition-1}$$

In this statement, an elementary item (name-1) is varied from its initially designated value (numeric-literal-1 or name-2) by a specified increment (numeric-literal-2 or name-3) until a specified condition (condition-1) is attained. The name must be numeric computational. The initial value of the elementary item (numeric-literal-1 or name-2) must be an unsigned integer. Numeric-literal-2 or name-3 can be either positive or negative, integer or fractional.

Similar to version 3 of the PERFØRM statement, the range of the statement is executed until the specified condition is attained. This condition may involve data either controlled by the VARYING option or, like version 3 of the statement, independent of the rest of the statement.

Illustration 1. If the following PERFØRM statement were executed,

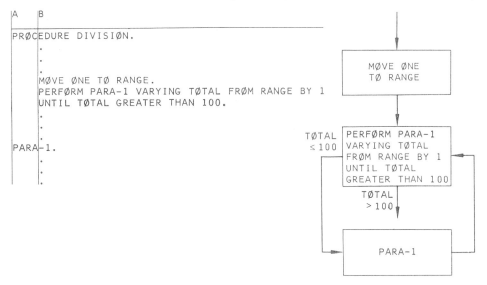

the computer would execute the statements in PARA-1 until the contents of TØTAL are greater than 100. Prior to each iteration of the statements, the contents of TØTAL are incremented by 1, and a test is made to determine if the condition is true of false. Similar to version 3 of the statement, if the test is false, the statements in the range (PARA-1) are executed. If the test is true, the statement immediately following the PERFØRM statement is executed instead of the statements in the PER-FØRM's range.

Illustration 2. If the following PERFØRM statement were executed,

```
A    B
DATA DIVISIØN.
FILE SECTIØN.
     .
     .
     .
01  IN-RECØRD.
     .
     .
     .
    02 NUMBER     PICTURE 99.
     .
     .
     .
PRØCEDURE DIVISIØN.
     .
     .
     .
    PERFØRM PARA-1 THRU PARA-3 VARYING CØUNTER FRØM 0
    BY 3 UNTIL CØUNTER EQUAL NUMBER.
     .
     .
PARA-1.
     .
     .
PARA-2.
     .
     .
PARA-3.
     .
     .
```

CØUNT ≠ NUMBER

PERFØRM PARA-1 THUR PARA-3 VARYING CØUNT FRØM 0 BY 3 UNTIL CØUNTER EQUAL NUMBER

CØUNTER = NUMBER

PARA-1

PARA-2

PARA-3

the computer would execute the statements in PARA-1 through PARA-3 until the contents of CØUNTER equaled the contents of NUMBER. Prior to each iteration of the statements, the contents of CØUNTER are incremented by 3, and a test is made to determine if the condition is true or false.

COMMON CHARACTERISTICS OF THE PERFORM STATEMENT

All four versions of the PERFØRM statement have certain common characteristics unique to this statement. These are

1. A transfer can be made outside a PERFØRM's range during execution of the statements within that range. For example, an IF statement within the range could have as either its true or false branch a statement that transfers control to statements located outside the PERFØRM's range. If desirable, reentry to the PERFØRM's range is possible.

The value of any index maintained in the PERFØRM's range is available for use outside the range, whether the range was left either because of branching or because execution of the PERFØRM's range was completed. For example, if a certain condition is to be attained before the PERFØRM's range can be left, an index can be established within the range to indicate the iteration on which the condition is attained. The following is an illustration of this characteristic:

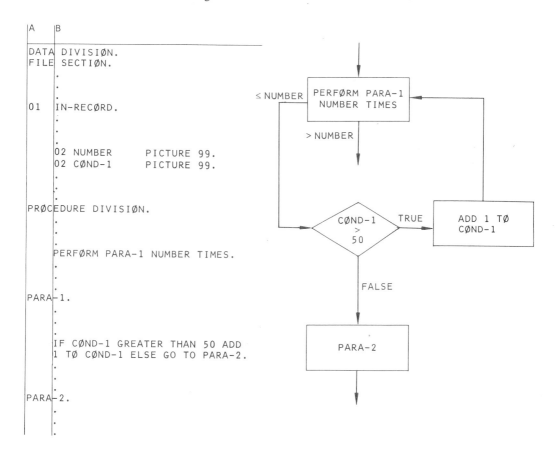

2. The range of a PERFØRM statement ends with the last statement in either the section or paragraph name specified as section-name-1 or paragraph-name-1 or, if present, section-name-2 or paragraph-name-2. The PERFØRM statement controls execution of the statements within its range. Thus, the last statement should not be a GØ TØ statement unless it is desired to break the PERFØRM's control of execution of the program, as control would be transferred to a statement outside the PERFØRM's range.

If a PERFØRM's range contains several branches, they must be rejoined prior to the last statement in the range being executed. However, in certain instances the logical execution of the program prevents the recombining of several branches. For example, the program may proceed along two mutually exclusive paths. In such a situation, a separate paragraph can be created that contains only the statement EXIT, and each branch is transferred to this paragraph. The general format of this paragraph is

paragraph-name. *EXIT.*

This paragraph is mentioned as paragraph-name-2 in the PERFØRM statement and thus is the last statement in the PERFØRM's range. The following is an illustration of this characteristic:

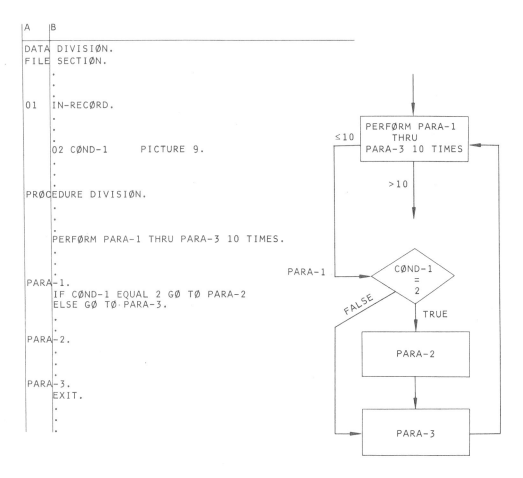

3. Several PERFØRM statements can be used in a program. If appropriate, several of them can refer to the same section(s) and/or paragraph(s). In each instance, the particular PERFØRM referencing the range will control execution of the statements, and when execution of them is completed, control will be returned to the statement

immediately following the referencing PERFØRM statement. The following is an illustration of this characteristic:

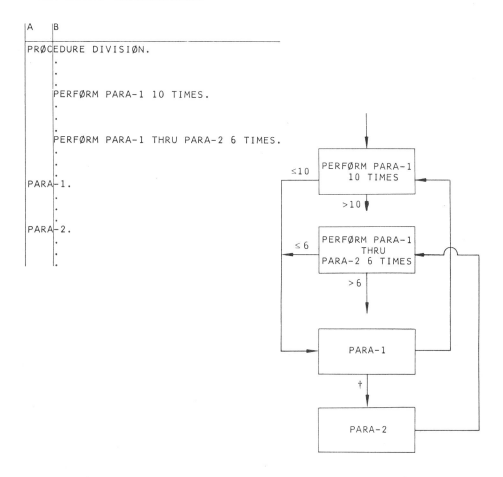

4. A PERFØRM statement can include in its range one or more PERFØRM statements. When this occurs, each inner PERFØRM statement is said to be "nested" in the next outer PERFØRM statement.

The following three rules must be observed when one is using nested PERFØRM statements:

a. The range of each PERFØRM statement must terminate with a different section or paragraph name.

b. An embedded PERFØRM statement must have its range either totally inside or totally outside the range of each of its outer PERFØRM statement. That is, the statement in the range of a PERFØRM statement cannot be continued within the range of the next embedded PERFØRM statement. The following is an illustration of this characteristic:

---

†Executed only when second PERFØRM has control of execution.

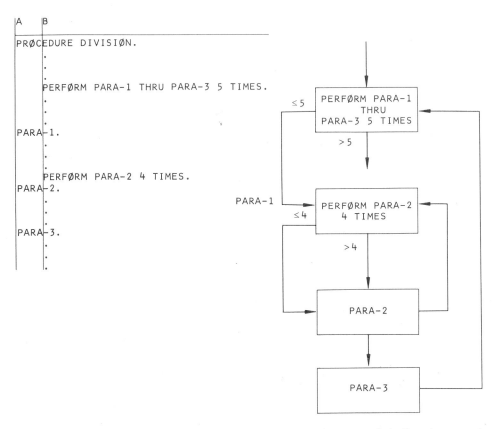

c. The ranges of two PERFØRM statements can overlap, provided that the second PERFØRM statement is not located within the range of the first PERFØRM statement.

Although the ability to nest PERFØRM statements provides the programmer with great execution capability and flexibility, it is complicated and thus should be carefully used.

TABLE HANDLING

In certain instances, it is necessary to similarly process several related numbers. In such situations, it is desirable to reflect in a program the fact that these numbers are related and to simultaneously retain each number's identity in the computer's memory for processing purposes. In COBOL, a table is the means through which this can be accomplished.

The Nature of a Table

A table is an ordered set of computer memory storage spaces identified by a table name. The entire set of storage spaces, a particular set of storage spaces, or a specific storage space within the table can be referenced.

Referencing Table Data

A subscript is either one, two, or three unsigned numeric integer literals and/or names with an unsigned numeric computational integer stored under each of them enclosed in a set of parentheses. The left parenthesis may or may not be immediately preceded by at least one space; however, the right parenthesis must be followed by at least one space.

The first literal or name of a subscript represents the specific *row* storage space, the second literal or name, if present, represents the specific *column* storage space, and the third literal or name, if present, represents the specific *rank* storage space. A name used as a subscript must be described in the DATA DIVISIØN. If there is more than one numeric literal and/or name, they must be separated by a space and, if desirable, also by a comma. A subscript contains one literal and/or name if a single-dimensional table is referenced; two literals and/or names if a two-dimensional table is referenced; and three literals and/or names if a three-dimensional table is referenced. (Unlike FORTRAN, BASIC, and PL/1, a literal or numeric computational integer stored under a name cannot be an arithmetic expression.) A subscript follows a name. The name and accompanying subscript are called a table element; a table element is a particular storage space in a table.

Single—Dimensional Tables. A table can contain a single column of numbers. A single-column table is referred to as single dimensional. For example, the number of each type of inventory item on hand at the end of a month might be stored in a single – dimensional table called INVENTØRY-LEVEL as follows:

$$117$$
$$225$$
$$309$$
$$416$$
$$523$$

Each row storage space in the table can be referenced by using the appropriate table element. For example, assume that the name LEVEL is assigned to the elementary items in the table. To reference the third storage space (row), the table element LEVEL (3) would be used. If the table element LEVEL (N) were used, the particular storage space in the table referenced would be dependent upon the number stored under the subscript named N.

Two-Dimensional Tables. A table can contain several columns of numbers. A two-or-more-column table is referred to as two dimensional. For example, assume a table called INVENTØRY, composed of five categories of items with each category, in turn, composed of six types of items. A two-dimensional table consisting of five rows and six columns similar to Table 7-1 could be created in the computer's memory to store the inventory information:

Table 7-1: A Two-dimensional Table

Makes

		1	2	3	4	5	6
	1	47	19	32	94	00	62
	2	27	07	21	43	56	74
Categories	3	63	87	63	01	47	31
	4	14	23	16	94	57	13
	5	06	45	37	61	11	29

Similar to the single dimensional table, each storage space in the table can be referenced by using the appropriate table element. For example, assume that the name MAKE is assigned to the elementary items in the table. To reference the fifth type of item (column) of the fourth category (row), the table element MAKE (4, 5) would be used.

Describing a Table

Similar to most data used in a COBOL program, before a table is used, it must be described in either the FILE SECTIØN or the WØRKING-STØRAGE SECTIØN of the DATA DIVISIØN. In every instance, because a table is subdivided into several elementary items, the table elements must be described as part of a group item.

The OCCURS Clause. As just mentioned, a table must be described in the DATA DIVISIØN prior to referencing it in the PRØCEDURE DIVISIØN. An ØCCURS clause is used to reflect the fact that a table is composed of several elementary items having the same format. The general format of this statement is

<u>ØCCURS</u> numeric-literal TIMES.

The numeric literal must be an unsigned integer. The clause can be assigned any level number 02 through 49 and can be located either immediately prior to or immediately after the PICTURE clause.

1.   Single-Dimensional Tables. To illustrate the use of the ØCCURS clause in describing a single-dimensional table, assume that the following statements concerning the previously discussed table, INVENTØRY-LEVEL, are written:

```
A    B

WØRKING-STØRAGE SECTIØN.
01   INVENTORY-LEVEL.
     02 LEVEL    PICTURE 999 ØCCURS 5 TIMES.
```

The name INVENTØRY-LEVEL is assigned to the table. The ØCCURS clause causes the computer to allocate five data fields in its memory, each named LEVEL. The overall size of the storage area LEVEL can be computed by multiplying the indicated size of one data field (999) times the number of occurrences (5). The PICTURE clause specifies that each of these five fields is to be a three-position numeric computational data field.

If necessary, an ØCCURS clause can be used with a group item instead of an elementary item. For example, assume that the first character of each of the elementary items composing the table INVENTØRY-LEVEL is a warehouse code, and the last two characters are the number of inventory items in that warehouse. It is desirable to separate the warehouse code from the number of inventory items for processing purposes. The following statements could be written to accomplish this:

```
A    B

WØRKING-STØRAGE SECTIØN.
01   INVENTØRY-LEVEL.
     02 LEVEL ØCCURS 5 TIMES.
        03 WAREHØUSE-CØDE       PICTURE 9.
        03 INVENTØRY-NUMBER     PICTURE 99.
```

The name INVENTØRY-LEVEL is assigned to the table. The ØCCURS clause appears in a statement containing the group item, LEVEL, as indicated by the absence of the PICTURE clause. It causes the computer to allocate, in its memory, storage space for five sets of the two fields WAREHØUSE-CØDE and INVENTØRY-NUMBER.

The storage spaces composing a table can be referenced by either the table name or a subgroup or elementary item name. When a table name (INVENTØRY-LEVEL) is used the contents of the entire table are referenced. However, when either a subgroup name, such as LEVEL, or an elementary item name, such as WAREHØUSE-CØDE or INVENTØRY-NUMBER, is referenced, the reference *must* include either the subgroup or elementary item name and a subscript. A subscript must be used to indicate the desired storage space within the table, as a subgroup or a elementary item name refers to several values rather than a specific value. For instance, in the previous example, to reference the INVENTØRY-NUMBER of the third LEVEL, the following would have to be specified:

INVENTØRY-NUMBER (3)

2. *Two-Dimensional Tables.* Similarly, to illustrate the use of the ØCCURS clause in describing a two-dimensional table, assume that the following statements concerning the previously discussed table, INVENTØRY, are written:

```
A     B
      |
WORK|ING-STØRAGE SECTIØN.
01  |INVENTØRY.
    |02 CATEGØRY   ØCCURS 5 TIMES.
    |   03 MAKE   PICTURE 99   ØCCURS 6 TIMES.
```

The name INVENTØRY is assigned to the table. The ØCCURS clause appears in both the statement containing the subgroup item, as indicated by the absence of a PICTURE clause, and the statement containing the elementary item, as indicated by the use of a PICTURE clause. The computer will allocate in its memory storage space for five subgroups, each called CATEGØRY, and six elementary items, each called MAKE, within each subgroup for a total of thirty individual items (five CATEGØRY times six MAKE of inventory items within each category).

Similiar to a single-dimensional table, the entire contents of a two-dimensional table are referenced by using the table name (INVENTØRY). If a particular subgroup name, such as CATEGØRY (3), is referenced the six values of (in this case) the third row are processed.

A particular item of a two-dimensional table can also be referenced. For example, in order to reference the fourth MAKE of the third CATEGØRY of the table INVENTØRY, the following statement would have to be specified:

MAKE (3, 4)

3. *Three-Dimensional Tables.* The ØCCURS clause can also be used to describe a three-dimensional table. For example, assume that the following statements concerning a three-dimensional table are written:

```
A    B
     |
WORKING-STØRAGE SECTIØN.
01   ACCØUNTS.
     02 DEPARTMENT   ØCCURS 5 TIMES.
       03 SECTIØN   ØCCURS 4 TIMES.
         04 BALANCE   PICTURE 9999V99   ØCCURS 6 TIMES.
```

The name ACCØUNTS is assigned to the table. Referencing ACCØUNTS will result in all 120 values (five DEPARTMENT times four SECTIØN within each department times six BALANCE within each section) being processed.

A reference to a particular subgroup department, such as DEPART-MENT (2), will result in the four sections and the six balances within the second department being processed.

Similarly, a reference to a particular subgroup section, such as SECTIØN (3, 1) will result in the six balances within the first section of the third department being processed.

Finally, to reference a particular elementary item, such as the BALANCE of the first SECTIØN of the fourth DEPARTMENT of the table ACCØUNTS, the following statement would have to be specified:

BALANCE (4, 1, 5)

Version 4—Extended: The PERFORM VARYING TABLE ELEMENT Statement

To simplify the processing of tables of data, the fourth version of the PERFØRM statement can be extended to the following general format:

$$\underline{PERFØRM} \quad \begin{matrix} \text{section-name-1} \\ \text{paragraph-name-1} \end{matrix} \quad \left[\underline{THRU} \quad \left\{ \begin{matrix} \text{section-name-2} \\ \text{paragraph-name-2} \end{matrix} \right\} \right]$$

$$\underline{VARYING} \quad \left\{ \begin{matrix} \text{subscript-1} \\ \text{name-1} \end{matrix} \right\} \quad \underline{FRØM} \quad \left\{ \begin{matrix} \text{subscript-2} \\ \text{numeric-literal-1} \\ \text{name-2} \end{matrix} \right\}$$

$$\underline{BY} \quad \left\{ \begin{matrix} \text{numeric-literal-2} \\ \text{name-3} \end{matrix} \right\} \quad \underline{UNTIL} \quad \text{condition-1}$$

$$\left[\underline{AFTER} \quad \left\{ \begin{matrix} \text{subscript-3} \\ \text{name-4} \end{matrix} \right\} \quad \underline{FRØM} \quad \left\{ \begin{matrix} \text{subscript-4} \\ \text{numeric-literal-3} \\ \text{name-5} \end{matrix} \right\} \right.$$

$$\underline{BY} \quad \left\{ \begin{matrix} \text{numeric-literal-4} \\ \text{name-6} \end{matrix} \right\} \quad \underline{UNTIL} \quad \text{condition-2}$$

$$\left[\underline{AFTER} \quad \left\{ \begin{array}{l} \text{subscript-5} \\ \text{name-7} \end{array} \right\} \quad \underline{FR\emptyset M} \quad \left\{ \begin{array}{l} \text{subscript-6} \\ \text{numeric-literal-5} \\ \text{name-8} \end{array} \right\} \right.$$

$$\left. \underline{BY} \quad \left\{ \begin{array}{l} \text{numeric-literal-6} \\ \text{name-9} \end{array} \right\} \quad \underline{UNTIL} \quad \text{condition-3} \right] \right]$$

In the above form, either subscript-1 or name-1 is the name of an elementary item that is used as a subscript in section-name-1 through section-name-2 or paragraph-name-1 through paragraph-name-2.

The elements composing the statement can be divided into three groups. The elements through the first UNTIL can be thought of as the controls necessary to control the outer range of a nested PERF∅RM; the elements from the first AFTER through the second UNTIL can be thought of as the controls necessary to control the middle range of a nested PERF∅RM; and the elements from the second AFTER through the last UNTIL can be thought of as the controls necessary to control the innermost range of a nested PERF∅RM. The middle range of a PERF∅RM is satisfied for each iteration of the outer range, and the innermost range is satisfied for each iteration of the middle range.

Illustration 1. Assume that the following PERF∅RM statement is executed:

```
A    B
DATA DIVISI∅N.
FILE SECTI∅N.
        .
        .
        .
01   IN-REC∅RD.
        .
        .
        .
     02 ELEMENT-∅NE     PICTURE 999V99.
     02 ELEMENT-TW∅     PICTURE 99V999.
        .
        .
        .
W∅RKING-ST∅RAGE SECTI∅N.
77   N                  PICTURE 9.
        .
        .
        .
01   TABLE-REC∅RD-LIST.
     02   TABLE-ELEMENT  PICTURE 999V999   ∅CCURS 5 TIMES.
        .
        .
        .
```

```
PRØCEDURE DIVISIØN.
    .
    .
    .
    PERFØRM PARA-1 VARYING N FRØM 1 BY 1 UNTIL N GREATER
    THAN 5.
    .
    .
    .
PARA-1.
    .
    .
    .
    READ IN-FILE.
    .
    .
    .
    ADD ELEMENT-ØNE, ELEMENT-TWØ GIVING
    TABLE-ELEMENT (N).
    .
    .
```

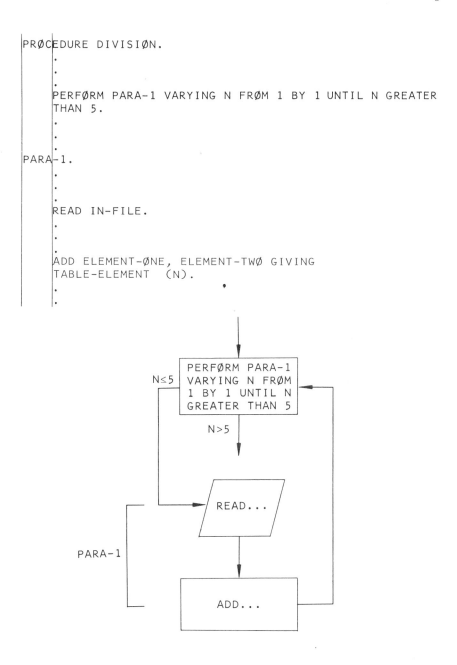

The computer will execute the statements in PARA-1 until N is greater than five. The elementary item N is initially assigned the value of 1. With each subsequent execution of the statements within PARA-1, the value of N will be incremented by 1. Thus, each of the five numbers previously indicated as being in the single dimensional table INVENTØRY-LEVEL could be referenced by specifying LEVEL (N).

Illustration 2. Assume that the following PERFØRM statement is executed:

PERFØRM PARA-1 THRU PARA-3 VARYING N FRØM 1 BY 1 UNTIL
N GREATER THAN 5 AFTER I FRØM 1 BY 1 UNTIL I GREATER THAN 6.

The computer will execute the statements in PARA-1 through PARA-3 until N is greater than five. Each time N is incremented, the value of I will be reset from a value of six to a value of one. Then I will be incremented by one until it is greater than six.

A SUMMARY OF THE FOUR VERSIONS OF THE PERFORM STATEMENT

The following are the four versions of the PERFØRM statement:

1. The Basic PERFØRM. General format:

$$\underline{PERF\text{\O}RM} \quad \left\{ \begin{array}{l} \text{section-name-1} \\ \text{paragraph-name-1} \end{array} \right\} \quad \left[\underline{THRU} \quad \left\{ \begin{array}{l} \text{section-name-2} \\ \text{paragraph-name-2} \end{array} \right\} \right]$$

This causes the statement range to be executed once. It is quite useful when one is writing special routines or for steering the program along general lines.

2. PERFØRM n TIMES. General format:

$$\underline{PERF\text{\O}RM} \quad \left\{ \begin{array}{l} \text{section-name-1} \\ \text{paragraph-name-1} \end{array} \right\} \quad \left[\underline{THRU} \quad \left\{ \begin{array}{l} \text{section-name-2} \\ \text{paragraph-name-2} \end{array} \right\} \right]$$

$$\left\{ \begin{array}{l} \text{numeric-} \\ \text{literal-1} \\ \text{name-1} \end{array} \right\} \quad \underline{TIMES}$$

This version causes the statement's range to be executed a set of determinable number of times.

3. PERFØRM UNTIL. General format:

$$\underline{PERF\text{\O}RM} \quad \left\{ \begin{array}{l} \text{section-name-1} \\ \text{paragraph-name-1} \end{array} \right\} \quad \left[\underline{THRU} \quad \left\{ \begin{array}{l} \text{section-name-2} \\ \text{paragraph-name-2} \end{array} \right\} \right]$$

$$\underline{UNTIL} \quad \text{condition-1}$$

This version causes the statement's range to be repeated until the condition specified in the statement is attained.

4. PERFØRM VARYING. General format:

$$\underline{PERF\emptyset RM} \quad \begin{Bmatrix} \text{section-name-1} \\ \text{paragraph-name-1} \end{Bmatrix} \quad \left[\underline{THRU} \quad \begin{Bmatrix} \text{section-name-2} \\ \text{paragraph-name-2} \end{Bmatrix} \right]$$

$$\underline{VARYING} \quad \text{name-1} \quad \underline{FR\emptyset M} \quad \begin{Bmatrix} \text{numeric-} \\ \text{literal-2} \\ \text{name-3} \end{Bmatrix} \quad \underline{BY} \quad \begin{Bmatrix} \text{numeric-} \\ \text{literal-2} \\ \text{name-3} \end{Bmatrix}$$

$$\underline{UNTIL} \quad \text{condition-1}$$

This version incorporates a name and allows the statement to establish its initial value and its increment. The program leaves the statement's range when the condition specified in the statement is attained.

4–Extended. PERFORM VARYING TABLE ELEMENT. General format:

$$\underline{PERF\emptyset RM} \quad \begin{Bmatrix} \text{section-name-1} \\ \text{paragraph-name-1} \end{Bmatrix} \quad \left[\underline{THRU} \quad \begin{Bmatrix} \text{section-name-2} \\ \text{paragraph-name-2} \end{Bmatrix} \right]$$

$$\underline{VARYING} \quad \begin{Bmatrix} \text{subscript-1} \\ \text{name-1} \end{Bmatrix} \quad \underline{FR\emptyset M} \quad \begin{Bmatrix} \text{subscript-2} \\ \text{numeric-literal-1} \\ \text{name-2} \end{Bmatrix}$$

$$\underline{BY} \quad \begin{Bmatrix} \text{numeric-literal-2} \\ \text{name-3} \end{Bmatrix} \quad \underline{UNTIL} \quad \text{condition-1}$$

$$\left[\underline{AFTER} \quad \begin{Bmatrix} \text{subscript-1} \\ \text{name-4} \end{Bmatrix} \quad \underline{FR\emptyset M} \quad \begin{Bmatrix} \text{subscript-4} \\ \text{numeric-literal-3} \\ \text{name-5} \end{Bmatrix} \right.$$

$$\underline{BY} \quad \begin{Bmatrix} \text{numeric-literal-4} \\ \text{name-6} \end{Bmatrix} \quad \underline{UNTIL} \quad \text{condition-2}$$

$$\left[\underline{AFTER} \quad \begin{Bmatrix} \text{subscript-5} \\ \text{name-7} \end{Bmatrix} \quad \underline{FR\emptyset M} \quad \begin{Bmatrix} \text{subscript-6} \\ \text{numeric-literal-5} \\ \text{name-8} \end{Bmatrix} \right.$$

$$\left. \left. \underline{BY} \quad \begin{Bmatrix} \text{numeric-literal-6} \\ \text{name-9} \end{Bmatrix} \quad \underline{UNTIL} \quad \text{condition-3} \right] \right]$$

This version, an extension of version 4, permits the construction of as many as three nested PERF∅RM statements. This extension of version 4 is often used for controlling programs dealing with 1-, 2-, or 3-level tables, in which case this statement can be used to set up and modify subscripts. However, this statement is not limited to this use.

TABLE SEARCHING

The processing of data often requires the searching of a table for a particular data item.

The SEARCH Statement

The SEARCH statement can be used in these situations to search a table for an element that satisfies a specified condition. The statement has two formats.

Format 1:   SEARCH identifier-1 [VARYING $\begin{Bmatrix} \text{index-name-1} \\ \text{identifier-2} \end{Bmatrix}$]

[AT END imperative-statement-1]

WHEN condition-1 $\begin{Bmatrix} \text{imperative-statement-2} \\ \underline{\text{NEXT}}\ \underline{\text{SENTENCE}} \end{Bmatrix}$

[WHEN condition-2 $\begin{Bmatrix} \text{imperative-statement-3} \\ \underline{\text{NEXT}}\ \underline{\text{SENTENCE}} \end{Bmatrix}$] . . .

This format is used when the table to be searched is *not* sorted. Identifier-1 is a data item described in the DATA DIVISIØN. The description must contain an ØCCURS clause followed by an INDEXED BY clause. An index is a programmer-supplied name present in each ØCCURS clause defining a table to be searched. An illustration of these clauses follows:

```
A    B
01   ACCØUNTS
     02    DEPARTMENT    ØCCURS 40 TIMES    INDEXED BY N.
           03   SECTIØN    PICTURE XXX.
           03   BALANCE    PICTURE 9999.
```

The ACCØUNTS table is indexed by N (which can be either a name with an unsigned integer number stored under it or an unsigned integer number). As the sequential search of the table occurs, the index name is automatically increased after each comparison.

When the VARYING option is used, index-name-1 is varied in the same way as the index specified in the relevant INDEXED BY clause. If identifier-2 is used, it must be either an elementary item specified as USAGE IS INDEX in the DATA DIVISIØN or an unsigned integer number. For example, in the following illustration

```
77.    TABLE-ELEMENT-NUMBER    USAGE IS INDEX.
```

the elementary item TABLE-ELEMENT-NUMBER is an INDEX name. Note the absence of any other clauses, such as the PICTURE and VALUE clauses. The reason for this is that the size of the field is always the same and the purpose of an index name is to store an index value for later use.

If the AT END option is included, imperative-statement-1 should terminate with a GØ TØ statement. The option will be executed if no match is found. If the AT END option is included and imperative-statement-1 does not terminate with a GØ TØ statement, a branch will be made to the next sentence, thus bypassing the WHEN option(s), if present. If the AT END clause is omitted, the computer will branch to the next sentence when the table has been searched and no match is found.

The WHEN option(s) is a conditional expression. The search of the table ends when the conditional is satisfied. If both WHEN options are used, the table search is terminated when either of the conditions is met. Similar to the AT END option, if the WHEN option(s) imperative-statement-2 does not terminate with a GØ TØ statement a branch will be made to the next sentence whether or not a match is found.

In the following illustration,

```
SEARCH EMPLØYEE-TABLE AT END GØ TØ NØT-FØUND-PARAGRAPH
   WHEN EMPLØYEE-ID-NUMBER EQUAL ØLD-NUMBER
   (TABLE-ELEMENT-NUMBER) GØ TØ FØUND-MATCH-PARAGRAPH
   WHEN EMPLØYEE-ID-NUMBER GREATER THAN ØLD-NUMBER
   (100) GØ TØ INVALID-EMPLØYEE-ID-NUMBER-PARAGRAPH.
```

the search of the table will end when either of the two conditional expressions are satisfied. If neither conditional is satisfied, the AT END option will be executed.

Format 2:   SEARCH ALL identifier-1 [AT END imperative-statement-1]

$$\text{WHEN condition-1} \quad \begin{Bmatrix} \text{imperative-statement-2} \\ \underline{\text{NEXT}} \ \underline{\text{SENTENCE}} \end{Bmatrix}$$

This format is used when the table to be searched *is* sorted. A sorted table requires the KEY clause to be present in the ØCCURS clause in addition to the INDEXED BY clause. Thus, the format of the ØCCURS clause is:

$$\text{OCCURS integer TIMES} \\ \left[\begin{Bmatrix} \underline{\text{ASCENDING}} \\ \underline{\text{DESCENDING}} \end{Bmatrix} \quad \text{KEY IS data-name-1 [data-name-2]} \ \ldots \right]$$

[INDEXED BY index-name-1 [index-name-2] ...]

For example, in the following illustration

```
01    ACCØUNTS.
      02    DEPARTMENT    ØCCURS 40 TIMES    ASCENDING KEY IS
            MØNTH, DAY    INDEXED BY N.
            03    MØNTH         PICTURE 99.
            03    DAY           PICTURE 99.
```

there are two keys, MONTH and DAY. Keys are listed in decreasing order of importance. Thus, the days are sorted in ascending sequence within the months, which is also in ascending sequence.

While only one WHEN option is available, multiple AND conditions are allowed. Thus, in the following illustration

```
SEARCH EMPLØYEE-TABLE AT END GØ TØ NØT-FOUND-PARAGRAPH
   WHEN EMPLØOYEE-ID-NUMBER EQUAL ØLD NUMBER
   (TABLE-ELEMENT-NUMBER) AND ØLD-NUMBER
   (TABLE-ELEMENT-NUMBER) EQUAL 65 GØ TØ
   MANAGER-PARAGRAPH.
```

the branch to MANAGER-PARAGRAPH will not occur until both conditional tests concerning the key fields (employee number and old number) are satisfied.

The SET Statement

The SET statement is a variation of the MØVE statement. It establishes reference points for table handling operations by setting index-names to values associated with table elements. The SET statement must be used when initializing index-name values before execution of a SEARCH statement; it can also be used to transfer values between index-names and other elementary items.

The statement has two formats:

$$\text{Format 1:} \quad \underline{\text{SET}} \left\{ \begin{array}{l} \text{index-name-1 [index-name-2] ...} \\ \text{identifier-1} \quad \text{[identifier-2] ...} \end{array} \right\} \quad \underline{\text{TO}} \left\{ \begin{array}{l} \text{index-name-3} \\ \text{identifier-3} \\ \text{literal-1} \end{array} \right\}$$

Index-name-1 can be set to equal index-name-3, indentifier-3, or literal-1. Identifier-3 must be defined in the DATA DIVISIØN as an elementary integer number. Literal-1 must be an unsigned integer number. If identifier-1 has not been defined in a USAGE IS INDEX clause, it only can be set to index-name-3. For example, in the following illustration

SET CØUNTER TØ TABLE–ELEMENT–NUMBER.

the only value of the TABLE-ELEMENT-NUMBER is also stored under CØUNTER.

Format 2: SET index-name-1 [index-name-2] ... $\begin{Bmatrix} \underline{\text{UP BY}} \\ \underline{\text{DOWN BY}} \end{Bmatrix} \begin{Bmatrix} \text{identifier-1} \\ \text{literal-1} \end{Bmatrix}$

By using this format, the value of index-name-1 can be either increased (UP BY) or decreased (DOWN BY) by either the value of identifier-1 or an unsigned integer number. Indentifier-1 cannot be defined in a USAGE IS INDEX clause.

A COMPLETE COBOL PROGRAM

The complete COBOL program in Figure 7-3 illustrates the use of the PERFØRM statement with table elements.

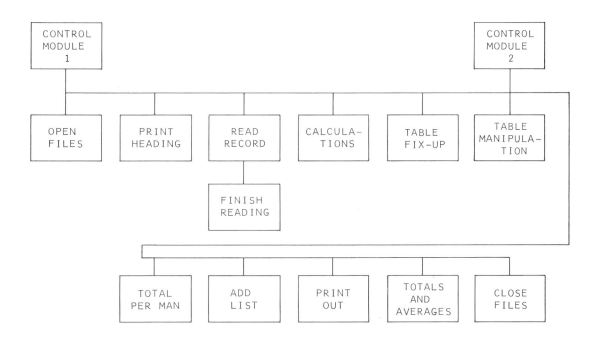

Figure 7-1: Structure chart for the following COBOL program

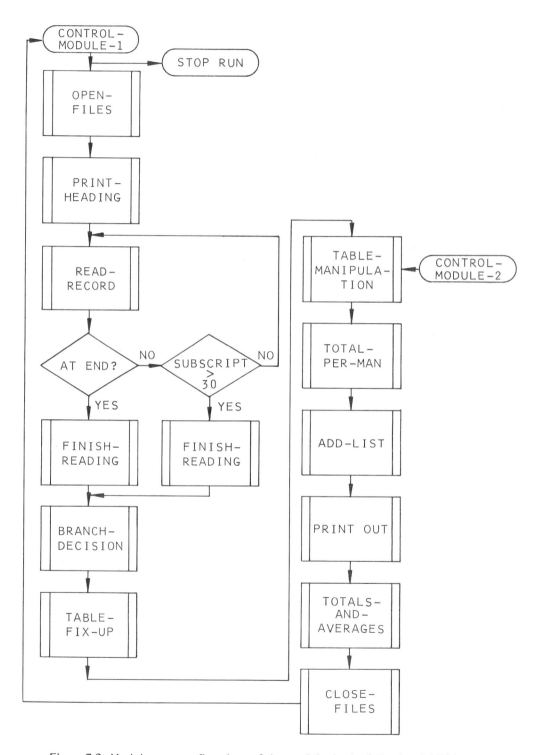

Figure 7-2: Module program flowchart of the modules in the following COBOL program

IBM

COBOL Coding Form

GX28-1464-5 U/M 050*
Printed in U.S.A.

SYSTEM	IBM-370-148		PUNCHING INSTRUCTIONS		PAGE 0010F010
PROGRAM	THE USE OF TABLE ELEMENTS		GRAPHIC	CARD FORM #	*
PROGRAMMER	V. THOMAS DOCK	DATE	PUNCH		

COBOL STATEMENT

SEQUENCE	CONT	B	COBOL STATEMENT	IDENTIFICATION
01			IDENTIFICATION DIVISION.	
02			PROGRAM-ID. HOURS.	
03			AUTHOR. V. THOMAS DOCK.	
04			INSTALLATION. THE XYZ COMPANY.	
05			DATE-WRITTEN. 6/1/77.	
06			DATE-COMPILED.	
07	*		THIS PROGRAM PRINTS A REPORT OF THE NUMBER OF HOURS WORKED BY	
08	*		EACH EMPLOYEE OF THE XYZ COMPANY. THE REPORT SHOWS THE TOTAL	
09	*		NUMBER OF HOURS WORKED PER WEEK, THE NUMBER OF OVERTIME HOURS	
10	*		WORKED PER WEEK, AND THE AVERAGE NUMBER OF HOURS WORKED BY	
11	*		EACH EMPLOYEE. THE REPORT ALSO SHOWS THE TOTAL NUMBER OF	
12	*		HOURS WORKED EACH DAY BY ALL EMPLOYEES AND THE AVERAGE	
13	*		NUMBER OF HOURS WORKED FOR ALL EMPLOYEES PER DAY.	
14			ENVIRONMENT DIVISION.	
15			CONFIGURATION SECTION.	
16			SOURCE-COMPUTER. IBM-370-148.	
17			OBJECT-COMPUTER. IBM-370-148.	
18			INPUT-OUTPUT SECTION.	
19			FILE-CONTROL.	
20			SELECT EMPLOYEE-TIME-CARDS ASSIGN TO UR-2540R-S-CARDIN.	
21			SELECT EMPLOYEE-WORK-SCHEDULE ASSIGN TO UR-1403-S-PROUT.	
22			DATA DIVISION.	
23			FILE SECTION.	
24			FD EMPLOYEE-TIME-CARDS	

*A standard card form, IBM Electro C61897, is available for punching source statements from this form. Instructions for using this form are given in any IBM COBOL reference manual. Address comments concerning this form to IBM Corporation, LDS Publishing, Dept. J04, 1501 California Ave., Palo Alto, Ca. 94304

*No. of forms per pad may vary slightly

Figure 7-3: A COBOL Program

IBM

COBOL Coding Form

GX28-1464-5 U/M 050*
Printed in U.S.A.

SYSTEM	IBM-370-148		PAGE 002 OF 010
PROGRAM	THE USE OF TABLE ELEMENTS	PUNCHING INSTRUCTIONS	
PROGRAMMER	V. THOMAS DUCK	GRAPHIC	CARD FORM #
	DATE	PUNCH	*

```
SEQUENCE  A B              COBOL STATEMENT
01           LABEL RECORD IS OMITTED.
02        01 TIME-CARDS.
03           02 EMPLOYEE-NAME        PICTURE A(15).
04           02 HOURS-MONDAY         PICTURE 99.
05           02 HOURS-TUESDAY        PICTURE 99.
06           02 HOURS-WEDNESDAY      PICTURE 99.
07           02 HOURS-THURSDAY       PICTURE 99.
08           02 HOURS-FRIDAY         PICTURE 99.
09           02 FILLER               PICTURE X(55).
10        FD EMPLOYEE-WORK-SCHEDULE
11        01 LABEL RECORD IS OMITTED.
12           LINE-OF-PRINT           PICTURE X(133).
13        WORKING-STORAGE SECTION.
14        77 SUBSCRIPT               PICTURE 99.
15        77 COMPUTATION-SUBSCRIPT   PICTURE 99.
16        77 REPEAT                  PICTURE 99.
17        77 MONDAY-TOTAL            PICTURE 999 VALUE ZERO.
18        77 TUESDAY-TOTAL           PICTURE 999 VALUE ZERO.
19        77 WEDNESDAY-TOTAL         PICTURE 999 VALUE ZERO.
20        77 THURSDAY-TOTAL          PICTURE 999 VALUE ZERO.
21        77 FRIDAY-TOTAL            PICTURE 999 VALUE ZERO.
22        77 GRAND-TOTAL             PICTURE 999 VALUE ZERO.
23        77 OVERTIME-TOTAL          PICTURE 999 VALUE ZERO.
24        77 MORE-DATA-CARDS         PICTURE AA VALUE SPACES.
```

*A standard card form, IBM Electro C61897, is available for punching source statements from this form. Instructions for using this form are given in any IBM COBOL reference manual. Address comments concerning this form to IBM Corporation, LDS Publishing, Dept. J04, 1501 California Ave., Palo Alto, Ca. 94304

*No. of forms per pad may vary slightly

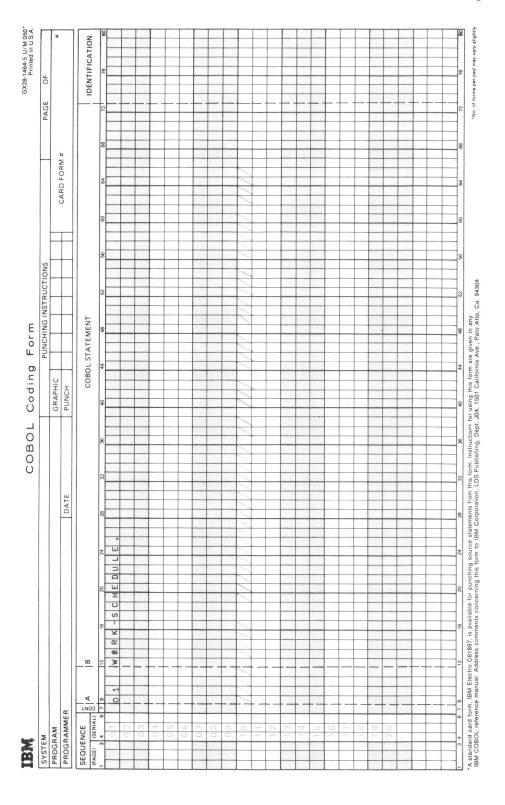

COBOL Coding Form

IBM

SYSTEM	IBM-370-148				PUNCHING INSTRUCTIONS		PAGE 0003 OF 010
PROGRAM	THE USE OF TABLE ELEMENTS			GRAPHIC			CARD FORM #
PROGRAMMER	V. THOMAS DOCK	DATE		PUNCH			

GX28-1464-5 U/M 050*
Printed in U.S.A.

*

```
        01  PRINT-LINE.
            02  NUMBER-OF-EMPLOYEES OCCURS 30 TIMES.
                03  NAME-OF-EMPLOYEE   PICTURE A(15).
                03  MONDAY-HOURS       PICTURE 99V9.
                03  TUESDAY-HOURS      PICTURE 99V9.
                03  WEDNESDAY-HOURS    PICTURE 99V9.
                03  THURSDAY-HOURS     PICTURE 99V9.
                03  FRIDAY-HOURS       PICTURE 99V9.
                03  TOTAL              PICTURE 99V9.
                03  OVERTIME           PICTURE 99V9.
                03  AVERAGE-PER-DAY    PICTURE 99V99.
        01  PRINT-LINE.
            02  FILLER            PICTURE X(5)  VALUE SPACES.
            02  NAME-EMPLOYEE     PICTURE A(15).
            02  FILLER            PICTURE X(4)  VALUE SPACES.
            02  MONDAY            PICTURE ZZ9.99.
            02  FILLER            PICTURE X(4)  VALUE SPACES.
            02  TUESDAY           PICTURE ZZ9.99.
            02  FILLER            PICTURE X(4)  VALUE SPACES.
            02  WEDNESDAY         PICTURE ZZ9.99.
            02  FILLER            PICTURE X(4)  VALUE SPACES.
            02  THURSDAY          PICTURE ZZ9.99.
            02  FILLER            PICTURE X(4)  VALUE SPACES.
            02  FRIDAY            PICTURE ZZ9.99.
            02  FILLER            PICTURE X(4)  VALUE SPACES.
```

*A standard card form, IBM Electro C61897, is available for punching source statements from this form. Instructions for using this form are given in any
IBM COBOL reference manual. Address comments concerning this form to IBM Corporation, LDS Publishing, Dept. J04, 1501 California Ave., Palo Alto, Ca. 94304

*No. of forms per pad may vary slightly

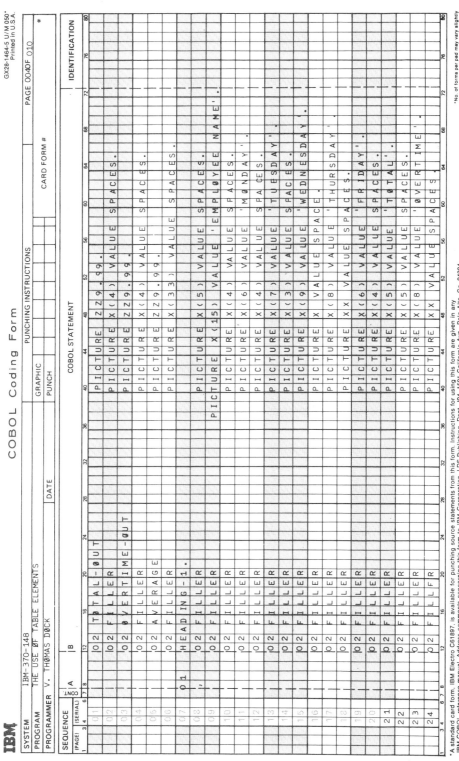

COBOL Coding Form

GX28-1464-5 U/M 050*
Printed in U.S.A.

SYSTEM	IBM-370-148		PAGE005 OF 010
PROGRAM	THE USE OF TABLE ELEMENTS	PUNCHING INSTRUCTIONS	CARD FORM #
PROGRAMMER	V. THOMAS DUCK	DATE	

```
SEQUENCE
(PAGE)  (SERIAL)  CONT  A   B                                      COBOL STATEMENT
01                      02  FILLER    PICTURE  X(7)  VALUE  'AVERAGE'.
02                      02  FILLER    PICTURE  X(32)  VALUE  SPACES.
03            PROCEDURE DIVISION.
04      *
05            CONTROL-MODULE-1.
06                PERFORM OPEN-FILES.
07                PERFORM PRINT-HEADING.
08                PERFORM READ-RECORD THRU FINISH-READING
09                    UNTIL MORE-DATA-CARDS EQUAL 'NO'.
10                PERFORM BRANCH-DECISION.
11                PERFORM TABLE-FIX-UP
12                    VARYING COMPUTATION-SUBSCRIPT
13                    UNTIL COMPUTATION-SUBSCRIPT GREATER THAN 30.
14      *
15            CONTROL-MODULE-2.
16                PERFORM TABLE-MANIPULATION.
17                PERFORM TOTAL-PER-MAN
18                    VARYING SUBSCRIPT FROM 1 BY 1
19                    UNTIL SUBSCRIPT GREATER THAN REPEAT.
20                PERFORM ADD-LIST
21                    VARYING SUBSCRIPT FROM 1 BY 1
22                    UNTIL SUBSCRIPT GREATER THAN REPEAT.
23                PERFORM PRINT-OUT
24                    VARYING SUBSCRIPT FROM 1 BY 1
```

GRAPHIC / PUNCH — IDENTIFICATION

*A standard card form, IBM Electro C61897, is available for punching source statements from this form. Instructions for using this form are given in any IBM COBOL reference manual. Address comments concerning this form to IBM Corporation, LDS Publishing, Dept. J04, 1501 California Ave., Palo Alto, Ca. 94304

*No. of forms per pad may vary slightly

IBM

COBOL Coding Form

GX28-1464-5 U/M 050*
Printed in U.S.A.

SYSTEM	IBM-370-148
PROGRAM	THE USE OF TABLE ELEMENTS
PROGRAMMER	V. THOMAS DOCK

PUNCHING INSTRUCTIONS — GRAPHIC / PUNCH — DATE

PAGE 006 OF 010 — CARD FORM #

IDENTIFICATION (73–80)

```
01          UNTIL SUBSCRIPT GREATER THAN REPEAT.
02          PERFORM TOTALS-AND-AVERAGES.
03          PERFORM CLOSE-FILES.
04          STOP RUN.
05 *    OPEN-FILES.
06          OPEN INPUT EMPLOYEE-TIME-CARDS
07              OUTPUT EMPLOYEE-WORK-SCHEDULE.
08 *
09      PRINT-HEADING.
10          MOVE ZEROS TO HEADING-1.
11          MOVE HEADING-1 TO PRINT.
12          WRITE LINE-OF-PRINT AFTER ADVANCING PAGE.
13 *
14      READ-RECORD.
15          READ EMPLOYEE-TIME-CARDS AT END
16              MOVE 30 TO MORE-DATA-CARDS
17              GO TO FINISH-READING.
18          IF SUBSCRIPT GREATER THAN NAME GO TO FINISH-READING.
19          MOVE EMPLOYEE-NAME TO EMPLOYEE-NAME (SUBSCRIPT).
20          MOVE EMPLOYEE-MONDAY-HOURS TO HOURS (SUBSCRIPT).
21          MOVE EMPLOYEE-TUESDAY-HOURS TO HOURS (SUBSCRIPT).
22          MOVE EMPLOYEE-WEDNESDAY-HOURS TO HOURS (SUBSCRIPT).
23          MOVE EMPLOYEE-THURSDAY-HOURS TO HOURS (SUBSCRIPT).
24          MOVE EMPLOYEE-FRIDAY-HOURS TO HOURS (SUBSCRIPT).
```

*A standard card form, IBM Electro C61897, is available for punching source statements from this form. Instructions for using this form are given in any IBM COBOL reference manual. Address comments concerning this form to IBM Corporation. LDS Publishing, Dept. J04, 1501 California Ave., Palo Alto, Ca. 94304

*No. of forms per pad may vary slightly

COBOL Coding Form

GX28-1464-5 U/M 050*
Printed in U.S.A.

SYSTEM	IBM-370-148		PAGE 007 OF 010
PROGRAM	THE USE OF TABLE ELEMENTS	PUNCHING INSTRUCTIONS	
PROGRAMMER	V. THOMAS DOCK	GRAPHIC / PUNCH	CARD FORM #

```
SEQUENCE
01   MOVE HOURS-FRIDAY TO FRIDAY-HOURS.
02   FINISH-READING.
03       EXIT.
04
05   BRANCH-DECISION.
06       IF SUBSCRIPT NOT EQUAL 30
07           NEXT SENTENCE
08       ELSE GO TO CONTROL-MODULE-2.
09       ADD 1 TO SUBSCRIPT.
10
11   TABLE-FIX-UP.
12       MOVE SPACES TO NAME-OF-EMPLOYEE (COMPUTATION-SUBSCRIPT).
13       MOVE ZERO TO MONDAY-HOURS (COMPUTATION-SUBSCRIPT).
14       MOVE ZERO TO TUESDAY-HOURS (COMPUTATION-SUBSCRIPT).
15       MOVE ZERO TO WEDNESDAY-HOURS (COMPUTATION-SUBSCRIPT).
16       MOVE ZERO TO THURSDAY-HOURS (COMPUTATION-SUBSCRIPT).
17       MOVE ZERO TO FRIDAY-HOURS (COMPUTATION-SUBSCRIPT).
18       MOVE ZERO TO TOTAL-COMPUTATION-SUBSCRIPT.
19       MOVE ZERO TO OVERTIME (COMPUTATION-SUBSCRIPT).
20       MOVE ZERO TO AVERAGE-PER-DAY (COMPUTATION-SUBSCRIPT).
21
22   TABLE-MANIPULATION.
23       SUBTRACT 1 FROM SUBSCRIPT GIVING REPEAT.
24
```

*A standard card form, IBM Electro C61897, is available for punching source statements from this form. Instructions for using this form are given in any IBM COBOL reference manual. Address comments concerning this form to IBM Corporation, LDS Publishing, Dept. J04, 1501 California Ave., Palo Alto, Ca. 94304

*No. of forms per pad may vary slightly

COBOL Coding Form

SYSTEM	IBM-370 148		PAGE 008 OF 010
PROGRAM	THE USE OF TABLE ELEMENTS		CARD FORM #
PROGRAMMER	V. THOMAS DOCK	DATE	

PUNCHING INSTRUCTIONS — GRAPHIC / PUNCH

```
01  TOTAL-PER-MAN.
02      ADD MONDAY-HOURS (SUBSCRIPT) TUESDAY-HOURS (SUBSCRIPT)
03          WEDNESDAY-HOURS (SUBSCRIPT) THURSDAY-HOURS (SUBSCRIPT)
04          FRIDAY-HOURS (SUBSCRIPT) GIVING TOTAL (SUBSCRIPT).
05      IF TOTAL (SUBSCRIPT) LESS THAN 40
06          MOVE ZEROS TO OVERTIME (SUBSCRIPT)
07      ELSE SUBTRACT 40 FROM TOTAL (SUBSCRIPT) GIVING
08          OVERTIME (SUBSCRIPT).
09      DIVIDE TOTAL (SUBSCRIPT) BY 5 GIVING AVERAGE-PER-DAY
10          (SUBSCRIPT).
11  ADD-LIST.
12      ADD MONDAY-HOURS (SUBSCRIPT) TO MONDAY-TOTAL.
13      ADD TUESDAY-HOURS (SUBSCRIPT) TO TUESDAY-TOTAL.
14      ADD WEDNESDAY-HOURS (SUBSCRIPT) TO WEDNESDAY-TOTAL.
15      ADD THURSDAY-HOURS (SUBSCRIPT) TO THURSDAY-TOTAL.
16      ADD FRIDAY-HOURS (SUBSCRIPT) TO FRIDAY-TOTAL.
17      ADD TOTAL (SUBSCRIPT) TO GRAND-TOTAL.
18      ADD OVERTIME (SUBSCRIPT) TO OVERTIME-TOTAL.
19  PRINT-OUT.
20      MOVE NAME-OF-EMPLOYEE (SUBSCRIPT) TO NAME-EMPLOYEE.
        MOVE MONDAY-HOURS (SUBSCRIPT) TO MONDAY.
        MOVE TUESDAY-HOURS (SUBSCRIPT) TO TUESDAY.
```

GX28-1464-5 U/M 050
Printed in U.S.A.

*A standard card form. IBM Electro C61897, is available for punching source statements from this form. Instructions for using this form are given in any IBM COBOL reference manual. Address comments concerning this form to IBM Corporation, LDS Publishing, Dept. J04, 1501 California Ave., Palo Alto, Ca. 94304

*No. of forms per pad may vary slightly

COBOL Coding Form

GX28-1464-5 U/M 050*
Printed in U.S.A.

SYSTEM	IBM-370-148		PUNCHING INSTRUCTIONS	PAGE 0090 OF 010
PROGRAM	THE USE OF TABLE ELEMENTS		GRAPHIC	CARD FORM #
PROGRAMMER	V. THOMAS DUCK	DATE	PUNCH	

IDENTIFICATION

SEQUENCE (PAGE) (SERIAL)	CONT	A	B	COBOL STATEMENT
01			MOVE WEDNESDAY-HOURS (SUBSCRIPT) TO WEDNESDAY.
02			MOVE THURSDAY-HOURS (SUBSCRIPT) TO THURSDAY.
03			MOVE FRIDAY-HOURS (SUBSCRIPT) TO FRIDAY.
04			MOVE TOTAL (SUBSCRIPT) TO TOTAL-OUT.
05			MOVE OVERTIME (SUBSCRIPT) TO OVERTIME-OUT.
06			MOVE AVERAGE-PER-DAY (SUBSCRIPT) TO AVERAGE.
07			MOVE PRINT-LINE TO LINE-OF-PRINT.
08			WRITE LINE-OF-PRINT AFTER ADVANCING 2 LINES.
09	*		
10			TOTALS-AND-AVERAGES.
11			MOVE TOTAL TO NAME-EMPLOYEE.
12			MOVE MONDAY-TOTAL TO MONDAY.
13			MOVE TUESDAY-TOTAL TO TUESDAY.
14			MOVE WEDNESDAY-TOTAL TO WEDNESDAY.
15			MOVE THURSDAY-TOTAL TO THURSDAY.
16			MOVE FRIDAY-TOTAL TO FRIDAY.
17			MOVE GRAND-TOTAL TO TOTAL-OUT.
18			MOVE OVERTIME-TOTAL TO OVERTIME-OUT.
19			MOVE ZERO TO AVERAGE.
20			MOVE PRINT-LINE TO LINE-OF-PRINT.
21			WRITE LINE-OF-PRINT AFTER ADVANCING 3 LINES.
22			DIVIDE MONDAY-TOTAL BY REPEAT GIVING MONDAY.
23			DIVIDE TUESDAY-TOTAL BY REPEAT GIVING TUESDAY.
24			DIVIDE WEDNESDAY-TOTAL BY REPEAT GIVING WEDNESDAY.

* A standard card form, IBM Electro C61897, is available for punching source statements from this form. Instructions for using this form are given in any IBM COBOL reference manual. Address comments concerning this form to IBM Corporation, LDS Publishing, Dept. J04, 1501 California Ave., Palo Alto, Ca. 94304

*No. of forms per pad may vary slightly

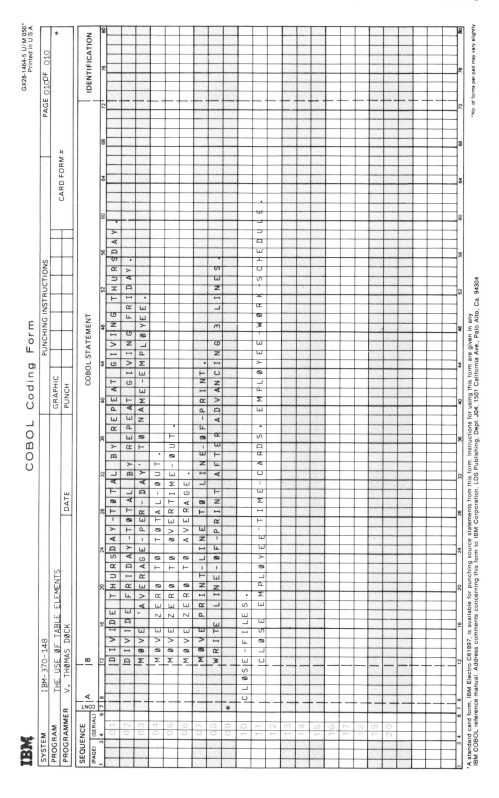

QUESTIONS

1. What is the function of the PERFØRM statement?
2. Discuss some of the common characteristics of the PERFØRM statement.
3. What is meant by a *table* in COBOL and what is its function?
4. How is a single dimensional table referenced, and how is it differentiated from a two-dimensional table? A three-dimensional table?
5. Discuss the ØCCURS clause and how it is used in table handling.

EXERCISES

1. Explain the operation of the following PERFØRM statements:
   a. PERFØRM FIRST–PARAGRAPH.
   b. PERFØRM FIRST–PARAGRAPH THRU SECØOND–PARAGRAPH.
   c. PERFØRM FIRST–PARAGRAPH VARIABLE–NUMBER TIMES.
   d. PERFØRM FIRST–PARAGRAPH UNTIL ACCUMULATØR GREATER THAN 50.
   e. PERFØRM FIRST–PARAGRAPH VARYING QUANTITY FRØM 2 BY 4 UNTIL QUANTITY GREATER THAN 40.
   f. PERFØRM FIRST–PARAGRAPH VARYING QUANTITY FRØM 1 BY 1 UNTIL QUANTITY GREATER THAN 10 AFTER AMØUNT FRØM 1 BY 2 UNTIL AMØUNT EQUAL FINAL–AMØUNT.

2. Given the following ØCCURS clause(s), define the size of the table(s):

	A	B

a. | 01 | FIRST-TABLE.
02 TABLE-ELEMENT ØCCURS 30 TIMES PICTURE 99V99.

b. | 01 | SECØND-TABLE.
02 ELEMENTS ØCCURS 6 TIMES.
   03 FIRST-ELEMENT   PICTURE 9(5).
   03 SECØND-ELEMENT   PICTURE XXX.
   03 THIRD-ELEMENT   PICTURE 9V99.
   03 FØURTH-ELEMENT   PICTURE X(20).

c. | 01 | THIRD-TABLE.
02 FIRST-ELEMENT ØCCURS 7 TIMES.
   03 SECØND-ELEMENT ØCCURS 10 TIMES   PICTURE $99.99.

d. | 01 | FØURTH-TABLE.
02 FIRST-ELEMENT ØCCURS 3 TIMES.
   03 SECØND-ELEMENT ØCCURS 5 TIMES.
      04 FIRST-SUB-ELEMENT   PICTURE 9.
      04 SECØND-SUB-ELEMENT   PICTURE X(5).
      04 THIRD-SUB-ELEMENT   PICTURE 9(4).

e. | 01 | FIFTH-TABLE
02 FIRST-ELEMENT ØCCURS 4 TIMES.
   03 SECØND-ELEMENT ØCCURS 6 TIMES.
      04 THIRD-ELEMENT ØCCURS 10 TIMES   PICTURE A(20).

*

8

ADVANCED COBOL STATEMENT

In the first seven chapters, those statements necessary to process most COBOL programs are presented. There are several additional statements that provide the capability to process a program more efficiently and to process more sophisticated programs. These "advanced" statements are presented in this chapter.

Several statements presented in the first seven chapters have one or more options that provide the statement with additional capability. While these options are only used in certain situations, their absence from the language would make programming these situations much more difficult.

The organization of this chapter is designed to aid the programmer when it is desirable to use the advanced statements. Thus, the chapter is broken into two parts. First, the advanced statements that can be used in the DATA DIVISIØN will be discussed in the order in which they would appear and the frequency with which they are used. Second, the advanced statements of the PRØCEDURE DIVISIØN will be discussed in the order in which they would appear and the frequency with which they are used.

DATA DIVISION

The REDEFINES Clause

The REDEFINES clause allows the same computer storage area either to be referred to by more than one name or to provide an alternative description of the same name. That is, this clause specifies the redefinition of a storage area rather than of the elementary items occupying the storage area. The general format of this clause is

level-number   name-1   <u>REDEFINES</u>   name-2

The level number of name-1 and name-2 must be the same; it cannot be level number 88. Name-1 is the alternate name for the previously described storage area represented by name-2. Name-2 is the name of the previously described elementary item. The REDEFINES clause must be the first clause following name-1. There can be no sentences between the sentences describing name-1 and name-2 with a level number less than the level number assigned name-1 and name-2. For example,

```
A    B

     .
     .
     .
02 ITEM-1.
   03 NUM-1    PICTURE X.
   03 NUM-2    PICTURE XXX.
   03 NUM-3    PICTURE 99.
02 ITEM-2 REDEFINES ITEM-1        PICTURE X(6).

     .
     .
     .
```

In this example, ITEM-2 is name-1 and ITEM-1 is name-2. When ITEM-2 redefines ITEM-1, the redefinition includes all of the elementary items subordinate to ITEM-1 (NUM-1, NUM-2, and NUM-3).

The sentence describing name-2 cannot contain an ∅CCURS clause, nor can name-2 be subordinate to a sentence that contains an ∅CCURS clause. When name-1 has a level number assigned it other than 01, the specified storage area must be the same size as the storage area specified for name-2.

When the SYNCHR∅NIZED clause is specified for an elementary item that contains a REDEFINES clause, the elementary item that is redefined must have the proper boundary alignment for the elementary item that REDEFINES it. For example,

```
A    B
     .
     .
     .
02 ITEM-1      PICTURE X(4).
02 ITEM-2 REDEFINES ITEM-1    PICTURE S9(9) CØMPUTATIØNAL SYNCHRØNIZED.
```

care must be taken to insure that ITEM-1 begins on a fullword boundary.

When the SYNCHRØNIZED clause is specified for a numeric computational elementary item that is the first elementary item subordinate to an elementary item that contains a REDEFINES clause, the numeric computational elementary item cannot require the addition of slack bytes.

Except for condition-name sentences, sentences giving the new description of the storage area cannot contain a VALUE clause.

Sentences giving the new description of a storage area must follow the sentences describing the area being redefined without intervening sentences that define new storage areas. Multiple redefinitions of the same storage area should all use the name of the elementary item that originally defined the area. For example,

```
A    B
     .
     .
     .
02 ITEM-1      PICTURE 9(4).
02 ITEM-2 REDEFINES ITEM-1    PICTURE 9V999.
02 ITEM-3 REDEFINES ITEM-1    PICTURE 99V99.
     .
     .
     .
```

Elementary items within an area can be redefined without the size of their storage areas being changed. For example, the following sentences

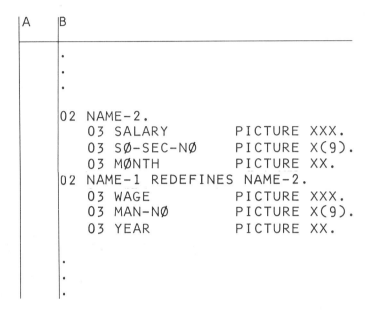

```
A   B

    .
    .
    .
02 NAME-2.
    03 SALARY        PICTURE XXX.
    03 SØ-SEC-NØ      PICTURE X(9).
    03 MØNTH          PICTURE XX.
02 NAME-1 REDEFINES NAME-2.
    03 WAGE           PICTURE XXX.
    03 MAN-NØ         PICTURE X(9).
    03 YEAR           PICTURE XX.
    .
    .
    .
```

result in the following storage area layout:

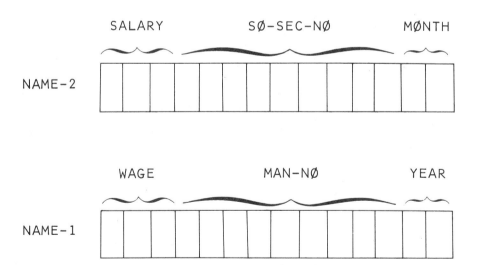

Elementary items can also be rearranged within a storage area. For example, the following sentences:

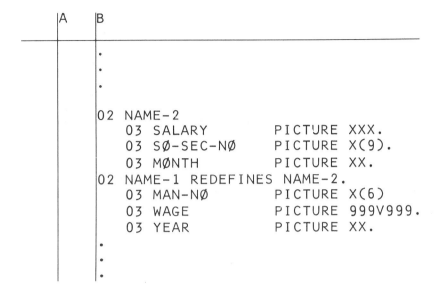

```
|A  |B
   | .
   | .
   | .
   | .
   |02 NAME-2
   |   03 SALARY          PICTURE XXX.
   |   03 SØ-SEC-NØ        PICTURE X(9).
   |   03 MØNTH           PICTURE XX.
   |02 NAME-1 REDEFINES NAME-2.
   |   03 MAN-NØ          PICTURE X(6)
   |   03 WAGE            PICTURE 999V999.
   |   03 YEAR            PICTURE XX.
   | .
   | .
   | .
```

result in the following storage area layout:

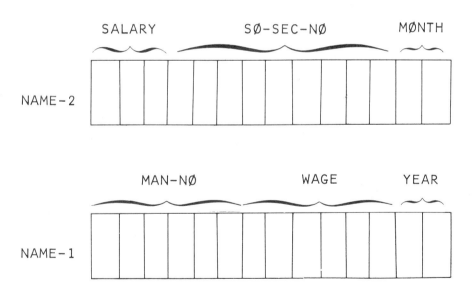

When a storage area is redefined, all descriptions of the area remain in effect. Thus, if ITEM-2 and ITEM-3 are two separate elementary items that share the same storage area due to redefinition, the statement "MØVE SUM TØ ITEM-2" or "MØVE TØTAL TØ ITEM-3" could be executed at any point in the program. In the first case, ITEM-2 would assume the value of SUM and take the form specified by the description of ITEM-2. In the second case, the same physical area would receive TØTAL according to the description of ITEM-3. It should be noted, however, that if both of the foregoing statements are executed successively in the order specified, the **value** TØTAL will overlay the value SUM. However, redefinition in itself does not cause any data to be erased and does not supersede a previous description.

The REDEFINES clause can also be used to initialize a table. For example, in the following illustration:

```
A      B
       .
       .
       .
01     DAY-VALUES.
       02 MØN   PICTURE A(9)   VALUE 'MØNDAY'.
       02 TUE   PICTURE A(9)   VALUE 'TUESDAY'.
       02 WED   PICTURE A(9)   VALUE 'WEDNESDAY'.
       02 THUR  PICTURE A(9)   VALUE 'THURSDAY'.
       02 FRI   PICTURE A(9)   VALUE 'FRIDAY'.
       02 SAT   PICTURE A(9)   VALUE 'SATURDAY'.
       02 SUN   PICTURE A(9)   VALUE 'SUNDAY'.
01     DAY-TABLE REDEFINES DAY-VALUES.
       02 DAY-OF-WEEK PICTURE A(9)   ØCCURS 7 TIMES.
       .
       .
       .
```

the group item DAY-VALUES, which has the name of a day of the week stored under each of its elementary items, is redefined such that the day names can be proceeded in a single-dimensional array named DAY-TABLE.

The Condition-Name Condition

The IF statement can be used to test the contents of a conditional variable to determine if the contents are equal to one of the values assigned to one of the condition-names representing each desired alternative of a particular condition associated with the conditional variable. A conditional variable and its associated condition-names are described in the DATA DIVISIØN. The condition-names must be described immediately following the conditional variable. For example,

```
A    B
     |
     | 02 MARITAL-STATUS   PICTURE 9.
     |    88 SINGLE VALUE 1.
     |    88 MARRIED VALUE 2.
     |    88 DIVØRCED VALUE 3.
     |
```

MARITAL-STATUS, which is the conditional variable, must be an elementary item. To reflect the fact that a name is a condition-name, it is assigned the level number 88. The condition-names SINGLE, MARRIED, and DIVØRCED do not represent a *data field,* but rather represent a *condition.* Thus, while a PICTURE clause must be used to describe MARITAL-STATUS, it cannot be used to describe the condition-names SINGLE, MARRIED, and DIVØRCED.

A VALUE clause is always associated with each condition name. The literal must be a type consistent with its description in the PICTURE clause describing the conditional variable.

The conditional variable MARITAL-STATUS is tested in the PRØCEDURE DIVISIØN by use of the three condition-names assigned above. Thus, the following simple conditional and unconditional transfer statements could be used to determine the condition of the marital status and to transfer to the appropriate paragraph in the program.

IF SINGLE GØ TØ PARA-1 IF MARRIED GØ TØ PARA-2 ELSE GØ TØ PARA-3.

While the conditional variable MARITAL-STATUS is being tested, it is not specified in the PRØCEDURE DIVISIØN. Rather, only the condition-names are used.

The JUSTIFIED RIGHT Clause

As indicated in Footnote b of Table 6-1, an alphabetic or alphanumeric elementary item is positioned in the receiving data field from left to right. Any unused positions to the right are filled with spaces. If the source data contain more characters than positions available in the receiving data field, the excess rightmost characters of the source data are truncated. These rules for positioning data in a receiving field can be altered by use of the following clause:

<u>JUSTIFIED</u> RIGHT

This clause can be used in any statement describing a nonnumeric elementary item receiving field in the DATA DIVISIØN. The clause is placed after either the PICTURE clause or, if present, the VALUE clause.

When this clause is used, the elementary item is positioned in the receiving data field from *right* to *left.* Any unused positions to the left are filled with spaces. If the source data contain more characters than positions available in the receiving data field, the excess leftmost characters of the source data are truncated. This clause cannot be used in a statement assigned a level number 88.

The SPECIAL-NAMES Paragraph

The CØNFIGURATIØN SECTIØN may contain a third paragraph called SPECIAL-NAMES. This paragraph provides the means to relate function-names (discussed below) to user-supplied mnemonic-names. It can also be used to specify the substitution character for the currency sign in the PICTURE clause. Finally, it can be used to exchange the functions of the comma and the period in the PICTURE clause and in numeric literals. The general format of this statement is

```
|A    |B
|     |
|SPECIAL-NAMES.
|     [function name IS mnemonic-name] . . .
|     [CURRENCY SIGN IS literal]
|     [DECIMAL-PØINT IS CØMMA] .
```

A function-name can be chosen from the following list:

1. SYSIN
2. SYSØUT
3. SYSPUNCH
4. CØNSØLE

Any one of these four function-names can be used in the DISPLAY and ACCEPT statements.

The literal specified in the CURRENCY SIGN IS option is used in the PICTURE clause to represent the currency sign ($). The literal must be a nonnumeric, single character which cannot be any of the following:

1. Alphabetic characters: A, B, C, D, Ø, P, R, S, V, X, Z, or the space
2. Numeric characters: 0 through 9
3. Special characters: * − , . ; ( ) + '

If the CURRENCY SIGN IS option is not present, only the $ can be used as the currency sign in the PICTURE clause.

The DECIMAL-PØINT IS CØMMA option causes the function of the comma and the period to be exchanged in the PICTURE clause and in numeric literals. Thus, whenever a decimal point must be used in a PIC-TURE clause or numeric literal, the comma must be used instead, and vice versa.

Illustration. Assume the following paragraph:

```
A   B
              .
              .
              .
ENVIRØNMENT DIVISIØN.
CØNFIGURATIØN SECTIØN.
SØURCE-CØMPUTER.    IBM-370-148.
ØBJECT-CØMPUTER.    IBM-370-148.
SPECIAL-NAMES.
      CØNSØLE IS KEYBØARD
      CURRENCY SIGN IS A
      DECIMAL-PØINT IS CØMMA.
              .
              .
              .
```

The use of KEYBØARD in either a DISPLAY and/or ACCEPT statement will cause the computer to either provide information on the console typewriter or accept data from the console typewriter, respectively. The alphabetic character A must be used instead of the $ wherever appropriate in the PICTURE clause, and the decimal point and comma must exchange their normal positions in the PICTURE clause and numeric literals.

The USAGE Clause

The USAGE clause specifies the form in which a data field is to be represented in the computer's memory. It is used in computers in which data can be stored in several different forms, one of which is more convenient for printing and punching (DISPLAY) and another of which is suitable for arithmetic operations (CØMPUTATIØNAL). While the USAGE clause does not have to be used in a COBOL program, it can in certain instances (discussed below) significantly affect the efficiency of the object program. The general format of this clause is

$$[\underline{USAGE} \text{ IS}] \left\{ \begin{array}{l} \underline{DISPLAY} \\ \underline{CØMPUTATIØNAL} \end{array} \right\}$$

This clause can be used in any statement in the DATA DIVISION assigned either a group or elementary item level number. If the clause is written at the group level, it applies to each elementary item in the group. At the elementary item level, the clause should be placed after either the PICTURE clause or, if present, the VALUE clause. The usage of an elementary item cannot contradict the usage of a group to which the elementary item is a member.

If the DISPLAY option is used, *one character is stored per byte.* This option should be used in all (1) punch card input and output data fields, (2) printer output data fields, (3) numeric data fields in the WØRKING-STØRAGE SECTIØN not involved in arithmetic and conditional operations, and (4) nonnumeric data fields in the WØRKING-STØRAGE SECTIØN. However, since the computer normally stores one character per byte (that is, the clause USAGE IS DISPLAY is automatically assumed by the computer), most programmers do not bother to use the USAGE IS DISPLAY option.

The CØMPUTATIONAL option can be used only with numeric computational data fields. When the option is used, the computer allocates either two, four, or eight bytes to the data field. The use of this option causes binary representation of the data. Thus, two characters are stored per byte. If the number being stored is one through four characters in length, two bytes are allocated; if the number being stored is five through nine characters in length, four bytes are allocated; and if the number being stored is ten through eighteen characters, eight bytes are allocated.

The CØMPUTATIØNAL option should be used only when a rather extensive series of calculations is going to be performed on a data field. Specifically, this option should be used only if a data field, such as a subscripted elementary item in a PERFØRM VARYING statement, is going to be arithmetically manipulated twelve or more times prior to being moved to a DISPLAY data field.

When the datum from a field of one form of USAGE is moved to a field of another form of USAGE, the datum is converted to the form of the receiving data field. Thus, if a datum from a DISPLAY data field is moved to a CØMPUTATIØNAL data field, approximately one-half as many bytes will be allocated in the computer's memory to the receiving data field. And if a datum from a CØMPUTATIØNAL data field is moved to a DISPLAY data field, approximately twice as many bytes will be allocated in the computer's memory to the receiving data field.

Illustration. Assume the following statements:

A	B		
77	AREA-1	PICTURE 9(5) USAGE IS DISPLAY.	
77	AREA-2	PICTURE 9(5) VALUE 12345 USAGE IS	
		CØMPUTATIØNAL.	

In the above examples, AREA-1 will be allocated five bytes and AREA-2 will be allocated four bytes in the computer's memory.

The SYNCHRONIZED Clause

When the USAGE IS CØMPUTATIØNAL clause is used with the description of an elementary item, the leftmost position of the data field must be aligned on either a halfword or a fullword boundary (storage address) prior to its being operated upon by an instruction.[†] Specifically, if the field size of an elementary item is S9 through S9(4), the item is aligned on a halfword (multiple of two) storage address; if the field size of an elementary item is S9(5) through S9(18), the item is aligned on a fullword (multiple of 4) storage address.

The boundary alignment of an elementary item can be automatically accomplished by the COBOL compiler. The compiler accomplishes this by compiling extra machine-language instructions that move the data field of an elementary item whose description includes a USAGE IS CØMPUTA-TIØNAL clause to the appropriate boundary each time the elementary item is referenced by a COBOL statement. However, these extra machine-language instructions take extra execution time.

The alternative to allowing the compiler to compile extra machine-language instructions is to use the SYNCHRØNIZED clause. This clause specifies the alignment of an elementary item on one of the proper boundaries in the computer's memory. That is, the contents of the elementary item are properly aligned prior to the compiling of the program. For example, in the following statement

```
A    B
77   GRAND-TØTAL  PICTURE S999V99 USAGE IS CØMPUTATIØNAL, SYNCHRØNIZED.
```

the elementary item GRAND-TØTAL is properly aligned prior to the compiling of the program. Thus, it will not have to be moved to a proper boundary prior to its being operated upon. For this reason, the SYNCHRØNIZED clause should always be used when the USAGE IS CØMPUTATIØNAL clause is used.

[†]A two-byte binary field is referred to as a *halfword* and a four-byte binary field is referred to as a *fullword*. These binary fields must have the proper *boundary alignment* before they can be operated upon by an instruction.

PROCEDURE DIVISION

The INTO Option

Generally, the contents of a record located on an input device are read into the computer's memory by means of an input record described in the FILE SECTIØN. However, the INTØ option can be used in the READ statement to cause the contents of the input record to also be transferred into another described area in either the WØRKING-STØRAGE SECTIØN or an output area in the FILE SECTIØN. The general format of the READ statement with the INTØ option included is

READ file-name RECØRD *INTØ* area-name   AT *END* imperative-statement.

The contents of the input record are available in both the regular input area described in the FILE SECTIØN and the area represented by area-name. Both areas must be appropriately described to accept the contents of the input record. The INTØ option cannot be used if the file being read contains more than one type of record image.

The use of the INTØ option has the same results as if a MØVE statement had been used to transfer the data from the regular input area to the other area. That is, the same data are located in two areas in the computer's memory.

Illustration. Assume that the following statement is executed:

READ INPUT-FILE INTØ AREA-1 AT END GØ TØ FINISH

This statement causes the contents of each record to be stored in the computer's memory in both the regular input area and AREA-1.

The WRITE Statement and LINAGE Clause

The use of an additional option of the WRITE statement combined with the LINAGE clause provides the means for automatic line spacing on a page. The expanded WRITE statement and the LINAGE clause formats are

The LINAGE Clause:

$$\underline{LINAGE} \text{ IS } \left\{ \begin{array}{l} \text{name-1} \\ \text{integer-1} \end{array} \right\} \text{ LINES } \left[\text{ ,WITH } \underline{FØØTING} \text{ AT } \left\{ \begin{array}{l} \text{name-2} \\ \text{integer-2} \end{array} \right\} \right]$$

$$\left[\text{ , LINES AT } \underline{TØP} \left\{ \begin{array}{l} \text{name-3} \\ \text{integer-3} \end{array} \right\} \right] \left[\text{ , LINES AT } \underline{BØTTØM} \left\{ \begin{array}{l} \text{name-4} \\ \text{integer-4} \end{array} \right\} \right]$$

The WRITE Statement:

WRITE record-name [FRØM name-1]

$$
\left[
\begin{Bmatrix} \underline{BEFØRE} \\ \underline{AFTER} \end{Bmatrix}
\quad ADVANCING \quad
\begin{Bmatrix}
\begin{Bmatrix} name\text{-}2 \\ integer \end{Bmatrix} & \begin{bmatrix} \underline{LINE} \\ \underline{LINES} \end{bmatrix} \\
\begin{Bmatrix} mnemonic\text{-}name \\ \underline{PAGE} \end{Bmatrix} &
\end{Bmatrix}
\right]
$$

$$
\left[
AT \begin{Bmatrix} \underline{END\text{-}ØF\text{-}PAGE} \\ \underline{EØP} \end{Bmatrix}
\quad imperative\text{-}statement
\right]
$$

The LINAGE clause, which is used in the FD statement describing the file of which the record indicated in the WRITE statement is a part, gives the line spacing specifications for the document to be printed. Integer-1 gives the maximum number of lines to be printed on each report, from the first heading line to the last total line. Integer-2 gives the maximum number of lines to be printed in the body of the report, not including any extra lines printed at the end of the report. As shown in Figure 8-1, the difference between integer-1 and integer-2 is the footing area (such as for totals) of the report.

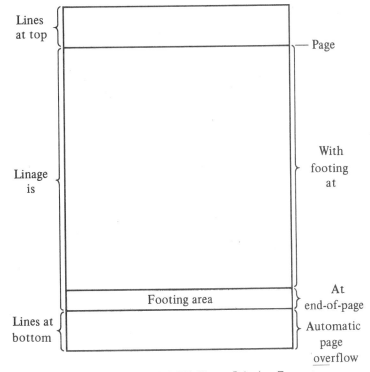

Figure 8-1: The LINAGE Clause Printing Format

Because integer-3 and integer-4 specify the number of blank lines at the top and bottom of the report, integer-1 plus integer-3 plus integer-4 should equal the number of available line on the report.

In place of integers, the values in the LINAGE clause can be represented by names. Thus, it is possible to vary the values used based on information received during execution of the program.

To illustrate the use of these statements, assume a report with the following format is to be printed.

LINE NUMBER	CONTENTS
1-5	Not used
6	The page header
7-58	The body of the report
59-61	The page totals
62-66	Not used

The **DATA DIVISIØN** would contain the following **LINAGE** clause:

```
A    B
DATA DIVISIØN.
     .
     .
     .
FD   PRINT FILE
     LABEL RECØRD IS ØMITTED
     LINAGE IS 56 LINES
          WITH FØØTING AT 53
          LINES AT TØP 5
          LINES AT BØTTØM 5.

01   PAYRØLL-RECORD.
     .
     .
     .
```

The page will consist of 66 lines which is the sum of the values referenced in each phase, except for the WITH FØØTING AT phrase. Five lines are unused at the top, and five at the bottom.

In the PRØCEDURE DIVISIØN, the statement:

```
WRITE PRINT-RECØRD FRØM PAGE-HEADER AFTER ADVANCING PAGE.
```

will cause printing of the header on line 6 because now **PAGE** is associated with line 6, since **LINES AT TØP 5** specifies that five lines be left blank at the top of the page.

Now consider these statements:

```
A     B
WRITE PAYRØLL-RECØRD
      AFTER ADVANCING 2 LINES
      AT END-ØF-PAGE PERFØRM REPØRT-TØTALS.



              .
              .
              .


REPØRT-TØTALS.
      WRITE PRINT-RECØRD FRØM REPØRT-TØTALS-RECØRD
          AFTER ADVANCING 3 LINES.
      WRITE PRINT-RECØRD FRØM PAGE-HEADER
          AFTER ADVANCING PAGE.
```

Report information will be printed from PAYRØLL-RECØRD until page line 58 (53 lines used + 5 unused top-of-page lines) is reached. Then the AT-END-ØF-PAGE phrase is executed. The program branches to the REPØRT-TØTALS paragraph and prints the REPØRT TØTALS RECØRD on the third line of the three-line footing area (56 minus 53). (Remember, this is page line 61.) Execution of the next WRITE statement results in a skip to line 6 of the next page to print PAGE-HEADER.

A special counter is used whenever the LINAGE clause is specified. It is called LINAGE-CØUNTER, a reserved word. It is set to 1 when the print file in which the LINAGE clause is used is opened or when an ADVANCING PAGE is encountered. The counter is automatically incremented the number of lines indicated when a WRITE statement is executed. When LINAGE-CØUNTER is equal to the value of the LINAGE specified an AT-END-ØF-PAGE condition occurs. The LINAGE-CØUNTER cannot be modified during execution of the program, but it can be accessed by another statement, such as the IF statement.

The Qualification of Names

A programmer-supplied name must be unique. Thus, the same name should not be used to represent different data in the same program. However, there are instances where for identification of the nature of the datum stored under it, it is desirable to use the same name to identify several data fields in the DATA DIVISIØN. In such a situation, the name can be made unique by referencing the name of some group to which the name is a member each time the name is used in the PRØCEDURE DIVISIØN. This is accomplished by the use of the following statement:

$$\text{name} \quad \left\{ \begin{array}{c} \underline{\text{ØF}} \\ \underline{\text{IN}} \end{array} \right\} \quad \text{group-name}$$

The reserved words ØF and IN can be used interchangeably when one is qualifying a name. A group name assigned a level number greater than the level number assigned the name being qualified can be used to qualify the name, so long as another data field with the same name does not exist within the group.

Illustration. Assume that the following two input files are described in a program.

```
|A    |B
|     |
| FD  |INPUT-FILE-1
|     |LABEL RECØRD IS ØMITTED.
| 01  |RECØRD-1.
|     |02 ID-NUMBER      PICTURE 9(5).
|     |  .
|     |  .
|     |  .
|     |
| FD  |INPUT-FILE-2
|     |LABEL RECØRD IS ØMITTED.
| 01  |RECØRD-2.
|     |02  ID-NUMBER      PICTURE 9(5).
|     |  .
|     |  .
|     |  .
```

The name ID-NUMBER exists in both RECØRD-1 and RECØRD-2. This name can be made unique in a MØVE statement by either "MØVE ID-NUMBER IN RECØRD-1 TØ IDENTIFICATIØN" or MØVE ID-NUMBER IN RECØRD-2 TØ IDENTIFICATIØN."

The MOVE CORRESPONDING Statement

In certain situations, it is desirable to simultaneously move several elementary items from one storage area to another storage area in the computer's memory. This can be accomplished by the use of the CØR-RESPØNDING option in the MØVE statement. The general format of the statement is

$$\underline{M\!\!\!\!/\,O\!VE} \quad \underline{C\!\!\!\!/\,ORRESP\!\!\!\!/\,ONDING} \quad \left\{ \begin{matrix} \text{group-name-1} \\ \text{record-name-1} \end{matrix} \right\} \underline{T\!\!\!\!/\,O} \left\{ \begin{matrix} \text{group-name-2} \\ \text{record-name-2} \end{matrix} \right\}$$

This statement causes the contents of the elementary items composing the name represented by group-name-1 or record-name-1 to be moved to those elementary items having the same name under the name represented by group-name-2 or record-name-2. Both the name represented by group-name-1 or record-name-1 and group-name-2 or record-name-2 can be either a group or record name. The contents of any elementary item in the receiving storage area not having the same name as an elementary item in the source storage area are not moved. In addition to having the same name, the source and receiving storage areas must be described according to the characteristics summarized in Table 6-1.

Illustration. Assume that the names shown in Table 8-1 each contain the indicated contents before and after a MØVE CØRRESPØNDING statement is executed.

Table 8-1: The Source Storage Area

A	B	Names		Before MØVE	After MØVE
01	RECØRD-1.				
	02 ITEM-A	PICTURE AAA.		SUM	Unchanged
	02 ITEM-B	PICTURE 9(5).		59372	Unchanged
	02 GRØUP-1.				
		03 ITEM-1	PICTURE X(5).	$5.25	Unchanged
		03 ITEM-2	PICTURE A(10).	BILL SMITH	Unchanged
		03 ITEM-3	PICTURE 9(5)V9(3).	74692372	Unchanged

The storage areas to which the contents are attempting to be moved are shown in Table 8-2. The contents of the storage areas are shown before and after the statement "MØVE CØRRESPØNDING RECØRD-1 TØ RECØRD-2" is executed.

Table 8-2: The Receiving Storage Area

A	B	Names		Before MØVE	After MØVE
01	RECØRD-2.				
	02 AMØUNT	PICTURE $9,999,99.		$2,163.25	Unchanged
	02 GRØUP-1.				
		03 ITEM-1	PICTURE X(5).	ABCDE	$5.25
		03 ITEM-2	PICTURE X(6).	THØMAS	BILL S
		03 ITEM-3	PICTURE $99.99	$64.35	$92.37
	02 ITEM-A	PICTURE X(5).			SUM

Since the elementary item ITEM-B and the elementary item AM∅UNT are not present in both the source and receiving storage areas, their contents are unchanged. However, the remaining elementary items in the receiving storage areas do have a name identical to the name of an elementary item in the source storage area. Thus, the contents of each name in the receiving area replace the contents of the appropriate name in the receiving area. It should be noted that the elementary items in the receiving area do not have to appear in the same sequence as the elementary items in the source area. Also, it is not necessary for the elementary items in the receiving area to have the same PICTURE clause as their counterparts in the source area. If the PICTURE clauses are not identical, the rules footnoted in Table 6-1 are followed.

The GO TO . . . DEPENDING ON Statement

The G∅ T∅ . . . DEPENDING ∅N statement is a conditional of the G∅ T∅ statement because it provides a multiple-branch capability based on a value. The general format of this statement is:

G∅ T∅ procedure-name-1 [procedure-name-2] . . .

DEPENDING ∅N identifier

The following is an illustration of the operational flow of this statement:

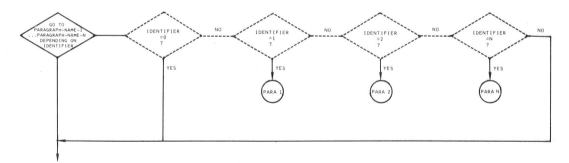

Figure 8-2: The Operational Flow of the G∅ T∅ . . . DEPENDING ∅N Statement

As indicated in the flow diagram, the branch to the beginning of a particular paragraph (or section) is based on the current value of the identifier. The identifier must be a positive, integer numeric literal with a PICTURE clause of four or less 9's. If the value of the identifier is outside the range of the nth paragraph, no branch occurs and control passes to the next sentence.

In the following illustration,

GØ TØ NEW-ØRDERS, IN-STØCK, ØUT-ØF-STØCK DEPENDING
ØN TRANSACTIØN-NUMBER.

if TRANSACTIØN-NUMBER has the number 2 stored under it a branch will
be made to the paragraph named IN-STØCK (the second paragraph name in
the series).

The ALTER Statement

The ALTER statement is used to substitute the paragraph named in a
GØ TØ statement, thus changing the paragraph branched to and executed.
The general format of this statement is:

ALTER procedure-name-1 TØ [PRØCEED TØ] procedure-name-2

[procedure-name-3 TØ [PRØCEED TØ] procedure-name-4] ...

Procedure-name-1 and, if used, procedure-name-3 must be the names of
paragraphs that contain one sentence consisting of only a GØ TØ statement.
Procedure-name-2 and, if used, procedure-name-4 must be the names of
either paragraphs of sections.

The effect of the ALTER statement is to replace the procedure-name
specified in the GØ TØ statement by the procedure-name specified in the
ALTER statement. In the following illustration,

```
A     B
PARAGRAPH-1
      GØ TØ BYPASS-PARAGRAPH.
PARAGRAPH-1A.
      .
      .
      .
BYPASS-PARAGRAPH.
      .
      .
      .
      ALTER PARAGRAPH-1 TØ PRØCEED TØ PARAGRAPH-2.
      .
      .
      .
PARAGRAPH-2.
      .
      .
      .
```

before the ALTER statement is executed, when control reaches PARA-GRAPH-1, the GØ TØ statement transfers control to **BYPASS-PARAGRAPH**. After execution of the ALTER statement, however, when control reaches PARAGRAPH-1, the GØ TØ statement transfers control to PARAGRAPH-2.

The INSPECT Statement

The INSPECT statement is used to count the number of times a specified character appears in a data field and/or to replace a character with another character. For example, the statement could be used to replace spaces with zeros in a data field prior to using the contents of the data field in an arithmetic computation. The general format of this statement is

Format 1:

$$\underline{\text{INSPECT}} \text{ data-name-1 } \underline{\text{TALLYING}} \left\{ , \text{data-name-2 } \underline{\text{FOR}} \left\{ , \left\{ \begin{array}{l} \underline{\text{ALL}} \\ \underline{\text{LEADING}} \\ \underline{\text{CHARACTERS}} \end{array} \right\} \left\{ \begin{array}{l} \text{data-name-3} \\ \text{literal-1} \end{array} \right\} \left[\left\{ \begin{array}{l} \underline{\text{BEFORE}} \\ \underline{\text{AFTER}} \end{array} \right\} \text{INITIAL} \left\{ \begin{array}{l} \text{data-name-4} \\ \text{literal-2} \end{array} \right\} \right] \right\} \dots \right\} \dots$$

Format 2:

$$\underline{\text{INSPECT}} \text{ data-name-1 } \underline{\text{REPLACING}} \left\{ \begin{array}{l} \underline{\text{CHARACTERS}} \underline{\text{BY}} \left\{ \begin{array}{l} \text{data-name-2} \\ \text{literal-1} \end{array} \right\} \left[\left\{ \begin{array}{l} \underline{\text{BEFORE}} \\ \underline{\text{AFTER}} \end{array} \right\} \text{INITIAL} \left\{ \begin{array}{l} \text{data-name-3} \\ \text{literal-2} \end{array} \right\} \right] \\ \left\{ \begin{array}{l} \underline{\text{ALL}} \\ \underline{\text{LEADING}} \\ \underline{\text{FIRST}} \end{array} \right\} \left\{ , \left\{ \begin{array}{l} \text{data-name-2} \\ \text{literal-1} \end{array} \right\} \underline{\text{BY}} \left\{ \begin{array}{l} \text{data-name-3} \\ \text{literal-2} \end{array} \right\} \left[\left\{ \begin{array}{l} \underline{\text{BEFORE}} \\ \underline{\text{AFTER}} \end{array} \right\} \text{INITIAL} \left\{ \begin{array}{l} \text{data-name-4} \\ \text{literal-3} \end{array} \right\} \right] \right\} \dots \end{array} \right\} \dots$$

Format 3:

$$\underline{\text{INSPECT}} \text{ data-name-1 } \underline{\text{TALLYING}} \left\{ , \text{data-name-2 } \underline{\text{FOR}} \left\{ , \left\{ \begin{array}{l} \underline{\text{ALL}} \\ \underline{\text{LEADING}} \\ \underline{\text{CHARACTERS}} \end{array} \right\} \left\{ \begin{array}{l} \text{data-name-3} \\ \text{literal-1} \end{array} \right\} \left[\left\{ \begin{array}{l} \underline{\text{BEFORE}} \\ \underline{\text{AFTER}} \end{array} \right\} \text{INITIAL} \left\{ \begin{array}{l} \text{data-name-4} \\ \text{literal-2} \end{array} \right\} \right] \right\} \dots \right\} \dots$$

$$\underline{\text{REPLACING}} \left\{ \begin{array}{l} \underline{\text{CHARACTERS}} \underline{\text{BY}} \left\{ \begin{array}{l} \text{data-name-5} \\ \text{literal-3} \end{array} \right\} \left[\left\{ \begin{array}{l} \underline{\text{BEFORE}} \\ \underline{\text{AFTER}} \end{array} \right\} \text{INITIAL} \left\{ \begin{array}{l} \text{data-name-4} \\ \text{literal-2} \end{array} \right\} \right] \\ \left\{ , \left\{ \begin{array}{l} \underline{\text{ALL}} \\ \underline{\text{LEADING}} \\ \underline{\text{FIRST}} \end{array} \right\} \left\{ , \left\{ \begin{array}{l} \text{data-name-5} \\ \text{literal-3} \end{array} \right\} \underline{\text{BY}} \left\{ \begin{array}{l} \text{data-name-6} \\ \text{literal-4} \end{array} \right\} \left[\left\{ \begin{array}{l} \underline{\text{BEFORE}} \\ \underline{\text{AFTER}} \end{array} \right\} \text{INITIAL} \left\{ \begin{array}{l} \text{data-name-7} \\ \text{literal-5} \end{array} \right\} \right] \right\} \dots \right\} \dots \end{array} \right\}$$

The statement's first format is used to count the number of times either a specified character or group of characters appear in a data field. The statement's *second format* is used to replace either a specified character with another character or group of characters with another group of characters. And the statement's *third format* is used to combine the capabilities of the first two formats.

Data-name must be described in the Data Division. If data-name represents a nonnumeric datum, the computer will successively examine each character in the datum, starting with the leftmost character. If data-name represents a numeric datum, the datum must consist of numeric characters and may possess an operational sign. As with the nonnumeric datum, the computer will successively examine each character in the datum starting with the leftmost character. The use of the alphabetic character S in the PICTURE clause to represent an assumed operational sign is ignored by the INSPECT statement.

Literal must be either a single character or group of characters whose type must be nonnumeric which must be consistent with that of the type of the datum stored under data-name. Literal also can be any figurative constant except "ALL literal."

When the ALL option is used, the contents of data-name-2 represents the number of occurrences of the specified character or group of characters. When the LEADING option is used, the contents of data-name-2 represent the number of occurrences prior to encountering a character other than the specified character or group of characters. And when the FIRST option is used, the contents of data-name-2 represent all characters encountered before the first occurrence of the specified character or group of characters.

The following replacement rules are followed when the REPLACING option is used:

1. When the ALL option is used, literal-2 is substituted for each occurrence of literal-1.
2. When the LEADING option is used, the substitution of literal-2 for each occurrence of literal-1 terminates as soon as either a character other than literal-1 or the rightmost position of the data field is encountered.
3. When the FIRST option is used, the first occurrence of literal-1 is replaced by literal-2.

Table 8-3 contains examples of the effect of several INSPECT statements.

Table 8-3: Illustrations of the INSPECT Statement

Statement	FIELD-1 (Before)	FIELD-1 (After)	COUNTER (After)	COUNT-1 (After)
1. INSPECT FIELD-1 TALLYING COUNTER FOR CHARACTERS BEFORE INITIAL ','.	456,3,9	456,3,9	3	N/A
2. INSPECT FIELD-1 REPLACING ALL ' ' BY '0'.	147 21	1470021	N/A	N/A
3. INSPECT FIELD-1 TALLYING COUNTER FOR LEADING ' ' REPLACING LEADING ' ' BY '*'.	bbbb456	****456	4	N/A
4. INSPECT FIELD-1 REPLACING FIRST '*' BY '$'.	****456	$***456	N/A	N/A
5. INSPECT FIELD-1 TALLYING COUNTER FOR CHARACTERS BEFORE '.', COUNT-1 FOR CHARACTERS AFTER '.'.	87323.4	87323.4	5	1
6. INSPECT FIELD-1 REPLACING ALL 'X' BY 'Y', 'B' BY 'Z', 'W' BY 'Q' AFTER INITIAL 'R'.	RXXBQWY ZACDWBR RAWRXEB	RYYZQQY ZACDWZR RAQRYEZ	N/A N/A N/A	N/A N/A N/A

The BLANK WHEN ZERO Clause

The BLANK WHEN ZERØ clause is used when it is desired that either a numeric computational or a numeric edited elementary item described in the DATA DIVISIØN is to be filled with blanks whenever its contents are zero. The general format of this clause is

BLANK WHEN *ZERØ*

The clause is placed after either the PICTURE clause or, if present, the VALUE clause. The clause cannot be used in a statement assigned a level number 88.

The ACCEPT Statement

The console typewriter can also be used as a slow input device. This input device can be used to enter small amounts of data to a program that is presently being executed.

To enter data into the computer's memory by means of this input device, the following statement is used:

ACCEPT name [*FRØM* mnemonic-name]

As in the DISPLAY statement, if the FRØM option is used, the message(s) will be read from the input device represented by mnemonic-name that is designated in the SPECIAL-NAMES paragraph of the CØNFIGURATIØN SECTIØN. If the FRØM option is not used, the data are entered on the card reader. An ACCEPT statement which includes the FRØM option should be preceded by a DISPLAY statement to inform the computer operator that he can expect to type something on the console typewriter.

When the ACCEPT statement is executed, the console typewriter automatically displays a system generated message code followed by the literal "AWAITING REPLY" on its keyboard. The computer system then waits until the computer operator types the appropriate reply on the keyboard. When the data are typed, it is stored in the computer's memory under the name in the ACCEPT statement. Whether it is or not, the data are treated as alphanumeric by the computer. As such, the data are left justified when it is stored. When the data are stored, the console typewriter is released and the execution of the program continues. For example, in the following statement,

ACCEPT RATE FRØM KEYBØARD.

the data typed on the keyboard are stored under the name RATE.

The Nested IF Statement

A simple conditional statement can be written as the true branch of a previous simple conditional statement. In such a situation, the latter simple conditional statement is "nested" in the former simple conditional statement. There is no specific limit to the number of simple conditional statements that may be nested. The only limitations are the size of the computer's memory and the fact that the logical structure of the statement quickly becomes confusing.

The nested conditional is, in fact, testing several conditionals in a single statement. It is a "short-cut" method of writing several simple or compound conditionals.

Figure 8-3 illustrates conditional statements with nested IF statements. (C stands for condition; S stands for any member of imperative statements; and the pairing of IF and ELSE is shown by the lines connecting them.)

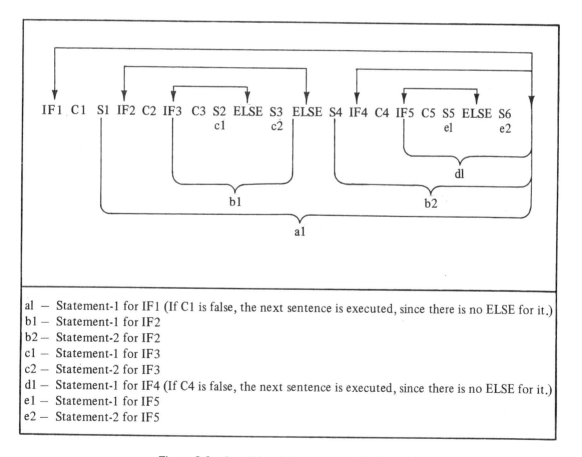

al — Statement-1 for IF1 (If C1 is false, the next sentence is executed, since there is no ELSE for it.)
b1 — Statement-1 for IF2
b2 — Statement-2 for IF2
c1 — Statement-1 for IF3
c2 — Statement-2 for IF3
d1 — Statement-1 for IF4 (If C4 is false, the next sentence is executed, since there is no ELSE for it.)
e1 — Statement-1 for IF5
e2 — Statement-2 for IF5

Figure 8-3: Conditional Statements with Nested IF Statements

Illustration. The following four simple conditional statements could be written to determine the classification of college students:

IF FRESHMAN ADD 1 TØ SUM-1.
IF SØPHØMØRE ADD 1 TØ SUM-2.
IF JUNIØR ADD 1 TØ SUM-3.
IF SENIØR ADD 1 TØ SUM-4.

The above four statements could also be written as the following nested IF statement:

IF FRESHMAN ADD 1 TØ SUM-1 IF SØPHØMØRE ADD 1 TØ SUM-2 IF JUNIØR ADD 1 TØ SUM-3 ELSE ADD 1 TØ SUM-4.

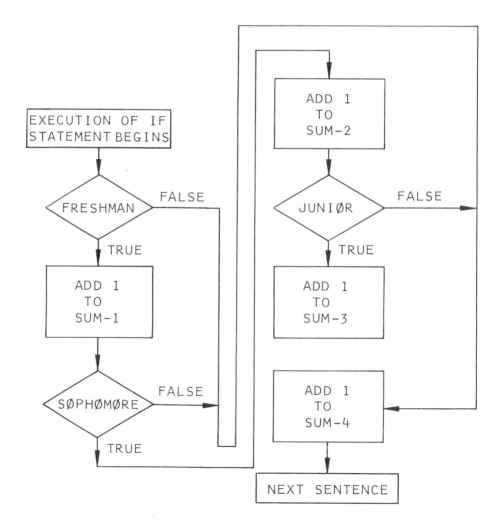

The ELSE option, if used, refers to the conditional statement immediately preceding it. If one or more ELSE options immediately follow the first ELSE option, the innermost IF and ELSE options are paired, then the next innermost IF and ELSE options, etc.

The STOP Statement

Occasionally, it is desirable to cause the computer to temporarily stop execution of a program. Such a situation when this temporary stop is desirable may be when certain types of errors are encountered, such as inaccurate input data or an improper computation, or so that the results of a test data can be verified. The general format of the statement to cause the temporary stop is

STØP literal

The literal can be either numeric or nonnumeric, or any figurative constant, except "ALL literal." When the statement is executed, the literal is printed on the console typewriter, and then the computer stops execution of the program. Execution of the program can be restarted only by the computer operator by means of the console typewriter. Upon restarting execution, the next statement is executed.

THE SORT STATEMENT

The records in a computer file usually are maintained in a sequence appropriate for the desired processing of the file. This sequence is generally based on a particular datum, such as social security number, account number, inventory number, etc. To update a file maintained in a particular order, the update transactions generally will be sorted into the same sequence as the file in order to achieve an efficient sequential file update. There are also frequent incidences in computing environments when the reporting of a particular file is required in a sequence other than the order in which the file is normally maintained. For example, an accounts receivable file normally would be maintained in account number sequence. For account collection purposes, it could be desirable to have a report listing of all accounts in the file in descending order on account balance. This would allow the credit department to place collection emphasis on those accounts with the greatest outstanding balances, which would provide the best return on time invested in the collection process.

COBOL provides the facilities to conveniently accomplish the sorting of both transaction and master files through the SØRT statement. The COBOL sorting process, though actually a quite complex multiphase operation, is externally straight forward and can be programmed easily by use of SØRT statement. Input to a SØRT procedure can consist of records from punched cards, magnetic tape, or magnetic disk. The actual sorting activity takes place on disk work areas under the control of the SØRT procedure. The final results of the SØRT process can be punched in cards, and/or written on tape, disk, or printer.

The actual sorting process consists of a sequence of events described as follows:

1. The file to be sorted and other necessary coding is identified in the COBOL program.
2. The SØRT procedure is invoked during the execution of the COBOL program.
3. Records are transferred to a "sort" file.
4. The sorting of the records occurs as per the specifications established by the SØRT statement.
5. The SØRT procedure transfers the sorted records back to the control of the COBOL program for continued processing.

At the discretion of the programmer, the transferring of records to and from the SØRT procedure can be under the direct control of the COBOL program, or can be handled automatically by the SØRT procedure. Direct control of the transferring of records to and from the sort file affords the programmer more flexibility in processing. For example, controlling record input to a SØRT procedure would allow a programmer to selectively exclude records from a sort. Records also can be modified before or after being transferred to or from the sort. However, direct control of record transfer does require more programming on the part of the programmer.

The SORT Statement Format

The ENVIRONMENT, DATA and PROCEDURE Divisions all require appropriate coding to utilize the SØRT procedure. The coding for the ENVIRONMENT Division is identical to the coding normally used for SELECT clauses for other files. The programmer must simply include a SELECT clause for the unsorted input file, the output file, and the actual sort file.

The general format of the SØRT procedure coding for the DATA and PRØCEDURE DIVISIØN is as follows:

<u>DATA DIVISIØN</u>

<u>SD</u> sort-file-name

$$[\underline{DATA} \quad \begin{Bmatrix} \underline{RECØRD} \text{ IS} \\ \underline{RECØRDS} \text{ ARE} \end{Bmatrix} \quad \text{data-name-1 (data-name-2) ...]}$$

[<u>RECØRD</u> CØNTAINS (integer-1 <u>TØ</u>) integer-2 CHARACTERS]

The letters "SD" are used to replace the usual letters, "FD". This modification simply indicates to the COBOL compiler that this file will be sorted. Accordingly, the file is automatically given the attributes defined by the SØRT procedure.

PRØCEDURE DIVISIØN

$$\underline{S\emptyset RT} \text{ file-name-1 } \emptyset N \quad \left\{ \begin{array}{l} \underline{DESCENDING} \\ \underline{ASCENDING} \end{array} \right\} \quad KEY \text{ (data-name-1)} \ldots$$

$$\left[\emptyset N \left\{ \begin{array}{l} \underline{DESCENDING} \\ \underline{ASCENDING} \end{array} \right\} \quad KEY \text{ (data-name-2)} \ldots \right] \ldots$$

$$\left\{ \begin{array}{l} \underline{INPUT} \ \underline{PR\emptyset CEDURE} \text{ IS section-name-1 } (\underline{THRU} \text{ section-name-2}) \\ \underline{USING} \text{ file-name-2} \end{array} \right\}$$

$$\left\{ \begin{array}{l} \underline{\emptyset UTPUT} \ \underline{PR\emptyset CEDURE} \text{ IS section-name-3 } (\underline{THRU} \text{ section-name-4}) \\ \underline{GIVING} \text{ file-name-3} \end{array} \right\}$$

The reserved word SØRT initiates the SØRT procedure. "File-name-1" is a required entry which must correlate with the appropriate SD file in the DATA Division. The file indicated by "file-name-1" is where the input file will be transferred to be sorted. The reserved work "ØN" is an optional entry followed by either the word "DESCENDING" or "ASCENDING" which establishes the sequencing of the file to be sorted. The optional reserved word KEY is followed by "data-name-1", which indicates the field upon which the file is to be sorted. Note that more than one SØRT key can be used—to a maximum of 12. The use of multiple SØRT keys allows hierarchical structuring of sorts. "Data-name-1" is the major sort key, with any additional keys becoming minor sort keys. This means that the file will be sorted on the last specified sort key first, and the SØRT procedure will sequentially work back, sorting on each key until a final sort is performed on the first specified sort field—"data-name-1". Characters are sorted in the following ascending order:

```
 1. . . . . . . . . . . . .    (SPACE)
 2. . . . . . . . . . . . . .  (PERIOD OR DECIMAL POINT)
 3. . . . . . . . . . . . . <  (LESS THAN)
 4. . . . . . . . . . . . . (  (LEFT PARENTHESIS)
 5. . . . . . . . . . . . . +  (PLUS SYMBOL)
 6. . . . . . . . . . . . . $  (CURRENCY SYMBOL)
 7. . . . . . . . . . . . . *  (ASTERISK)
 8. . . . . . . . . . . . . )  (RIGHT PARENTHESIS)
 9. . . . . . . . . . . . . ;  (SEMICOLON)
10. . . . . . . . . . . . . -  (HYPHEN OR MINUS SYMBOL)
11. . . . . . . . . . . . . /  (STROKE OR SLASH)
```

```
 12.  . . . . . . . . . . . . .  ,  (COMMA)
 13.  . . . . . . . . . . . . .  >  (GREATER THAN)
 14.  . . . . . . . . . . . . .  '  (APOSTROPHE OR SINGLE QUOTATION MARK)
 15.  . . . . . . . . . . . . .  =  (EQUAL SIGN)
 16.  . . . . . . . . . . . . .  "  (QUOTATION MARK)
17-42.  . . . . . . . . . . . .  A THROUGH Z
43-51.  . . . . . . . . . . . .  -9 THROUGH -1
52-61.  . . . . . . . . . . . .  0 THROUGH 9
```

This is the Extended Binary-Coded Decimal Interchange Code, or EBCDIC, sorting sequence. The apostrophe or single quotation mark is available only on IBM and WATBOL compilers.

As indicated previously, the programmer can allow the SØRT procedure to automatically control the transferring of records to and from the SØRT procedure. In this case, the USING and GIVING options are used.

The USING clause indicates the name of the input file (file-name-2) from which the records to be sorted are obtained. Records in the input file and the sort file must be the same length. The USING clause automatically opens the input file, reads the records, and closes the file after all of the records have been read. Therefore, these instructions are not written by the programmer.

The GIVING clause indicates the name of the output file (file-name-3) to which the output (records) of the SØRT statement is assigned. Records in the sort file and the output file must be the same length. The GIVING clause automatically opens the output file, writes the sorted records into it, and closes the file after all of the sorted records have been written. Thus, similar to the USING clause, these instructions are not written by the programmer.

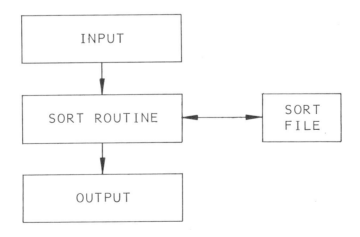

Figure 8-4: Sort Operation with USING and GIVING Clauses.

The USING and GIVING clauses should be used when the records of a file are to be read, sorted, and written without any other manipulation. There are situations, however, when other processing steps are necessary. When this is the case, the programmer must write either the input and/or output procedures by means of the INPUT PRØCEDURE and/or the ØUTPUT PRØCEDURE clauses. For example, "section-name-1" THRU "section-name-2" could consist of a sequence of COBOL statements which would: (1) ØPEN the input file, (2) READ the records, (3) exclude records based on certain criteria, (4) MØVE records to the appropriate fields of the record established in the SD, (5) RELEASE records to the SØRT procedure, (6) RETURN records from the SØRT procedure, (7) WRITE the records, and (8) CLØSE the input file after all of the records has been read.

The RELEASE Statement

The records from the programmer-written input procedure must be passed to the sort statements for processing. This is accomplished by means of the RELEASE statement, which is written as follows:

RELEASE sort-record-name [FRØM area-name].

"Sort-record-name" is the name of the sort record described in the sort file. When this statement is executed, a record to be sorted from the input file is "released" to the SØRT procedure. When the FRØM area-name option is also specified, the record first would be moved from the storage area represented by "area-name" to the sort-file name. Then the record would be released to the SØRT procedure. After a record has been released to the SØRT procedure, it can no longer be referred to in the INPUT PRØCEDURE.

The RETURN Statement

After the data records have been sorted by the SØRT statement, control must be "returned" from the SØRT statement to the output procedure. This is accomplished by means of the RETURN statement, which is written as follows:

RETURN sort-file RECØRD [INTØ area-name]
AT END imperative-statement.

This statement must be used in the ØUTPUT PRØCEDURE section. Execution of the statement results in a record being accessed from the sort-file in exactly the same manner as the READ statement accesses record from an input file. The contents of the "returned" record are assigned to the

appropriate elementary items composing the record described in the sort-file
(SD level). The INTØ option can be used to return the contents of a sort-file
record into either a group item described in the WØRKING-STØRAGE
SECTIØN or into a different record described in the FILE SECTIØN. The
AT END phrase is a required "conditional." It is executed only when there
are no more records to be returned from the sort-file.

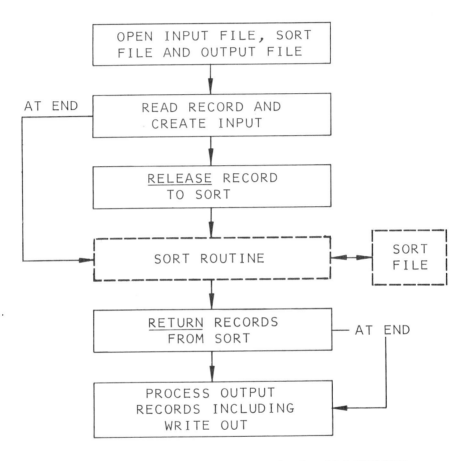

Figure 8-5: Sort Operation with INPUT and ØUTPUT PRØCEDURES.

The input and output procedures are executed under the control of the
SØRT statement. After the statements within the procedures are executed,
the program always branches back to the statement immediately following
the SØRT statement. Therefore, all branches within either of the two sections must be rejoined prior to the last statement in the section being executed. However, in certain instances the logical execution of the program
within the input or output procedure prevents the recombining of several
branches. For example, the program may proceed along two mutually
exclusive paths. In such a situation, a separate paragraph can be created that

contains only the statement EXIT, and each branch is tranferred to this paragraph. The general format of this paragraph is

    paragraph-name. <u>EXIT</u>.

In many instances, this is the last paragraph in the input or output procedure.

To illustrate the use of the SØRT statement, the appropriate COBOL program segments are shown in Figure 8-6 for sorting the accounts receivable file described earlier in descending order on account balance.

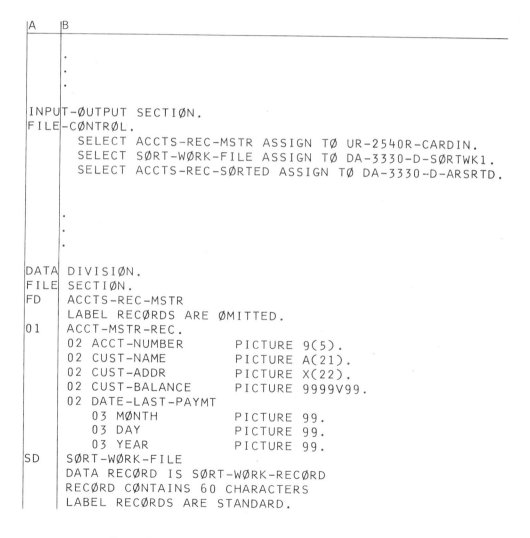

```
|A    |B
     |      .
     |      .
     |      .
     |
INPUT-ØUTPUT SECTIØN.
FILE-CØNTRØL.
     |      SELECT ACCTS-REC-MSTR ASSIGN TØ UR-2540R-CARDIN.
     |      SELECT SØRT-WØRK-FILE ASSIGN TØ DA-3330-D-SØRTWK1.
     |      SELECT ACCTS-REC-SØRTED ASSIGN TØ DA-3330-D-ARSRTD.
     |
     |      .
     |      .
     |      .
     |
DATA DIVISIØN.
FILE SECTIØN.
FD   | ACCTS-REC-MSTR
     | LABEL RECØRDS ARE ØMITTED.
01   | ACCT-MSTR-REC.
     |      02 ACCT-NUMBER        PICTURE 9(5).
     |      02 CUST-NAME          PICTURE A(21).
     |      02 CUST-ADDR          PICTURE X(22).
     |      02 CUST-BALANCE       PICTURE 9999V99.
     |      02 DATE-LAST-PAYMT
     |         03 MØNTH           PICTURE 99.
     |         03 DAY             PICTURE 99.
     |         03 YEAR            PICTURE 99.
SD   | SØRT-WØRK-FILE
     | DATA RECØRD IS SØRT-WØRK-RECØRD
     | RECØRD CØNTAINS 60 CHARACTERS
     | LABEL RECØRDS ARE STANDARD.
```

Figure 8-6: Sort Operation with USING and GIVING Clauses.

```
01    SØRT-WØRK-RECØRD.
      02 ACCT-NUMBER        PICTURE 9(5).
      02 CUST-NAME          PICTURE A(21).
      02 CUST-ADDR          PICTURE X(22).
      02 CUST-BALANCE       PICTURE 9999V99.
      02 DATE-LAST-PAYMT.
         03 MØNTH           PICTURE 99.
         03 DAY             PICTURE 99.
         03 YEAR            PICTURE 99.
FD    ACCTS-REC-SØRTED
      DATA RECØRD IS SØRTED-REC
      RECØRD CØNTAINS 60 CHARACTERS
      LABEL RECØRDS ARE STANDARD.
01    SØRTED-RECØRD.
      02 ACCT-NUMBER        PICTURE 9(5).
      02 CUST-NAME          PICTURE A(21).
      02 CUST-ADDR          PICTURE X(22).
      02 CUST-BALANCE       PICTURE 9999V99.
      02 DATE-LAST-PAYMT.
         03 MØNTH           PICTURE 99.
         03 DAY             PICTURE 99.
         03 YEAR            PICTURE 99.
PRØCEDURE DIVISIØN.

          .
          .
          .


SØRT-ACC-REC-FILE.
      SØRT SØRT-WØRK-FILE
      ØN DESCENDING KEY CUST-BALANCE
      USING ACCTS-REC-MSTR
      GIVING ACCTS-REC-SØRTED.

          .
          .
          .
```

Figure 8-6: Sort Operation with USING and GIVING Clauses. (continued)

The preceding series of program statements would create a new disk file of the accounts receivable master file. The new file would be sequenced in descenidng order keyed on CUST-BALANCE.

For a more complex example, the sort process could be modified as follows:

1. All accounts with zero balances could be excluded. This would be appropriate since, for collection purposes, including those accounts is of little, if any, value. This modification would also save sort time.

2. The sorting could be keyed on customer balance (descending) with year and month (ascending) of last payment. This would allow placing collection emphasis on those accounts with the greatest delinquency, starting with the largest balances within each delinquency category.

3. The output from the program could be written by the printer rather than being written on to disk.

The statement modifications necessary to achieve this new sort are shown in Figure 8-7.

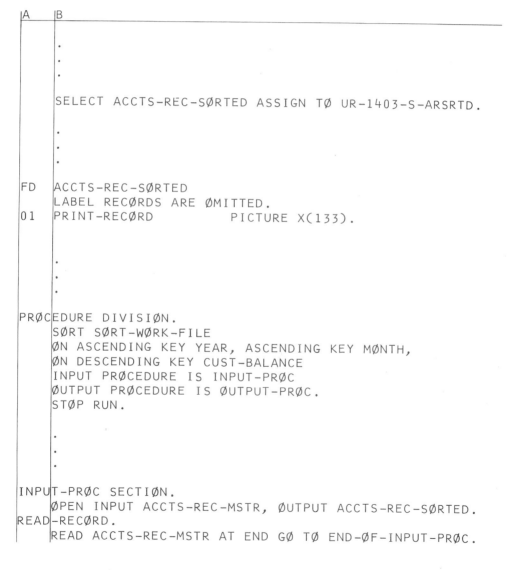

```
|A    |B
     |  .
     |  .
     |  .
     |SELECT ACCTS-REC-SØRTED ASSIGN TØ UR-1403-S-ARSRTD.
     |  .
     |  .
     |  .
|FD  |ACCTS-REC-SØRTED
     |LABEL RECØRDS ARE ØMITTED.
|01  |PRINT-RECØRD          PICTURE X(133).
     |  .
     |  .
     |  .
|PRØCEDURE DIVISIØN.
     |SØRT SØRT-WØRK-FILE
     |ØN ASCENDING KEY YEAR, ASCENDING KEY MØNTH,
     |ØN DESCENDING KEY CUST-BALANCE
     |INPUT PRØCEDURE IS INPUT-PRØC
     |ØUTPUT PRØCEDURE IS ØUTPUT-PRØC.
     |STØP RUN.
     |  .
     |  .
     |  .
|INPUT-PRØC SECTIØN.
     |ØPEN INPUT ACCTS-REC-MSTR, ØUTPUT ACCTS-REC-SØRTED.
|READ-RECØRD.
     |READ ACCTS-REC-MSTR AT END GØ TØ END-ØF-INPUT-PRØC.
```

Figure 8-7: Sort Operation with INPUT and ØUTPUT PRØCEDURES

```
      IF CUST-BALANCE EQUALS 0 GØ TØ READ-RECØRD.
      MØVE ACCT-MSTR-REC TØ SØRT-WØRK-RECØRD.
      RELEASE SØRT-WØRK-RECØRD.
      GØ TØ READ-RECØRD.
END-ØF-INPUT-PRØC.
      EXIT.
ØUTPUT-PRØC SECTIØN.
WRITE-RECØRD.
      RETURN SØRT-WØRK-FILE RECØRD AT END GØ TØ CLØSE-FILE.
      MØVE SØRT-WØRK-RECØRD TØ PRINT-RECØRD.
      WRITE PRINT-RECØRD AFTER ADVANCING 2 LINES.
      GØ TØ WRITE-RECØRD.
CLØSE-FILE.
      CLØSE ACCTS-REC-MSTR, ØUTPUT ACCTS-REC-SØRTED.
```

Figure 8-7: Sort Operation with INPUT and ØUTPUT PRØCEDURES. (Continued)

Note that YEAR and MØNTH are sorted on ascending order while CUST-BALANCE is sorted on descending order. The result of the sort will be that each customer balance will be listed in descending order within ascending ordered years and ascending ordered months within each year.

QUESTIONS

1. Discuss the function of the REDEFINES clause.

2. What signifies an elementary item as being a condition name? What is the function of a condition name?

3. What is the function of the JUSTIFIED RIGHT clause and of what use is it to a programmer?

4. Where is a SPECIAL-NAMES paragraph located in a COBOL program and what SPECIAL-NAMES options are available to the programmer?

5. What is the function of the INTØ option of a READ statement?

6. Discuss the function of the FRØM option of a WRITE statement.

7. How does the MØVE CØRRESPØNDING statement differ from the simple MØVE statement?

8. Discuss the INSPECT statement in relation to how the TALLYING option might be used. What is the use of the REPLACING option?

*

DISK AND TAPE STATEMENTS

The medium of punched cards for input and printer printout for output has been discussed or implied in the first eight chapters. There are several other common storage media, such as direct-access devices (magnetic disk and drum) and magnetic tape, that can be used as either input and/or output medium. This chapter will focus on the magnetic disk and magnetic tape as an input and output medium.

The storage of data on and the reading of data from a magnetic disk or magnetic tape involves only the minor addition of several statements and the modification of one or more statements already discussed. These additional and modified statements are discussed in this chapter. This is accomplished within the framework of each of the four divisions composing a COBOL program.

THE IDENTIFICATION DIVISION

This division requires neither any additional statements nor the expansion of statements already discussed if either a magnetic disk or a magnetic tape is being referenced in the program. The division is prepared according to the rules and procedures discussed in Chapter 3.

FILE ORGANIZATION and FILE ACCESS

The files discussed in the previous chapters have been read and written in sequence. Punched cards were read in the sequence in which they were arranged in the data deck; the records were generally processed serially (one after another) in the same order. However, alternative file processing methods are available in COBOL.

In describing the use of files, it is important to distinguish between file organization and file access. File organization refers to the *way* the records of a file are organized for use. COBOL supports three file organizations:

File organization	Explanation
Sequential	The records in the file are organized logically in sequence based on a record key.
Relative	The records in the file are stored in logical locations, each of which has an integer number associated with it.
Indexed	Often termed indexed sequential or ISAM (indexed sequential access method) the records in the file are organized logically in the sequence written (based on a record key), and a separate index is automatically established by the computer which allows the storage address of any record to be identified by the "key" associated with the record.

File organization refers to logical organization rather than the physical organization. For files on punched cards or magnetic tape, logical and physical organization are the same. For files on direct-access devices (such as magnetic disk), the logical and physical organization can be the same or different. For example, an indexed file is logically organized sequentially. But physically, it could be stored on a magnetic disk in a number of non-contiguous storage locations. The sequence would in this case be maintained by a data item in each record, called a pointer, which points to the next record in the sequence. However, the programmer should be concerned only with the logical organization.

In contrast to file organization, file access mode refers to *how* the records of a file are to be obtained from the storage medium. There are three access modes supported by COBOL:

Access mode	Explanation
Sequential	The records are written or read one at a time in the sequence in which they are logically organized; in order to read the third record, the first and second must first be read.

Random	The records can be obtained in any order, regardless of the order in which they were written or the physical or logical order of the records in the file.
Dynamic	The records are accessed in both sequential and random mode during the same processing of the file.

The organization and access methods available for use depend, in part, on the storage medium.

Type of storage	Type of organization	Mode of access
Serial-access (punched cards and magnetic tape)	Sequential	Sequential
Direct-access (disk, drum, mass storage subsystems)	Sequential	Sequential
	Relative	Sequential Random Dynamic
	Indexed	Sequential Random Dynamic

Sequential organization with sequential access is available when using either serial-access and direct-access storage devices. Relative and indexed sequential organizations require the use of a direct-access storage device such as magnetic disk.

THE ENVIRONMENT DIVISION

The first section within this division, the CØNFIGURATIØN SECTIØN, is prepared according to the rules and procedures discussed in Chapter 4. The second section, the INPUT-ØUTPUT SECTIØN, however, must be assigned several additional clauses in addition to the SELECT and ASSIGN clauses. The specific additional clauses depend upon the particular program. The following is a discussion of four of these additional clauses.

The ORGANIZATION Clause

The ∅RGANIZATI∅N clause defines the *way* the records of a file as organized for use. The general format of this clause is

$$\underline{\text{∅RGANIZATI∅N}} \text{ IS } \left\{ \begin{array}{l} \underline{\text{SEQUENTIAL}} \\ \underline{\text{RELATIVE}} \\ \underline{\text{INDEXED}} \end{array} \right\}$$

The absence of this clause or the specification of ∅RGANIZATI∅N IS SEQUENTIAL indicates the records will be either sequentially written into a file when a WRITE statement is executed or sequentially read from a file when a READ statement is executed.

In certain situations, however, the records to be processed will not be (are not) sequentially organized. In such situations, either ∅RGANIZATI∅N IS RELATIVE or ∅RGANIZATI∅N IS INDEXED is used, depending upon whether the records of the file will be (are) organized relative or indexed.

The ACCESS MODE Clause

The ACCESS M∅DE clause defines how the records of a file are to be obtained from the storage medium. The general format of this clause is

$$\underline{\text{ACCESS}} \text{ M∅DE } \underline{\text{IS}} \left\{ \begin{array}{l} \underline{\text{SEQUENTIAL}} \\ \underline{\text{RAND∅M}} \\ \underline{\text{DYNAMIC}} \end{array} \right\}$$

The absence of this clause or the specification of ACCESS IS SEQUENTIAL indicates the record will be either sequentially written into a file when a WRITE statement is executed or sequentially read from a file when a READ statement is executed.

In certain situations, however, the records will not be processed sequentially. In such situations, the process made of either random or dynamic must be used.

When ACCESS IS RAND∅M is specified, the storage and retrieval of records are based upon a "key" associated with each record.† Thus, the RELATIVE KEY clause (discussed next) must also be used. When ACCESS IS DYNAMIC is specified, the storage and retrieval of records are based upon an index and "key" associated with each record. Thus, the REC∅RD KEY clause (discussed after the RELATIVE KEY clause) must be used.

---

†A key is a programmer-selected, unique data field within each record.

The RELATIVE KEY Clause

The RELATIVE KEY clause is optional if the access mode is sequential and required if the access mode is RANDØM. Its function is to contain the storage address for either a particular record to be accessed (written or read) or the record that was last accessed. The general format of the RELATIVE KEY clause is

RELATIVE KEY IS name

The "name" specified in the clause must be described as an unsigned numeric data field in the WØRKING-STØRAGE SECTIØN. However, the name cannot be contained in the file for which it is the key.

If the access mode is sequential, a relative record number from one through the number of records in the file is stored in the RELATIVE KEY field prior to accessing a record. For example, when creating the file, the records are written in successively higher relative record locations, starting with relative record location 1.

However, if the random access mode is used, the records are written (read) in the relative record location indicated by the RELATIVE KEY field. Any unused record locations are indicated at the beginning of the file when the file is created so that when subsequent reference is made to a record location in the file, it can be immediately determined whether or not the location contains an active record. If a referenced record location does not contain an active record, it will be indicated on the printer printout.

The RECORD KEY Clause

The RECØRD KEY clause must be used whenever the dynamic process mode of either storing or retrieving records is used. This is due to the fact that a RECØRD KEY (record identifier, which serves as a unique symbolic identifier for a record and is associated with the record itself) is located in an index (automatically created by the computer when the file is first stored on the direct-access medium and associated with the storage address of the record.

The general format of the RECØRD KEY clause is

RECØRD KEY IS name

THE DATA DIVISION

The second section within this division, the WØRKING-STØRAGE SECTIØN, is prepared according to the rules and procedures discussed in

Chapter 5. The first section, the FILE SECTIØN, however, may be assigned one or more additional clauses in addition to the LABEL RECØRDS clause, which must be expanded upon. The specific additional clauses depend upon the particular program. The clauses may appear in any sequence. The last clause is terminated by a period.

For readability, each clause should be placed on a separate line. More than one clause, however, may be placed on the same line.

The following is a discussion of each of the clauses that can be assigned to the FILE SECTIØN.

The BLOCK CONTAINS Clause

The BLØCK CØNTAINS clause is used to specify the size of a physical record.[†] The general format of this clause is

$$\underline{BL\emptyset CK} \text{ C\emptyset NTAINS } [\text{integer-1 } \underline{T\emptyset}] \text{ integer-2 } \begin{Bmatrix} \underline{\text{CHARACTERS}} \\ \underline{\text{REC\emptyset RDS}} \end{Bmatrix}$$

The BLØCK CØNTAINS clause is unnecessary when a physical record contains only one complete logical record. However, if a physical record contains several complete logical records, this clause is required.

The BLØCK CØNTAINS clause need not be specified for direct-access files whose records have a recording mode of either F, V, or U.[‡] Also, the clause need not be specified for magnetic tape files whose records are specified as having a recording mode of U.

When both integer-1 and integer-2 appear, they must be positive integers. The RECØRDS option may be used unless one of the following situations exists, in which case the CHARACTERS option should be used:

1. The physical record contains padding [area(s) not contained in a logical record composing the physical record].

[†] A record may be classified as being one of two types: physical or logical. A physical record contains one or more logical records. A logical record is one record.

[‡] A record assigned a recording mode of F indicates that the record is *fixed* in length (every record within the file contains the same number of bytes).

A record assigned a recording mode of V indicates that the record is *variable* in length (the records within the file do not contain the same number of bytes).

A record assigned a recording mode of U indicates that the record is *unspecified* in length (a particular record within the file may be either fixed or variable in length).

2. The logical records are grouped in such a manner that an inaccurate physical record size would be implied.

3. The logical records extend across physical records; that is, the recording mode is S (spanned).

The use of the RECØRDS option causes the COBOL compiler to assume that the block size provides for integer-2 logical records of maximum size. The compiler provides additional space for any required control bytes.

When the CHARACTERS option is used, the physical record size reflects the number of bytes occupied in the computer's memory by the characters composing the physical record, regardless of the number of characters used to represent the elementary item within the physical record. (The number of bytes occupied in the computer's memory by an elementary item is included as part of the discussion of the USAGE clause in Chapter 8.) Integer-1 and integer-2 must include slack bytes and control bytes contained in the physical record.

If the CHARACTERS option is used and only integer-2 is included and it is not defined as zero, integer-2 represents the exact size of the physical record. However, if both integer-1 and integer-2 are included, they refer to the minimum and maximum size of the physical record respectively.

If the BLØCK CØNTAINS clause is omitted, the computer assumes that the records are not blocked. When neither the CHARACTERS nor the RECORDS option is specified, the computer assumes the CHARAC-TERS option.

The RECORD CONTAINS Clause

The RECØRD CØNTAINS clause is used to specify the size of a particular type of record in a file. The general format of this clause is

RECØRD CØNTAINS [integer-1 TØ] integer-2 CHARACTERS

Integer-1 and integer-2 must be positive integers. The following three factors should be considered when one is using this clause:

1. If both integer-1 and integer-2 are used, they refer to the number of characters in the smallest record and the number of characters in the largest record, respectively.

2. Integer-2 should not be used by itself unless each record in the file is the same size. If integer-2 is used by itself, it represents the exact number of characters composing each record in the file.

3. The size of the record must reflect the number of bytes occupied in the computer's memory by the characters composing the record, regardless of the number of characters used to represent the elementary item within the record. (The number of bytes occupied in the computer's memory by an elementary item is included as part of the discussion of the USAGE clause in Chapter 8.)

The RECØRD CØNTAINS clause is never required. However, the author recommends that this clause always be used, as it provides a convenient way of checking on the size of the records being processed.

The LABEL RECORDS Clause

The LABEL RECØRDS clause specifies whether or not labels are assigned to the file; if they are assigned, it identifies them. It is the only clause required in every File Description.

Data stored on either mass storage or magnetic tape devices are invisible to the naked eye, and as such the computer must be given some means of knowing where the first data record of a particular file begins and where the last data record of that file ends. This is accomplished by means of a *header label* and a *trailer label* record. A header label record is an 80-byte record that precedes the first data record of a file. It contains information identifying the file and control information that helps to prevent the file from accidently being erased. A trailer label record is an 80-byte record that follows the last record of a file. The record contains control information, such as the number of records in the file. The two label records are created by the COBOL compiler when the file is written onto the output device and checked by the COBOL compiler when the file is read. Data stored on punched cards, however, are visible, and as such labels are not necessary. The general format of this clause is

$$\underline{\text{LABEL}} \quad \left\{ \begin{array}{l} \underline{\text{RECØRD}} \text{ IS} \\ \underline{\text{RECØRDS}} \text{ ARE} \end{array} \right\} \quad \left\{ \begin{array}{l} \underline{\text{ØMITTED}} \\ \underline{\text{STANDARD}} \end{array} \right\}$$

If the clause LABEL RECØRD IS ØMITTED is used, the file either is or will be stored on either punched cards or printer printout. The presence of this clause implies that no labels are assigned to the file. Occasionally, it is unnecessary to assign labels to a particular file located on a magnetic tape device. In such instances, the clause LABEL RECØRD

IS ∅MITTED can be used. If it is used, label records will be neither created nor checked by the COBOL compiler.

If the clause LABEL REC∅RDS ARE STANDARD is used, the file either is or will be stored on either a mass storage or magnetic tape device, labels are assigned to the file, and the labels conform to system specifications.

The DATA RECORDS Clause

The DATA REC∅RDS clause identifies the type of record(s) in a file. This clause serves only as documentation and is never required. The general format of this clause is

$$\text{DATA} \quad \left\{ \begin{array}{l} \underline{REC\emptyset RD} \text{ IS} \\ \underline{REC\emptyset RDS} \text{ ARE} \end{array} \right\} \quad \text{record-name-1} \quad [\text{record-name-2}] \quad \ldots$$

If a file contains only one type of record, the DATA REC∅RD IS record-name-1 format is used. However, if a file contains several types of records, the DATA REC∅RDS ARE record-name-1, record-name-2, etc. format is used. The record names do not have to be listed in any particular order.

THE PROCEDURE DIVISION

Several of the statements discussed in earlier chapters require additional elements to be used when one is referencing either a magnetic disk or a magnetic tape. The discussion of these statements will be primarily concerned with the factors that should be considered when one is using these additional elements.

The OPEN Statement

The basic format of the ∅PEN statement was also discussed in Chapter 6. The complete general format of this statement is

$$\underline{\emptyset PEN} \quad \left[\underline{INPUT} \left\{ \text{file-name} \left[\begin{array}{l} \underline{REVERSED} \\ \text{WITH } \underline{N\emptyset} \underline{REWIND} \end{array} \right] \right\} \quad \ldots \right]$$

$$\left[\underline{\emptyset UTPUT} \text{ file-name} \quad [\text{WITH } \underline{N\emptyset} \underline{REWIND}] \quad \ldots \right]$$

The REVERSED and the WITH NØ REWIND options can be used only when a file being referenced either will be or is stored on a single reel of magnetic tape. When the REVERSED option is specified, execution of the ØPEN statement causes the file to be positioned at the end of the file. The NØ REWIND option has no effect on the positioning of the file. Rather, the option appears only for language consistency. When either the WITH NØ REWIND option or no option is specified, the file is positioned by the operating system.

The OPEN I-O Statement

The Øpen I-Ø statement is used when a file must be specified as both an input and an output file. The reason for this is that several updated records will be written back onto the direct-access device in the same storage location from which they were read. The general format of this statement is

ØPEN I-Ø file-name

The START Statement

Generally, the processing of a relative or indexed file organization sequentially begins with the first record of the file. However, if processing is to begin with some record other than the first one in the file, the START statement must be used. The general format of this statement is

$$
\underline{\text{START}} \text{ file-name}
\left[
\underline{\text{KEY}}
\left\{
\begin{array}{l}
\text{IS } \underline{\text{EQUAL}} \text{ TO} \\
\text{IS } = \\
\text{IS } \underline{\text{GREATER}} \text{ THAN} \\
\text{IS } > \\
\text{IS } \underline{\text{NOT}} \underline{\text{LESS}} \text{ THAN} \\
\text{IS } \underline{\text{NOT}} <
\end{array}
\right\}
\text{name-1}
\right]
$$

$\underline{\text{INVALID}}$ KEY imperative-statement.

When the START statement is executed, the appropriate record is readied for processing based upon the key stored under name-1—which is described in the DATA DIVISIØN—and the preceding relational operator. Assuming the key is associated with a record, execution of the READ statement after the START statement has been executed will result in normal sequential processing. If there is no record associated with the key, however, the INVALID KEY option is executed.

The READ Statement

The basic format of the READ statement was discussed in Chapter

6, and the INTØ option was discussed in Chapter 8. Another option not yet discussed is the INVALID KEY. The general format of the READ statement with this option included is

$$\underline{\text{READ}} \text{ file-name REC}\cancel{\text{O}}\text{RD} \quad [\underline{\text{INT}\cancel{\text{O}}} \text{ area-name}] \begin{Bmatrix} \text{AT } \underline{END} \\ \underline{INVALID} \text{ KEY} \end{Bmatrix}$$

imperative-statement

The AT END option must be specified when a reference is made to a file stored in the sequential access mode.

The INVALID KEY option must be specified when a reference is made to a file that has been stored in either the random or dynamic access mode. If either ACCESS IS RANDOM or ACCESS IS DYNAMIC is specified for the file being referenced, the contents of either the RELATIVE KEY or the RECØRD KEY for the file must be set to the desired value before the execution of the READ statement.

The imperative statement following the INVALID KEY option is executed if the contents of the RELATIVE or RECØRD KEY field are invalid. The contents of the RELATIVE or RECØRD KEY field are considered invalid if the record cannot be found in the file.

The WRITE Statement

The basic format of the WRITE statement was also discussed in Chapter 6. Similar to the READ statement, another option not yet discussed is the INVALID KEY. The general format of the WRITE statement with this option included is

$$\underline{\text{WRITE}} \text{ record-name } [\underline{\text{FR}\cancel{\text{O}}\text{M}} \text{ name-1}] \ \underline{INVALID} \text{ KEY}$$
imperative-statement

The WRITE record-name [FRØM name-1] format is used when the file is to be stored on a magnetic tape.

The INVALID KEY option must be specified when a reference is made to a file that is (1) to be sequentially stored on, or (2) to add a record to an existing file on a direct-access device. The imperative statement following the INVALID KEY option is executed if

1. An output record being written in the sequential access mode is either out of sequence or if a record already stored in the file has the same key.

2. An output record being added to an existing file in the direct-access mode has the same key as a record already stored in the file.

The REWRITE Statement

The REWRITE statement is used when updating (I-∅) an existing file. The general format of this statement is

<u>REWRITE</u> record-name [FR∅M name-1]
<u>INVALID</u> KEY imperative-statement

When the REWRITE statement is executed, the record is written in the same storage location that it was read from by the last executed READ statement. The INVALID KEY option is used only when the access mode is either random or dynamic.

The DELETE Statement

The DELETE statement is used when it is desirable to delete a record from a relative or indexed organized file. The general format of this statement is

<u>DELETE</u> file-name REC∅RD
<u>INVALID</u> KEY imperative-statement

Execution of this statement does not delete the record from the magnetic disk file. Rather, any future reference to the record via a key is ignored by the program. If the file is being accessed sequentially, execution of the DELETE statement must follow a READ statement. The record read is the one deleted.

The CLOSE Statement

Finally, the basic format of the CL∅SE statement was discussed in Chapter 6. The complete general format of this statement is

$$\underline{CL\emptyset SE} \quad \text{file-name-1} \quad \begin{bmatrix} \underline{REEL} \\ \underline{UNIT} \end{bmatrix} \quad \begin{bmatrix} \text{WITH} & \begin{Bmatrix} \underline{N\emptyset\ REWIND} \\ \underline{L\emptyset CK} \end{Bmatrix} \end{bmatrix}$$

$$\begin{bmatrix} \text{file-name-2} & \begin{bmatrix} \underline{REEL} \\ \underline{UNIT} \end{bmatrix} & \begin{bmatrix} \text{WITH} & \begin{Bmatrix} \underline{N\emptyset\ REWIND} \\ \underline{L\emptyset CK} \end{Bmatrix} \end{bmatrix} \end{bmatrix}$$

The REEL, WITH N∅ REWIND, and L∅CK options are applicable only if the file being referenced is stored on magnetic tape. If the N∅ REWIND option is not specified, the magnetic tape reel on which the referenced file is located will be rewound. If just the L∅CK option is specified, the reel will be rewound in such a way as to prevent its re-use without operator intervention. The UNIT option is applicable only if the file being referenced is a mass storage file in sequential access mode.

If the WITH NØ REWIND option is specified, the magnetic tape reel on which the referenced file is located will not be rewound, as would normally be done. Rather, the magnetic tape reel will remain in its present position. This option is commonly used when one is processing several files located on one magnetic tape reel on which the referenced file is located to be rewound. In addition, the file cannot be further referenced in the program without operator intervention.

THE CREATION OF A SEQUENTIAL ACCESS MODE FILE

The program in Figure 9-3 creates a 15-record master tape file. The contents of each record are then printed double spaced.

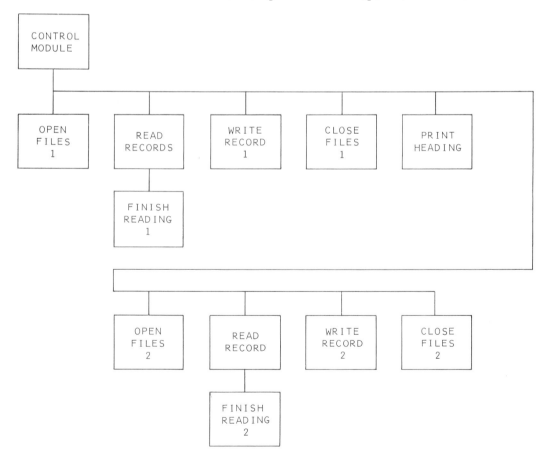

Figure 9-1: Structure chart for the following COBOL Program

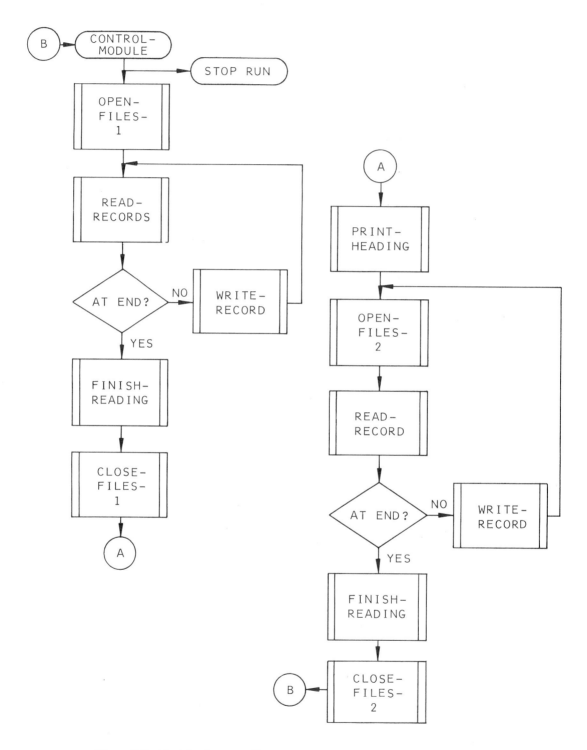

Figure 9-2: Modular Program Flowchart of the Modules in the following COBOL Program

IBM   COBOL Coding Form

GX28-1464-5 U/M 050*
Printed in U.S.A.

SYSTEM	IBM-370-148				
PROGRAM	THE CREATION OF A SEQUENTIAL ACCESS MODE FILE	PUNCHING INSTRUCTIONS			PAGE 01 OF 007
PROGRAMMER	V. THOMAS DOCK	GRAPHIC		CARD FORM #	*
	DATE	PUNCH			

```
01   IDENTIFICATION DIVISION.
02   PROGRAM-ID. TAPEFILE.
03 * ILLUSTRATION OF THE CREATION OF A SEQUENTIAL FILE.
04   ENVIRONMENT DIVISION.
05   CONFIGURATION SECTION.
06   SOURCE-COMPUTER. IBM-370-148.
07   OBJECT-COMPUTER. IBM-370-148.
08   INPUT-OUTPUT SECTION.
09   FILE-CONTROL.
10     SELECT CARD-FILE ASSIGN TO UR-2540-S-CARDIN.
11     SELECT DETAIL-FILE ASSIGN TO UT-3400-S-DETAIL.
12     SELECT PRINT-FILE ASSIGN TO UR-1403-S-PROUT.
13   DATA DIVISION.
14   FILE SECTION.
15   FD CARD-FILE
16       LABEL RECORDS ARE OMITTED.
17   01 CARD-RECORD-1.
18     02 EMPLOYEE-NAME           PICTURE A(25).
19     02 FILLER                  PICTURE X(4).
20     02 SOCIAL-SECURITY-NUMBER  PICTURE X(11).
21     02 FILLER                  PICTURE X(4).
22     02 ADDRESS                 PICTURE X(36).
23   01 CARD-RECORD-2.
24     02 HOURS-WORKED            PICTURE 99.
```

*A standard card form, IBM Electro C61897, is available for punching source statements from this form. Instructions for using this form are given in any IBM COBOL reference manual. Address comments concerning this form to IBM Corporation, LDS Publishing, Dept. J04, 1501 California Ave., Palo Alto, Ca. 94304

*No. of forms per pad may vary slightly

Figure 9-3: A COBOL Program

COBOL Coding Form

GX28-1464-5 U/M 050*
Printed in U.S.A.

SYSTEM	IBM-370-148
PROGRAM	THE CREATION OF A SEQUENTIAL ACCESS MODE FILE
PROGRAMMER	V. THOMAS DUCK

PUNCHING INSTRUCTIONS — GRAPHIC / PUNCH — CARD FORM #

PAGE 002 OF 007   *

IDENTIFICATION

```
SEQUENCE  CONT  A  B          COBOL STATEMENT
01              02 FILLER                      PICTURE XX.
02              02 WAGE-PER-HOUR               PICTURE 99V99.
03              02 FILLER                      PICTURE X(6).
04              02 YEARS-WITH-COMPANY          PICTURE 99.
05              02 FILLER                      PICTURE XXX.
06              02 MARITAL-STATUS              PICTURE A.
07              02 FILLER                      PICTURE X(4).
08              02 NUMBER-OF-CHILDREN          PICTURE 99.
09              02 FILLER                      PICTURE X(54).
10       FD  DETAIL-FILE
11           LABEL RECORDS ARE STANDARD
12           BLOCK CONTAINS 15 RECORDS
13           RECORD CONTAINS 83 CHARACTERS.
14       01  TAPE-REC.
15              02 EMPLOYEE-NAME               PICTURE A(25).
16              02 SOCIAL-SECURITY-NUMBER      PICTURE X(11).
17              02 ADDRESS                     PICTURE X(36).
18              02 HOURS-WORKED                PICTURE 99.
19              02 WAGE-PER-HOUR               PICTURE 99V99.
20              02 YEARS-WITH-COMPANY          PICTURE 99.
21              02 MARITAL-STATUS              PICTURE A.
22              02 NUMBER-OF-CHILDREN          PICTURE 99.
23       FD  PRINT-FILE
24           LABEL RECORDS ARE OMITTED.
```

*A standard card form, IBM Electro C61897, is available for punching source statements from this form. Instructions for using this form are given in any IBM COBOL reference manual. Address comments concerning this form to IBM Corporation, LDS Publishing, Dept. J04, 1501 California Ave., Palo Alto, Ca. 94304

*No. of forms per pad may vary slightly

IBM

COBOL Coding Form

GX28-1464-5 U/M 050
Printed in U.S.A.

SYSTEM	IBM-370-148		PAGE 003DF OC7
PROGRAM	THE CREATION OF A SEQUENTIAL ACCESS MODE FILE	PUNCHING INSTRUCTIONS	CARD FORM #
PROGRAMMER	V. THOMAS DOCK	DATE	

GRAPHIC
PUNCH

COBOL STATEMENT

```
01   01  DETAIL-LINE.
02       02  FILLER                    PICTURE X.
03       02  EMPLOYEE                  PICTURE A(25).
04       02  SOCIAL-SECURITY-NUMBER    PICTURE X(11).
05       02  FILLER                    PICTURE X(7).
06       02  ADDRESS                   PICTURE X(20).
07       02  HOURS-WORKED              PICTURE 99.
08       02  FILLER                    PICTURE X(12).
09       02  WAGE-PER-HOUR             PICTURE $$9.99.
10       02  FILLER                    PICTURE X(12).
11       02  YEARS-WITH-COMPANY        PICTURE 99.
12       02  FILLER                    PICTURE X(17).
13       02  MARITAL-STATUS            PICTURE A.
14       02  FILLER                    PICTURE X(12).
15       02  NUMBER-OF-CHILDREN        PICTURE 99.
16       02  FILLER                    PICTURE XXX.
17   01  PRINT-LINE                    PICTURE X(133).
18   WORKING-STORAGE SECTION.
19   77  MORE-DATA-CARDS               PICTURE AA VALUE SPACES.
20   77  MORE-TAPE-RECORDS             PICTURE AA VALUE SPACES.
21   01  HEAD-1.
22       02  FILLER                    PICTURE X(2)  VALUE SPACES.
23       02  FILLER                    PICTURE A(13) VALUE EMPLOYEE NAM
24   E.
```

*A standard card form, IBM Electro C61897, is available for punching source statements from this form. Instructions for using this form are given in any IBM COBOL reference manual. Address comments concerning this form to IBM Corporation, LDS Publishing, Dept. J04, 1501 California Ave., Palo Alto, Ca. 94304

*No. of forms per pad may vary slightly

COBOL Coding Form

GX28-1464-5 U/M 050*
Printed in U.S.A.

SYSTEM	IBM-370-148
PROGRAM	THE CREATION OF A SEQUENTIAL ACCESS MODE FILE
PROGRAMMER	V. THOMAS DOCK

PUNCHING INSTRUCTIONS — GRAPHIC / PUNCH — CARD FORM # — PAGE 004 OF 007

```
01   02 FILLER            PICTURE X(5)  VALUE SPACES.
02   02 SOCIAL-SECURITY-NUM PICTURE A(22) VALUE 'SOCIAL SECUR
03 -   ITY NUMBER'.
04   02 FILLER            PICTURE X(5)  VALUE SPACES.
05   02 ADRES             PICTURE A(7)  VALUE 'ADDRESS'.
06   02 FILLER            PICTURE X(5)  VALUE SPACES.
07   02 HOURS-WORK        PICTURE A(12) VALUE 'HOURS WORKED
08 -   '.
09   02 FILLER            PICTURE X(5)  VALUE SPACES.
10   02 WAG-PER-HOUR      PICTURE X(11) VALUE 'HOURLY WAGE'
11 .
12   02 FILLER            PICTURE X(5)  VALUE SPACES.
13   02 YEARS-WITH-COMP   PICTURE X(11) VALUE 'TOTAL YEARS'
14 .
15   02 FILLER            PICTURE X(5)  VALUE SPACES.
16   02 MARITAL-STAT      PICTURE X(14) VALUE 'MARITAL STAT
17 -   US'.
18   02 FILLER            PICTURE X(3)  VALUE SPACES.
19   02 NUMBER-OF-CHILD   PICTURE A(8)  VALUE 'CHILDREN'.
20   PROCEDURE DIVISION.
21 * CONTROL-MODULE.
22   PERFORM OPEN-FILES-1.
23   PERFORM READ-RECORDS THRU FINISH-READING-1
24   PERFORM
```

*A standard card form, IBM Electro C61897, is available for punching source statements from this form. Instructions for using this form are given in any IBM COBOL reference manual. Address comments concerning this form to IBM Corporation, LDS Publishing, Dept. J04, 1501 California Ave., Palo Alto, Ca. 94304

*No. of forms per pad may vary slightly

IDENTIFICATION

COBOL Coding Form

GX28-1464-5 U/M 050*
Printed in U.S.A.

SYSTEM	
PROGRAM	THE CREATION OF A SEQUENTIAL ACCESS MODE FILE
PROGRAMMER	V. THOMAS DOCK

PUNCHING INSTRUCTIONS — GRAPHIC / PUNCH
CARD FORM #
PAGE 005 OF 007
IDENTIFICATION

COBOL STATEMENT

```
SEQUENCE  CONT  B/COBOL STATEMENT

01              PERFORM UNTIL MORE-DATA-CARDS EQUAL 'NO'.
02              PERFORM CLOSE-FILES-1.
03              PERFORM PRINT-HEADING.
04              PERFORM OPEN-FILES-2.
05              PERFORM READ-RECORD THRU FINISH-READING-2
06                  UNTIL MORE-TAPE-RECORDS EQUAL 'NO'.
07              PERFORM CLOSE-FILES-2.
08              STOP RUN.
09      *
10          OPEN-FILES-1.
11              OPEN INPUT CARD-FILE
12                  OUTPUT DETAIL-FILE.
13      *
14          READ-RECORDS.
15              MOVE SPACES TO TAPE-REC.
16              READ CARD-FILE AT END
17                  MOVE 'NO' TO MORE-DATA-CARDS, GO TO FINISH-READING-1.
18              MOVE CORRESPONDING CARD-RECORD-1 TO TAPE-REC.
19              READ CARD-FILE AT END
20                  MOVE 'NO' TO MORE-DATA-CARDS, GO TO FINISH-READING-1.
21              MOVE CORRESPONDING CARD-RECORD-2 TO TAPE-REC.
22      *
23          WRITE-RECORD-1.
24              WRITE TAPE-REC.
```

*A standard card form, IBM Electro C61897, is available for punching source statements from this form. Instructions for using this form are given in any IBM COBOL reference manual. Address comments concerning this form to IBM Corporation, LDS Publishing, Dept. J04, 1501 California Ave., Palo Alto, Ca. 94304

*No. of forms per pad may vary slightly

IBM

COBOL Coding Form

GX28-1464-5 U/M 050*
Printed in U.S.A.

SYSTEM	IBM-370-148	PUNCHING INSTRUCTIONS		PAGE 006 OF 007
PROGRAM	THE CREATION OF A SEQUENTIAL ACCESS MODE FILE	GRAPHIC		CARD FORM # *
PROGRAMMER	V. THOMAS DECK	DATE	PUNCH	

```
SEQ   COBOL STATEMENT
01  *
02   FINIISH-READING-1.
03       EXIT.
04  *
05   CLOSE-FILES-1.
06       CLOSE CARD-FILE
07  *
08   PRINT-HEADING.
09       WRITE PRINT-LINE FROM HEAD-1 AFTER ADVANCING PAGE.
10  *
11   OPEN-FILES-2.
12       OPEN INPUT DETAIL-FILE
13            OUTPUT PRINT-FILE.
14  *
15   READ-RECORD.
16       READ DETAIL-FILE AT END
17           MOVE NO TO MORE-TAPE-RECORDS)
18           MOVE SPACES TO DETAIL-LINE.
19       MOVE CORRESPONDING TAPE-REC TO DETAIL-REC
20  *        GO TO FINISH-READING-2.
21   WRITE-RECORD-2.
22       WRITE DETAIL-LINE AFTER ADVANCING 2 LINES.
23  *  FINIISH-READING-2.
24     FINIISH-READING-2.
```

IDENTIFICATION

*A standard card form, IBM Electro C61897, is available for punching source statements from this form. Instructions for using this form are given in any IBM COBOL reference manual. Address comments concerning this form to IBM Corporation, LDS Publishing, Dept. J04, 1501 California Ave., Palo Alto, Ca. 94304

*No. of forms per pad may vary slightly

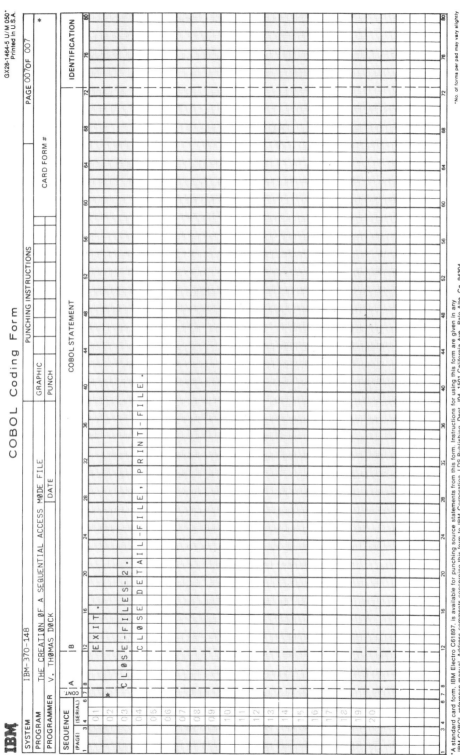

COBOL Coding Form

SYSTEM	IBM-370-148		PAGE 007 OF 007
PROGRAM	THE CREATION OF A SEQUENTIAL ACCESS MODE FILE		
PROGRAMMER	V. THOMAS DUCK	DATE	CARD FORM #

PUNCHING INSTRUCTIONS
GRAPHIC
PUNCH

```
01  *
02  *         EXIT.
03            CLOSE-FILES-2.
04                CLOSE DETAIL-FILE, PRINT-FILE.
05
06
07
08
09
10
11
12
13
14
15
16
17
18
19
20
```

*A standard card form, IBM Electro C61897, is available for punching source statements from this form. Instructions for using this form are given in any IBM COBOL reference manual. Address comments concerning this form to IBM Corporation, LDS Publishing, Dept. J04, 1501 California Ave., Palo Alto, Ca. 94304

*No. of forms per pad may vary slightly

THE CREATION OF A RANDOM ACCESS MODE FILE

The program in Fig. 9-6 creates a file via the random access mode. A data field in the WØRKING-STØRAGE SECTIØN (CD-ITEM-CØDE-1) is the RELATIVE KEY. Each record is written in the relative record location indicated by this key.

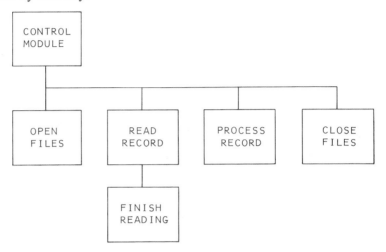

Figure 9-4: Structure Chart for the followng COBOL Program

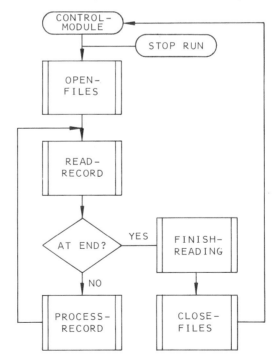

Figure 9-5: Modular Program Flowchart of the Modules in the following COBOL Program

IBM

COBOL Coding Form

GX28-1464-5 U/M 050*
Printed in U.S.A.

SYSTEM	IBM-370-148
PROGRAM	THE CREATION OF A RANDOM ACCESS MODE FILE
PROGRAMMER	V. THOMAS DOCK

PUNCHING INSTRUCTIONS — GRAPHIC / PUNCH — CARD FORM #

PAGE 001 OF 004

```
SEQUENCE  CONT
01  IDENTIFICATION DIVISION.
02  PROGRAM-ID. DISKFILE.
03* ILLUSTRATION OF THE CREATION OF A RANDOM ACCESS FILE.
04  ENVIRONMENT DIVISION.
05  CONFIGURATION SECTION.
06  SOURCE-COMPUTER. IBM-370-148.
07  OBJECT-COMPUTER. IBM-370-148.
08  INPUT-OUTPUT SECTION.
09  FILE-CONTROL.
10      SELECT CARD-FILE, ASSIGN TO UR-2540R-S-INFILE.
11      SELECT DA-FILE, ASSIGN TO DA-3330-D-MASTER, ORGANIZATION IS
12      RELATIVE, ACCESS IS RANDOM, ACTUAL KEY IS FILE-KEY.
13  DATA DIVISION.
14  FILE SECTION.
15  FD  CARD-FILE
16      LABEL RECORDS ARE OMITTED
17      RECORD CONTAINS 80 CHARACTERS
18  01  CARDS.
19      02  CD-ITEM-CODE       PICTURE 99999.
20
```

*A standard card form, IBM Electro C61897, is available for punching source statements from this form. Instructions for using this form are given in any IBM COBOL reference manual. Address comments concerning this form to IBM Corporation, LDS Publishing, Dept. J04, 1501 California Ave., Palo Alto, Ca. 94304

IDENTIFICATION

COBOL Coding Form

GX28-1464-5 U/M 050*
Printed in U.S.A.

SYSTEM	IBM-370-148
PROGRAM	THE CREATION OF A RANDOM ACCESS MODE FILE
PROGRAMMER	V. THOMAS DOCK

PUNCHING INSTRUCTIONS — GRAPHIC / PUNCH — CARD FORM # — PAGE002 OF OC-4

```
SEQUENCE  CONT
(PAGE)(SERIAL) A  B

 01          02  CD-ITEM-NAME         PICTURE  X(30).
 02          02  CD-STOCK-ON-HAND     PICTURE  9(6).
 03          02  CD-UNIT-PRICE        PICTURE  999V99.
 04          02  CD-STOCK-VALUE       PICTURE  9(7)V99.
 05          02  CD-ORDER-POINT       PICTURE  999.
 06          02  FILLER               PICTURE  X(20).
 07    FD  DA-FILE
 08        LABEL RECORDS ARE STANDARD
 09        RECORD CONTAINS 60 CHARACTERS.
 10    01  DISK.
 11          02  DISK-ITEM-CODE       PICTURE  999.
 12          02  DISK-ITEM-NAME       PICTURE  X(30).
 13          02  DISK-STOCK-ON-HAND   PICTURE  9(6).
 14          02  DISK-UNIT-PRICE      PICTURE  999V99.
 15          02  DISK-STOCK-VALUE     PICTURE  9(7)V99.
 16          02  DISK-ORDER-POINT     PICTURE  999.
 17    WORKING-STORAGE SECTION.
 18    77  QUOTIENT                   PICTURE  9999.
 19    77  MORE-DATA-CARDS            PICTURE  AAA VALUE SPACES.
 20    01  FILE-KEY.
 21          02  TRACK-ID             PICTURE  S9(5) USAGE IS COMPUTATIO
 22    NAL. SYNCHRONIZED.
 23          02  RECORD-ID            PICTURE  X(30).
```

*A standard card form, IBM Electro C61897, is available for punching source statements from this form. Instructions for using this form are given in any IBM COBOL reference manual. Address comments concerning this form to IBM Corporation, LDS Publishing, Dept. J04, 1501 California Ave., Palo Alto, Ca. 94304

*No. of forms per pad may vary slightly

IBM

COBOL Coding Form

GX28-1464-5 U/M 050*
Printed in U.S.A.

SYSTEM	IBM-370-148		PAGE 003 OF 004
PROGRAM	THE CREATION OF A RANDOM ACCESS MODE FILE		CARD FORM #
PROGRAMMER	V. THOMAS DUCK	DATE	

PUNCHING INSTRUCTIONS — GRAPHIC / PUNCH

```
SEQUENCE CONT    COBOL STATEMENT
(PAGE)(SERIAL)
 01          PROCEDURE DIVISION.
 02       *
 03          CONTROL-MODULE.
 04              PERFORM OPEN-FILES.
 05              PERFORM READ-RECORD THRU FINISH-READING
 06                  UNTIL MORE-DATA-CARDS EQUAL NO.
 07              PERFORM CLOSE-FILES.
 08              STOP RUN.
 09       *
 10          OPEN-FILES.
 11              OPEN INPUT CARD-FILE
 12                   OUTPUT DA-FILE.
 13       *
 14          READ-RECORD.
 15              READ CARD-FILE AT END
 16                  MOVE NO TO MORE-DATA-CARDS GO TO FINISH-READING.
 17       *
 18          PROCESS-RECORD.
 19              DIVIDE 175 INTO CD-ITEM-CODE GIVING QUOTIENT.
 20              MOVE QUOTIENT TO TRACK-ID.
 21              MOVE CD-ITEM-CODE TO RECORD-ID.
 22              MOVE CD-ITEM-CODE TO DISK-ITEM-CODE.
 23              MOVE CD-ITEM-NAME TO DISK-ITEM-NAME.
 24              MOVE CD-STOCK-ON-HAND TO DISK-STOCK-ON-HAND.
```

IDENTIFICATION

*A standard card form, IBM Electro C61897, is available for punching source statements from this form. Instructions for using this form and instructions for punching are given in any IBM COBOL reference manual. Address comments concerning this form to IBM Corporation, LDS Publishing, Dept. J04, 1501 California Ave., Palo Alto, Ca. 94304

*No. of forms per pad may vary slightly

COBOL Coding Form

SYSTEM	IBM-370-148					GX28-1464-5 U/M 050* Printed in U.S.A.
PROGRAM	THE CREATION OF A RANDOM ACCESS MODE FILE				PAGE 004 OF 004	
PROGRAMMER	V. THOMAS DOCK		DATE		CARD FORM #	*

PUNCHING INSTRUCTIONS — GRAPHIC / PUNCH

SEQUENCE (PAGE) (SERIAL)	CONT	A B	COBOL STATEMENT	IDENTIFICATION
01			MOVE CD-UNIT-PRICE TO DISK-UNIT-PRICE.	
02			MOVE CD-STOCK-VALUE TO DISK-STOCK-VALUE.	
03			MOVE CD-ORDER-POINT TO DISK-ORDER-POINT.	
04			WRITE DISK INVALID KEY DISPLAY 'UNABLE TO WRITE RECORD'	
05			TRACK-ID.	
06	*			
07			FINISH-READING.	
08			EXIT.	
09	*			
10			CLOSE-FILES.	
11			CLOSE CARD-FILE, DA-FILE.	
12				
13				
14				
15				
16				
17				
18				
19				
20				

*A standard card form, IBM Electro C61897, is available for punching source statements from this form. Instructions for using this form are given in any IBM COBOL reference manual. Address comments concerning this form to IBM Corporation, LDS Publishing, Dept. J04, 1501 California Ave., Palo Alto, Ca. 94304

*No. of forms per pad may vary slightly

THE CREATION OF A DYNAMIC ACCESS MODE FILE

The program in Figure 9-9 creates a 12-record master disk file and a 20-record transaction tape file. While the disk records *are* in sequence by transaction number, the tape records are *not* in sequence by transaction number.

In Figure 9-12, the transaction file is read and then the master file is searched for an identical transaction number (the master file transaction numbers are identical to 12 of the transaction file transaction numbers). If a transaction number match is found, the master record amount is updated. If no match is found, the following message is written: 'INVALID TAPE RECORD', followed by the contents of the transaction record.

This is an example of executing two programs with one job card. Thus, the ORGANIZATION and ACCESS clauses are not necessary in the second program (Figure 9-12).

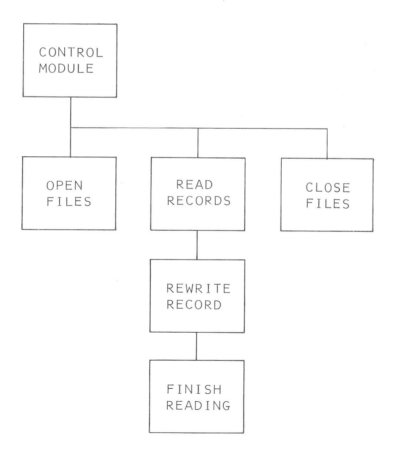

Figure 9-7: Structure Chart for the following COBOL Program

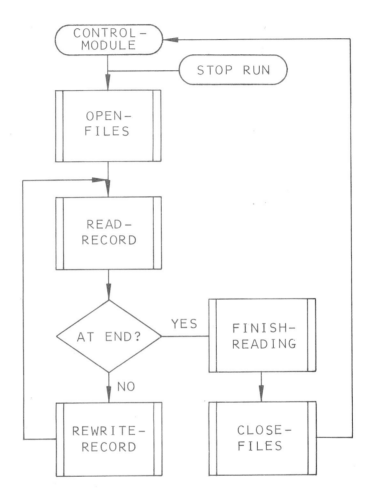

Figure 9-8: Modular Program Flowchart of the Modules in the following COBOL Program

IBM

COBOL Coding Form

GX28-1464-5 U/M 050*
Printed in U.S.A.

SYSTEM	IBM-370-148
PROGRAM	THE CREATION OF A DYNAMIC ACCESS MODE FILE
PROGRAMMER	V. THOMAS DOCK DATE

PAGE 001 OF 003   CARD FORM #   *

PUNCHING INSTRUCTIONS — GRAPHIC / PUNCH

```
SEQUENCE
(PAGE)(SERIAL)  CONT  B   COBOL STATEMENT

01      IDENTIFICATION DIVISION.
02      PROGRAM-ID. DISKFILE.
03    * ILLUSTRATION OF THE CREATION OF A DYNAMIC ACCESS FILE.
04      ENVIRONMENT DIVISION.
05      CONFIGURATION SECTION.
06      SOURCE-COMPUTER. IBM-370-148.
07      OBJECT-COMPUTER. IBM-370-148.
08      INPUT-OUTPUT SECTION.
09      FILE-CONTROL.
10          SELECT DETAIL-FILE ASSIGN TO UT-2400-S-DETAIL.
11          SELECT MASTER-FILE ASSIGN TO DA-3300-I-MASTER, ORGANIZATION
12              IS INDEXED, ACCESS IS DYNAMIC, RECORD KEY IS TRAN-NO-DISK.
13      DATA DIVISION.
14      FILE SECTION.
15      FD  DETAIL-FILE
16          LABEL RECORDS ARE STANDARD
17          BLOCK CONTAINS 20 RECORDS
18          RECORD CONTAINS 18 CHARACTERS.
19      01  TAPE-REC.
20          02 TRAN-NO-TAPE     PICTURE 9(5).
21          02 AMT              PICTURE 999V99.
22          02 FILLER           PICTURE X(8).
23      FD  MASTER-FILE
24          LABEL RECORDS ARE STANDARD
```

* A standard card form, IBM Electro C61897, is available for punching source statements from this form. Instructions for using this form are given in any IBM COBOL reference manual. Address comments concerning this form to IBM Corporation, LDS Publishing, Dept. J04, 1501 California Ave., Palo Alto, Ca. 94304

*No. of forms per pad may vary slightly

IBM

COBOL Coding Form

GX28-1464-5 U/M 050*
Printed in U.S.A.

SYSTEM	IBM-370-148
PROGRAM	THE CREATION OF A DYNAMIC ACCESS MODE FILE
PROGRAMMER	V. THOMAS DOCK DATE

PUNCHING INSTRUCTIONS — GRAPHIC / PUNCH — CARD FORM # — PAGE 002 OF 003 — IDENTIFICATION

```
01      BLOCK CONTAINS 12 RECORDS
02      RECORD CONTAINS 10 CHARACTERS.
03      DISK-REC.
04          02  TRAN-NO-DISK    PICTURE 9(5).
05          02  AMT             PICTURE 999V99.
06  WORKING-STORAGE SECTION.
07  77  MORE-TAPE-RECORDS       PICTURE AA VALUE SPACES.
08  PROCEDURE DIVISION.
09  *
10  CONTROL-MODULE.
11      PERFORM OPEN-FILES.
12      PERFORM READ-RECORDS THRU FINISH-READING
13          UNTIL-MORE TAPE-RECORDS EQUAL 'NO'.
14      PERFORM CLOSE-FILES.
15      STOP RUN.
16  OPEN-FILES.
17      OPEN INPUT DETAIL-FILE
18          I-O MASTER-FILE.
19  *
20  READ-RECORDS.
21      READ DETAIL-FILE AT END
22          MOVE 'NO' TO MORE-TAPE-RECORDS GO TO FINISH-READING.
23      MOVE TRAN-NO-TAPE TO TRAN-NO-DISK.
24      READ MASTER-FILE INVALID KEY DISPLAY 'INVALID TAPE RECORD'
```

*A standard card form. IBM Electro C61897, is available for punching source statements from this form. Instructions for using this form are given in any IBM COBOL reference manual. Address comments concerning this form to IBM Corporation, LDS Publishing, Dept. J04, 1501 California Ave., Palo Alto, Ca. 94304

*No. of forms per pad may vary very slightly

COBOL Coding Form

SYSTEM	IBM-370-148		GX28-1464-5 U/M 050*
PROGRAM	THE CREATION ØF A DYNAMIC ACCESS MØDE FILE		Printed in U.S.A.
PROGRAMMER	V. THØMAS DØCK	DATE	PAGE 003 OF 003

PUNCHING INSTRUCTIONS

| GRAPHIC | | CARD FORM # | |
| PUNCH | | | * |

SEQUENCE			B	COBOL STATEMENT	IDENTIFICATION
01			I TAPE-REC. GØ TØ FINISH-READING.	
02			MØVE AMT ØF TAPE-REC TØ AMØUNT ØF DISK-REC.	
03	*			
04			REWRITE-RECØRD.	
05			REWRITE DISK-REC INVALID KEY DISPLAY 'UNABLE TØ REWRITE ØN DI	
06	—		SK-'.	
07	*			
08			FINISH-READING.	
09			EXIT.	
10	*			
11			CLØSE-FILES.	
12			CLØSE DETAIL-FILE, MASTER-FILE.	
13				
14				
15				
16				
17				
18				
19				
20				

*A standard card form, IBM Electro C61897, is available for punching source statements from this form. Instructions for using this form are given in any IBM COBOL reference manual. Address comments concerning this form to IBM Corporation, LDS Publishing, Dept. J04, 1501 California Ave., Palo Alto, Ca. 94304

*No. of forms per pad may vary slightly

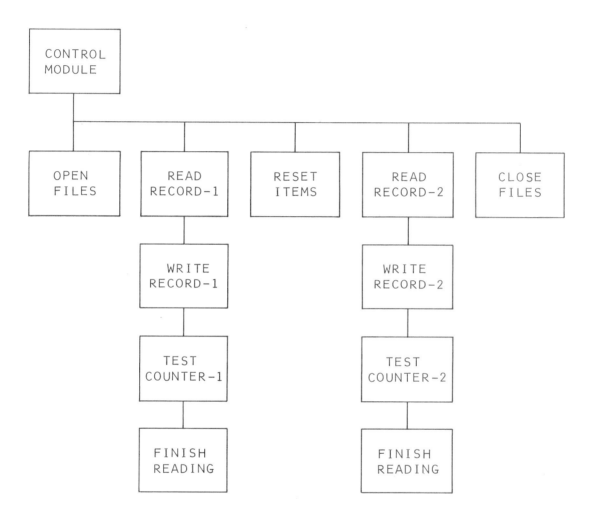

Figure 9-10: Structure Chart for the following COBOL Program

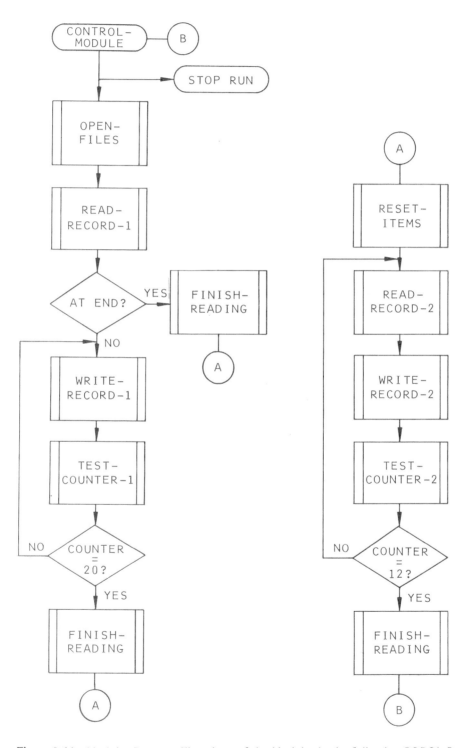

Figure 9-11: Modular Program Flowchart of the Modules in the following COBOL Program

COBOL Coding Form

GX28-1464-5 U/M 050*
Printed in U.S.A.

SYSTEM	IBM-370-148			PUNCHING INSTRUCTIONS				PAGE 0010F004
PROGRAM	THE PROCESSING OF A DYNAMIC ACCESS MODE FILE			GRAPHIC				CARD FORM #
PROGRAMMER	V. THOMAS DOCK		DATE	PUNCH				

SEQUENCE		CONT			COBOL STATEMENT															IDENTIFICATION
(PAGE)	(SERIAL)	6 7	8 A	12 B	16	20	24	28	32	36	40	44	48	52	56	60	64	68	72	76	80

```
01          IDENTIFICATION DIVISION.
02          PROGRAM-ID. DISKFILE.
03    *     ILLUSTRATION OF THE PROCESSING OF A DYNAMIC ACCESS FILE.
04          ENVIRONMENT DIVISION.
05          CONFIGURATION SECTION.
06          SOURCE-COMPUTER. IBM-370-148.
07          OBJECT-COMPUTER. IBM-370-148.
08          INPUT-OUTPUT SECTION.
09          FILE-CONTROL.
10              SELECT CARD-FILE ASSIGN TO UR-2540R-S-CARDIN.
11              SELECT DETAIL-FILE ASSIGN TO UT-3400-S-DETAIL.
12              SELECT MASTER-FILE ASSIGN TO DA-3330-I-MASTER, RECORD KEY
13                  IS TRAN-NO-DISK.
14          DATA DIVISION.
15          FILE SECTION.
16          FD  CARD-FILE
17              LABEL RECORDS ARE OMITTED.
18          CARD-RECORD.
19          02  TRAN-NO-CARD        PICTURE 9(5).
20          02  AMT                 PICTURE 999V99.
21          FD  DETAIL-FILE
22              LABEL RECORDS ARE STANDARD
23              BLOCK CONTAINS 20 RECORDS
24              RECORD CONTAINS 18 CHARACTERS.
```

*A standard card form, IBM Electro C61897, is available for punching source statements from this form. Instructions for using this form are given in any
IBM COBOL reference manual. Address comments concerning this form to IBM Corporation, LDS Publishing, Dept. J04, 1501 California Ave., Palo Alto, Ca. 94304

*No. of forms per pad may vary slightly

IBM

COBOL Coding Form

GX28-1464-5 U/M 050*
Printed in U.S.A.

SYSTEM	IBM-370-148			
PROGRAM	THE PROCESSING OF A DYNAMIC ACCESS MODE FILE		PUNCHING INSTRUCTIONS	PAGE 002 OF 004
PROGRAMMER	V. THOMAS DOCK	DATE	GRAPHIC / PUNCH	CARD FORM #

SEQUENCE	CONT	A	B — COBOL STATEMENT	IDENTIFICATION
01		01	TAPE-REC.	
02			02 TRAN-NO-TAPE PICTURE 9(5).	
03			02 AMT PICTURE 999V99.	
04			02 FILLER PICTURE X(8).	
05		FD	MASTER-FILE	
06			LABEL RECORDS ARE STANDARD	
07			BLOCK CONTAINS 12 RECORDS	
08			RECORD CONTAINS 10 CHARACTERS.	
09		01	DISK-REC.	
10			02 TRAN-NO-DISK PICTURE 9(5).	
11			02 AMT PICTURE 999V99.	
12			WORKING-STORAGE SECTION.	
13		77	COUNTER PICTURE 99 VALUE ZERO.	
14		77	MORE-DATA-CARDS PICTURE AA VALUE SPACES.	
15			PROCEDURE DIVISION.	
16	*			
17			CONTROL-MODULE.	
18			PERFORM OPEN-FILES.	
19			PERFORM READ-RECORD-FILES THRU FINISH-READING-1	
20			UNTIL MORE-DATA-CARDS EQUAL NO.	
21			PERFORM RESET-ITEMS.	
22			PERFORM READ-RECORD-2 THRU FINISH-READING-2	
23			UNTIL MORE-DATA-CARDS EQUAL NO.	
24			PERFORM CLOSE-FILES.	

COBOL Coding Form

SYSTEM	IBM-370-148
PROGRAM	THE PROCESSING OF A DYNAMIC ACCESS MODE FILE
PROGRAMMER	V. THOMAS DOCK

PUNCHING INSTRUCTIONS — GRAPHIC / PUNCH

CARD FORM #

PAGE 003 OF 004

GX28-1464-5 U/M 050*
Printed in U.S.A.

```
       A   B
01  *
02      STOP RUN.
03      OPEN-FILES.
04          OPEN INPUT CARD-FILE
05          OUTPUT DETAIL-FILE, MASTER-FILE.
06  *
07      READ-RECORD-1.
08          READ CARD-FILE AT END
09          MOVE 'NO' TO MORE-DATA-CARDS, GO TO FINISH-READING-1.
10  *
11      WRITE-RECORD-1.
12          WRITE TAPE-REC FROM CARD-RECORD.
13  *
14      TEST-COUNTER-1.
15          ADD 1 TO COUNTER.
16          IF COUNTER EQUAL TO 20
17          GO TO FINISH-READING-1
18  *       ELSE GO TO READ-RECORD-1.
19      FINISH-READING-1.
20          EXIT.
21  *
22  *
23      RESET-ITEMS.
24          MOVE 0 TO COUNTER.
```

* A standard card form, IBM Electro C61897, is available for punching source statements from this form. Instructions for using this form are given in any IBM COBOL reference manual. Address comments concerning this form to IBM Corporation, LDS Publishing, Dept. J04, 1501 California Ave., Palo Alto, Ca. 94304

*No. of forms per pad may vary slightly

GX28-1464-5 U/M 050*
Printed in U.S.A.

COBOL Coding Form

SYSTEM	
PROGRAM	THE PROCESSING OF A DYNAMIC ACCESS MODE FILE
PROGRAMMER	V. THOMAS DOCK

PUNCHING INSTRUCTIONS

| GRAPHIC | |
| PUNCH | |

DATE

CARD FORM #

PAGE 004 OF 004

```
01   MOVE SPACES TO MORE-DATA-CARDS.
02  *
03   READ-RECORD-2.
04       READ CARD-FILE AT END
05       MOVE 'NO' TO MORE-DATA-CARDS.
06  *
07   WRITE-RECORD-2.
08       WRITE DISK-REC FROM CARD-RECORD.
09  *
10   TEST-COUNTER-2.
11       ADD 1 TO COUNTER.
12       IF COUNTER EQUAL TO 12
13       GO TO FINISH-READING-2
14       ELSE GO TO READ-RECORD-2.
15  *
16   FINISH-READING-2.
17       EXIT.
18  *
19   CLOSE-FILES.
20       CLOSE CARD-FILE, DETAIL-FILE, MASTER-FILE.
```

*A standard card form, IBM Electro C61897, is available for punching source statements from this form. Instructions for using this form are given in any IBM COBOL reference manual. Address comments concerning this form to IBM Corporation, LDS Publishing, Dept. J04, 1501 California Ave., Palo Alto, Ca. 94304

*No. of forms per pad may vary slightly

EXERCISE

1. Write a program to create a 12-record master disk file and a 20-record transaction tape file. Then read the transaction file and search the master file for an identical transaction number (the master file transaction numbers are identical to 12 of the transaction file transaction numbers). If a transaction number match is found, update the master record amount. If no match is found, write the following message: 'INVALID TAPE RECORD', followed by the contents of the transaction record. The records composing the tape file have the following format:

   cc   1-5   Transaction number
         6-10   Amount xxx.xx
         11-18 Not used
   Labels are standard; blocking factor = 20.
   Transaction number is record identifier.

   The records composing the disk file have the following format:

   cc   1-5   Transaction number
         6-10   Amount xxx.xx
   Labels are standard; blocking factor 12.
   Transaction number is record identifier.

Note:

1. The disk file is to be created and updated via the random access mode. While the disk records *are* in sequence by transaction number, the tape records are *not* in sequence by transaction number.

AN INTRODUCTION TO
THE IBM 29 CARD PUNCH

The following is a brief discussion of both the operation of the IBM 29 Card Punch and the use of the various functional control switches and keys and punching keys.

All functional control keys are blue with white printing; all punching keys are gray with black printing. Only the information concerning the specific functional control switches and keys and punching keys that the reader will need to understand and apply to punch most program statements and data into punch cards is presented. For a more in-depth discussion of the IBM 29 Card Punch, the reader should refer to a copy of *Reference Manual IBM 29 Card Punch,* Reference Number GA24-3332-6.

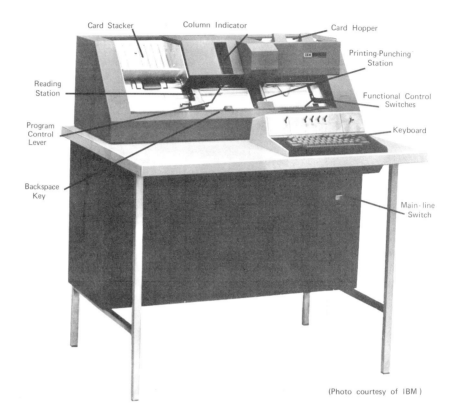

Card Stacker

Column Indicator

Card Hopper

Printing-Punching Station

Reading Station

Functional Control Switches

Program Control Lever

Keyboard

Backspace Key

Main-line Switch

(Photo courtesy of IBM)

Figure A-1

Functional Switches

Keyboard

(Photo courtesy of IBM)

Figure A-2

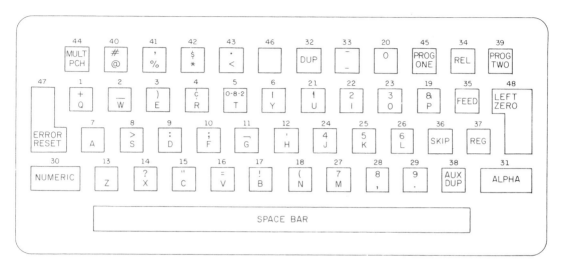

To Prepare the Card Punch for Operation

1. Flip the Main-Line Switch, which is located directly beneath the right side of the machine cabinet (Fig. A-1), to the "on" position. There is no warm-up period necessary before the machine is operative.

2. Place up to approximately 500 punch cards in the Card Hopper, which is located on the upper right side of the machine (Fig. A-1). Even though the reader may desire to use no more than one punch card, the author suggests that a minimum of two punch cards be placed in the Card Hopper at a time.

   The punch cards are placed into the Card Hopper 9 edge down and face forward. They are held in place by a pressure plate. This plate should be pushed back until the pressure plate can slide back no further. Then release the back portion of the pressure plate, and the pressure plate should lock in place. Next, place the punch cards in the Card Hopper. After the punch cards have been placed in the Card Hopper, release the pressure plate by again squeezing the two-piece top portion of the pressure plate and allowing the pressure plate slowly to slide toward the punch cards until it stops at the back of the last punch card placed in the Card Hopper.

   The punch cards, when the FEED functional control key (Fig. A-3, #35) is pressed, are fed from the front of the Card Hopper.

3. Flip the PRINT functional control switch (Fig. A-2) to the "on" position. This permits the printing of each card column as it is either being punched or duplicated. Whether the reader desires also to flip the AUTO FEED functional control switch (Fig. A-2), which

permits the feeding of punch cards from the Card Hopper automatically after the first two punch cards have been manually fed, to
the "on" position is optional. If the reader has had little experience
with this card punch machine, the author suggests that he leave this
switch in the "off" position.

The AUTO SKIP–DUP, TWO, PROG SEL, and L PRINT functional
control switches (Fig. A-2) should be rendered inoperative by flipping
the Program Control Lever, which is located at the bottom of the
Program Unit (Fig. A-1), to the right and thus raising the Starwheels.

To Prepare the Card Punch for Punching a Punch Card

4. When the FEED functional control key is pressed, a punch card is
   lowered from the Card Hopper to the Printing-Punching Station,
   which is located immediately beneath the Card Hopper (Fig. A-1).

5. When the REG (Fig. A-3, #37) functional control key is pressed, the
   first punch card located in the printing-Punching Station is registered
   and thus placed in position to be punched beginning with the first
   card column.

To Punch the Punch Card

6. Any punching key (Fig. A-3) having two character symbols illustrated
   on it may be thought of as similar to a typewriter key with two
   character symbols illustrated on it in reference to its operation. The
   keyboard is in ALPHA mode (Fig. A-3, #31) during its normal mode
   of operation and thus any punching key—and the DUP functional
   control key—that is pressed with a two-character symbol illustrated on
   it will punch into and print on (if it is assumed that the PRINT
   functional control switch is in the "on" position) the particular card
   column indicated by the Column Indicator, which is located at the base
   of the Program Drum holder (Fig. A-1), the illustrated lower-level
   character.

   Any punching key pressed with only one character symbol illustrated
   on it will punch and print (assuming the same situation as described
   above) the illustrated character into the particular card column
   indicated by the Column Indicator.

7. To punch an upper-level illustrated character when the card punch is
   in ALPHA mode, the reader must press the NUMERIC functional control
   key (Fig. A-3, #30) before pressing the punching key illustrating the
   desired character.

8. The Column Indicator indicates the card column under the punching
   and/or reading head that will be either read and/or punched the next

time either a punching key or the DUP functional control key is pressed.

9. If during the punching of a punch card, the reader desires to skip one or more punch card columns, this can be accomplished by pressing the Space Bar (Fig. A-3). Each time the Space Bar is pressed, the punch cards in both the Printing-Punching and Reading Stations (Fig. A-1) progress forward one card column.

10. If the reader desires to punch a character in one or more card columns of a punch card that has already passed the Print-Punching heads, he can back the punch card up to the desired card column or columns by pressing the Backspace functional control key, which is located just below the card bed (Fig. A-1), between the punching and reading heads. As long as the Backspace Key is held down, any registered punch cards at either the Printing-Punching and/or Reading Stations and the Program Drum will backspace one card column at a time until card column 1 is reached.

To Move the Completed Punch Card from the Printing-Punching Station to the Reading Station

11. When the punching of the punch card in the Printing-Punching Station is completed, the reader should press the REL functional control key (Fig. A-3, #34). This key moves the punch card in the Printing-Punching Station to the Reading Station and the punch card in the Reading Station (if any) into position to move into the Card Stacker.

The Reading Station

12. The Reading Station is located directly to the left of the Printing-Punching Station. Through use of the DUP functional control key (Fig. A-3), either all or part of the data punched on the punch card located in the Reading Station can be duplicated on the punch card that has been registered in the Printing-Punching Station.

Duplicating Punch Card Data

13. If the reader desires to duplicate either all or part of the data punched on a punch card located in the Reading Station onto a punch card that has been registered in the Printing-Punching Station, he must press the DUP functional control key. Consecutive columns of data punched in the punch card in the Reading Station will continue to be duplicated as long as the DUP functional control key is pressed.

If the reader should desire to change one or more characters punched in particular card columns of a punch card being duplicated, continue duplicating and/or spacing until the Column Indicator indicates each card column where the reader desires to change the character punched in it; then, using the previously discussed procedures, press the punching key illustrating the desired character.

The Terminal Location of the Punched Cards

14. The Card Stacker is located on the upper left side of the Card Punch (Fig. A-1). Like the Card Hopper, it can hold up to approximately 500 punched cards. The punched cards are stacked at an angle, 12 edge down and face backward, and are held in position by a card weight. When the punched cards are removed, they are in the same sequence as they were punched.

Terminating Operation of the Card Punch

15. When punching is completed, all punch cards that left the Card Hopper but are not in the Card Stacker can be moved to the Card Stacker by flipping the CLEAR functional control switch (Fig. A-2) to the "on" position until all the punch cards have cleared the card bed.

16. Remove all punch cards from the Card Hopper by using the same basic process that was used originally to place them in the Card Hopper.

17. Remove all punched cards from the Card Stacker.

18. The Card Punch is turned off by flipping the Main-line Switch to the "off" position.

B

A LIST OF ANS COBOL RESERVED WORDS

ACCEPT	BY	DATE-WRITTEN
ACCESS	CF	DE
ACTUAL	CH	DECIMAL-POINT
ADD	CHARACTERS	DECLARATIVES
ADDRESS	CLOCK-UNITS	DELETE
ADVANCING	CLOSE	DEPENDING
AFTER	COBOL	DESCENDING
ALL	CODE	DETAIL
ALPHABETIC	COLUMN	DISPLAY
ALTER	COMMA	DIVIDE
ALTERNATE	COMP	DIVISION
AND	COMPUTATIONAL	DOWN
ARE	COMPUTE	ELSE
AREA	CONFIGURATION	END
AREAS	CONTAINS	ENDING
ASCENDING	CONTROL	ENTER
ASSIGN	CONTROLS	ENVIRONMENT
AT	COPY	EQUAL
AUTHOR	CORR	ERROR
BEFORE	CORRESPONDING	EVERY
BEGINNING	CURRENCY	EXIT
BLANK	DATA	FD
BLOCK	DATE-COMPILED	FILE

229

FILE-CONTROL
FILE-LIMIT
FILE-LIMITS
FILLER
FINAL
FIRST
FOOTING
FOR
FROM
GENERATE
GIVING
GO
GREATER
GROUP
HEADING
HIGH-VALUE
HIGH-VALUES
I-O
I-O—CONTROL
IDENTIFICATION
IF
IN
INDEX
INDEXED
INDICATE
INITIATE
INPUT
INPUT-OUTPUT
INPUT PROCEDURE
INSPECT
INSTALLATION
INTO
INVALID
IS
JUST
JUSTIFIED
KEY
LABEL
LAST
LEADING
LEFT
LESS
LIMIT

LIMITS
LINAGE
LINAGE-COUNTER
LINE
LINE-COUNTER
LINES
LOCK
LOW-VALUE
LOW-VALUES
MEMORY
MODE
MODULES
MOVE
MULTIPLE
MULTIPLY
NEGATIVE
NEXT
NO
NOT
NUMBER
NUMERIC
OBJECT-COMPUTER
OCCURS
OF
OFF
OMITTED
ON
OPEN
OPTIONAL
OR
OUTPUT
OUTPUT PROCEDURE
PAGE
PAGE-COUNTER
PERFORM
PF
PH
PIC
PICTURE
PLUS
POSITION
POSITIVE
PROCEDURE

PROCEED
PROCESSING
PROGRAM-ID
QUOTE
QUOTES
RANDOM
RD
READ
RECORD
RECORDS
REDEFINES
REEL
RELEASE
REMAINDER
RENAMES
REPLACING
REPORT
REPORTING
REPORTS
RERUN
RESERVE
RESET
RETURN
REVERSED
REWIND
REWRITE
RF
RH
RIGHT
ROUNDED
RUN
SAME
SD
SEARCH
SECTION
SECURITY
SEEK
SEGMENT-LIMIT
SELECT
SENTENCE
SEQUENTIAL
SET
SIGN

SIZE	TALLY	USAGE
SØRT	TALLYING	USE
SØURCE	TAPE	USING
SØURCE-CØMPUTER	TERMINATE	VALUE
SPACE	THAN	VALUES
SPACES	THRØUGH	VARYING
SPECIAL-NAMES	THRU	WHEN
STANDARD	TIMES	WITH
START	TØ	WØRDS
STATUS	TYPE	WØRKING-STØRAGE
STØP	UNIT	WRITE
SUBTRACT	UNTIL	ZERØ
SUM	UP	ZERØS
SYNC	UPØN	ZERØES
SYNCHRØNIZED		

*

PROGRAM DEBUGGING

Unfortunately, most computer programs do not successfully execute the first time they are read into the computer by means of an input device. Rather, many computer programs contain one or more errors of three possible types of program errors the first several times they are read into the computer. The process of detecting and correcting these program errors is called "debugging."

The following is a brief discussion, in the order of their detection, of each of these three types of errors:

A. *Syntax errors.* A syntax error indicates that a COBOL program statement is not formed according to the rules of the COBOL language. For instance, a COBOL reserved word may be misspelled, or a required delimiter (for example, a comma or period) may be missing. This type of error is detected during compilation of the source program by the COBOL compiler program. The COBOL compiler program indicates its discovery of these errors to the programmer through the printing of the printer printout appropriate diagnostic error messages.

B. *Execution errors.* Execution errors are detected during execution of the object program; that is, after the source program has been compiled into an object program and the computer begins to execute the object program. An execution error indi-

233

cates that, for example, an attempt was made to divide a number by zero or a calculated number exceeds the memory storage capacity of the computer for that particular type of number. This type of error is also indicated by the printing on the printer printout appropriate diagnostic error messages.

C. *Logical errors.* Logical errors indicate that the computer program does not correctly express the problem it is attempting to solve and thus the results are incorrect. For example, a COBOL program statement may be executed out of sequence, or the program may transfer to the incorrect COBOL program statement under certain conditions. This type of error is the most difficult to discover, as they are not detected by the computer and thus no diagnostic error messages are printed on the printer printout.

In COBOL, four types of syntax errors may be detected during the process of compilation. These errors are listed in a diagnostic listing, which follows the source program listing. Each line in a diagnostic listing contains a detected error message. The following are four examples of possible error messages:

```
CARD                          ERROR MESSAGE
 14  IKF1010I-W   LEFT PAREN SHOULD NOT BE FOLLOWED BY A SPACE.
 21  IKF1031I-C   USE SENTENCE NOT PRECEDED BY SECTION-NAME.  SECTION-
                  NAME ASSUMED.
 47  IKF1023I-E   INVALID FILE-NAME.  USE IGNORED.
 63  IKF0020I-D   COMPILER ERROR.  COMPILATION WILL NOT BE COMPLETED.
```

An error message is composed of four parts. The *first* part is the card number assigned the statement in which the error has occurred. The card number is generated by the COBOL compiler during the printing of the source program listing. The *second* part is the error code assigned that particular error. Generally, additional information concerning the error and what steps must be taken to correct it can be obtained by referencing this error code in the appropriate COBOL manual. The *third* part is the level of diagnostic. The level is indicated by an alphabetic character (W, C, E, or D). The *fourth* part is the error message itself. In most instances, the error message will provide enough information to correct the error. Thus, it will usually not be necessary to use the error code to obtain additional information concerning the error from the appropriate COBOL manual.

Each of the four types of errors represents a level of severity. The first level of error, which is indicated by W, is a *warning* diagnostic. It indicates a potential problem, although the error is not serious enough to prevent the compilation process from being completed. In most instances, a warning diagnostic can be ignored.

The second level of error, which is indicated by a C, is a *conditional* diagnostic. It indicates an error that should be corrected. When the compiler encounters a conditional error, it usually makes an assumption and corrects the statement. Thus, although the compilation process can be completed, the results of the execution of the program usually will be incorrect.

The third level of error, which is indicated by an E, is an *error* diagnostic. This is a serious type of error. Although the compilation process is completed, the statement containing the error is not considered by the COBOL compiler as being part of the program. Thus, execution of the program should not be attempted until the error is corrected.

The fourth level of error, which is indicated by a D, is a *disaster* diagnostic. This is a serious type of error. The compilation process cannot be completed until the error is corrected.

When one is correcting error messages, the author recommends that the error messages be corrected in the order in which they appear in the diagnostic listing. The reason for this recommendation is that in many instances a particular coding error in a program statement will cause one or more other syntax errors. Thus, one or more error messages will be printed following the error message pertaining to the real coding error. By correcting the error messages in the order in which they appear in the source program listing, an error message caused by a previous real coding error will be more easily detected. In turn, time will not be spent attempting to correct an error that does not really exist.

The DISPLAY Statement

The DISPLAY statement can be useful in debugging a program. Either the computer console or the printer can be used to receive such monitoring and control information as error messages, control totals, etc. from a program without interrupting execution of the program.

To receive information from the computer by means of this output device, the following statement is used:

$$\underline{\text{DISPLAY}} \quad \begin{Bmatrix} \text{literal-1} \\ \text{name-1} \end{Bmatrix} \quad \begin{bmatrix} \text{literal-2} \\ \text{name-2} \end{bmatrix} \quad \ldots \quad [\underline{\text{UP}\emptyset\text{N}} \text{ mnemonic-name}]$$

The statement can be used to write either one or more numeric or nonnumeric literal messages and/or the contents of one or more particular storage areas by referencing the name of each of the desired storage areas. If the UPØN option is used, the message(s) will be written on the output device represented by mnemonic-name that is designated in the SPECIAL-NAMES paragraph of the CØNFIGURATIØN SECTIØN. For example, if the following SPECIAL-NAMES paragraph were established in a program:

```
A      B
|      |
ENVIRØNMENT DIVISIØN.
CØNFIGURATIØN SECTIØN.
SØURCE-CØMPUTER.  IBM-370-148.
ØBJECT-CØMPUTER.  IBM-370-148.
SPECIAL-NAMES
       CØNSOLE IS KEYBØARD.
```

Execution of the statement

DISPLAY 'SUM ØF A AND B CAUSED ØVERFLØW' UPØN
KEYBØARD.

will cause the nonnumeric literal specified in the DISPLAY statement to be written on the console typewriter.

If the UPØN option is *not* used, the message will be written on the printer. For example, execution of the following statement

DISPLAY CØUNTER.

will cause the contents of CØUNTER, a numeric literal data field described in the DATA DIVISIØN, to be written on the printer.

If the contents of a numeric computational data field that contains the alphabetic character S is displayed, the rightmost character of the number is written as an alphabetic letter. The particular alphabetic character written is the one that is the equivalent of the digit punch plus the zone punch in the Hollerith code. For example, the number +155 would be written as 15E, where E is a combination of the digit punch 5 and the zone punch 12 (a 12-punch represents a plus sign). The number −155 would be written as 15N, where N is a combination of the digit 5 and the zone punch 11 (an 11-punch represents a minus sign).

The READY TRACE Statement

Users of an IBM computer system can take advantage of the READY TRACE statement to assist them in tracing the execution of either all of the part of the PROCEDURE DIVISION. The statement is written as follows:

READY TRACE.

This statement can be located anywhere within the division.

After the READY TRACE statement is executed, each section name and paragraph name card encountered is printed—the card number automatically assigned by the printer and its contents—following the source program listing but prior to the output. An individual can trace the flow of execution of the sections and paragraphs within the entire division by placing the READY TRACE statement immediately following the division statement. If it is desirable to trace the flow of execution of only particular section(s) and/or paragraph(s), the statement should be located immediately proceeding them. In either case, it can be determined if each section and paragraph is being executed in the proper logical order and the correct number of times.

*

PROGRAM FLOWCHARTING

Regardless of the degree of complication of a program, flowcharting is an important step in the process of preparing it for execution by a computer. A flowchart is a graphical representation of the definition, analysis, or solution of a problem in which symbols are used to represent operations, data, flow, etc.[†]

Program Flowchart

A program flowchart is a detailed description of the operations and decisions required to solve a problem. Specifically, it shows how the data are to be processed, i.e., the sequential performance of the operations and decisions. Three uses of a program flowchart in computer applications are:[‡]

1. An aid to computer program development.

2. A guide for the coding of instructions that make up a computer program.

3. Part of the documentation of a computer program.

The following are some of the conventions and techniques that should be considered when one is preparing a program flowchart.

[†]*American National Standard Flowchart Symbols and Their Usage in Information Processing.* Business Equipment Manufacturers Association, Sponsor. New York, New York: American National Standards Institute, Inc., 1971, p.7.

[‡]*Introduction to IBM Data Processing Systems.* White Plains, New York: International Business Machines Corporation, 3rd ed., March 1969, p. 69.

239

1. A program flowchart is prepared to serve as a basis for actual program writing.

2. One of the most important uses of a program flowchart is its provision of a pictorial sequence of logic and arithmetic operations. As such, the relationship of one portion of a program to another should be recognizable both during development of the program and after its competion.

3. The program processing steps should start at the top of a page and move down and to the right to the lower right-hand corner. If the flow goes in a reverse direction, arrowheads are used on the flow lines. The arrowheads can also be used with normal flow to increase clarity and readability.

4. A program flowchart should be referenced to its corresponding written program. This greatly aids in program testing and debugging, maintenance, and modification. One way to cross-reference is to place a notation either above the symbol to either the right or the left of the vertical flow line or inside the symbol separated by a stripe.

5. Titles should be short but not confusing. For better understanding, the language in the flowchart should be English rather than a machine-oriented or problem-oriented language. Whenever the text pertaining to a symbol cannot be placed within a symbol, it should be

   a. Placed alongside.

   b. Referenced to a narrative located elsewhere on the flowchart.

   c. Placed within the annotation, comment symbol.

The following is an illustration and accompanying description of the more commonly used program flowchart symbols. The shape of each of these symbols and its accompanying description is recommended by the American National Standards Institute, Inc. (ANSI X3.5-1970):

	INPUT/OUTPUT	Represents the function of either making information available (input) or recording processed information (output).
	PROCESS	Represents any kind of processing function.
	FLOW LINE	Represents the function of linking symbols. It indicates the sequence of available information and executable operations.

CROSSING OF FLOW LINES   Represents the crossing of flow lines that have no logical inter-relation.

JUNCTION OF FLOW LINES   Represents the joining of two or more incoming flow lines with one outgoing flow line. (Every flow line entering and leaving a junction should have arrowheads near the junction point.)

ANNOTATION, COMMENT   Represents the function of adding descriptive comments or explanatory notes as clarification.) (The broken line is connected to any symbol at a point where the annotation is meaningful by extending the broken line in whatever fashion is appropriate.)

DECISION   Represents either a decision or switching-type operation that determines which of a number of alternative paths is to be followed.

PREDEFINED PROCESS   Represents a named process consisting of one or more operations or program steps that are not specified in this program unit (for example, a subroutine or module).

CONNECTOR   Represents either an exit to or an entry from another part of the flow chart. It is a junction in a line of flow. A set of two connectors is used to represent a continued flow direction when the flow is broken by any limitation of the flow chart. A set of two or more connectors is used to represent the junction of several flow lines with one flow line, or the junction of one flow line with one of several alternative flow lines.

TERMINAL   Represents a terminal point in a flow chart (start, stop, halt, delay, or interrupt).

ANSWERS TO QUESTIONS AND EXERCISES

ANSWERS TO CHAPTER 1 QUESTIONS

1. The first characteristic of a computer is that it is *electronic*; i.e., it has no internal moving parts and functions by electrical impulses. The second characteristic, *internal storage*, is the ability simultaneously to store the representations of source statements and data. Third, the principle of the *stored program* depicts the ability to store a series of statements that instruct the computer in its operation. Fourth, *execution modification* is the ability to make logical decisions based on stored data and/or the result of an arithmetic or logical operation.

2. A *stored program* is a series of statements internally stored within a computer.

3. An *analog computer* measures either continuous electrical impulses or physical magnitudes, and decimal digits may be obtained indirectly. A *digital computer* operates on decimal digits that may represent either discrete data or symbols in the process of obtaining desired objectives. The digital computer is also capable of obtaining greater degrees of accuracy than an analog computer.

4. The acronym COBOL represents COmmon Business Oriented Language.

5. *"Business-oriented" data processing* encompasses a wide variety of problems characterized basically by a large volume of input and output, and relatively few mathematical and/or logical operations.

6. COBOL is designed to handle business-oriented problems in data processing. It also allows a high degree of flexibility and is easily documented. It can be written in English-like words or combinations of letters, which may allow a person unfamiliar with programming to read and understand the basics of the program.

7. A *source program* is a series of program statements (in a humanly readable form such as COBOL) provided by a programmer.

8. An *object program* is a source program that has been translated by the compiler into a machine sensible form.

9. Generally, data cards can be distinguished from statement cards by their location and contents. Statement cards, in COBOL, normally appear first in the program, preceded only by the necessary JCL cards. Following the statement cards are another set of JCL cards and then the data cards. The contents of the statement cards will be COBOL statements which make up the source program, and they must conform to explicit card column requirements. Data cards contain the data on which the program is to execute, and there are no card column requirements beyond those imposed by the program itself.

ANSWERS TO CHAPTER 2 QUESTIONS AND EXERCISES

QUESTIONS

1. A COBOL coding form, while not absolutely essential, enables the programmer to organize the source statements, by card column, for any program. The coding form may also be used as a reference (by page and line or statement number) if the programmer desires to review a program or check the accuracy of the program against the initial coding. In addition, the keypunch operator, who generally punches the information into punch cards in a business environment, should be able easily to interpret the programmer's instructions. Finally, additional lines are provided at the bottom of each page to allow the programmer to insert additions or corrections to the initial program.

2. The coding form columns, which correspond to card columns, are provided for the following information:

   Columns 1-3:   the coding form page number or any other number the pro-grammer desires to insert[†]

   Columns 4-6:   the COBOL statement serial number or any other number the programmer desires to insert[†]

   Column 7:   the continuation (denoted by a hyphen) of the previous statement to an additional card

   Columns 8-72:   the program source statements; area A (columns 8-11) allocated for division, section, and paragraph headings and area B (columns 12-72) for the COBOL source statements

   Columns 73-80:   serves no function, but can be used for identification, sequencing, or any other purpose the programmer deems necessary

---

[†]It should be noted that even though the programmer may select any three numeric characters, the individual characters must be in ascending order.

3. The IDENTIFICATIØN DIVISIØN performs the primary function of identifying the program, and it contains many optional identification features. The ENVIRØN-MENT DIVISIØN performs the function of describing the type of computer on which the program is to be compiled and executed, and it describes the type of input and output device to be employed with the file names attached to each.

The DATA DIVISIØN gives a detailed description of the data to be processed and the relationships that exist among various data items.

The PRØCEDURE DIVISIØN contains the statements that instruct the computer as to the specific operations to be performed as well as the order of execution of the statements.

4. The COBOL program hierarchy represents a rough outline system which orders and organizes the contents of a COBOL program. The hierarchy from the highest order to the lowest are (1) divisions, (2) sections, (3) paragraphs, (4) sentences, and (5) statements, each level representing the components of the next higher level.

5. The COBOL hierarchical data structure is a logical organization of data to be either read and/or written. The hierarchy from highest level to lowest includes (1) files, (2) records, (3) group items, and (4) elementary items, each level representing the components of the next higher level.

6. The two types of data that can appear in a COBOL program are variables and constants. *Variables* are represented by programmer-supplied names, the value of which can change. *Constants* can be represented by programmer-supplied names, but it is not necessary. The value of a constant does not change.

EXERCISES

1. a. Valid

   b. Invalid, hyphen needed between NET and ASSETS

   c. Invalid, name begins with a special character ($)

   d. Invalid, ZERØ is a COBOL reserved word

   e. Valid

   f. Invalid, PRØDUCT and NAME separated by special character (.), which should be a hyphen

   g. Valid; even though the letter Ø is not slashed (which suggests the number zero), it is valid. However, it is suggested that the programmer refrain from using zeros in the place of the letter O to avoid confusion and potential future difficulties.

   h. Valid

2. a. Figurative constant

   b. Invalid; the currency sign ($) rules out the possibility of this being a numeric literal.

   c. Nonnumeric literal; even though the figurative constant QUØTES appears, it is used within quotation marks, which makes it a nonnumeric literal.

   d. Numeric literal

   e. Nonnumeric literal

    f. Invalid; the special character (,) rules out the possibility of this being a numeric literal.

    g. Figurative constant

    h. Numeric literal

ANSWERS TO CHAPTER 3 QUESTIONS AND EXERCISE

QUESTIONS

1. The only required paragraph within the IDENTIFICATIØN DIVISIØN is the PRØGRAM-ID, with the associated programmer-supplied name.

2. The rules governing the programmer-supplied PRØGRAM-ID name are

    a. It may contain from one to eight characters.

    b. It may be any combination of alphabetic and/or numeric characters.

    c. The first character should be alphabetic.

EXERCISE

Line	Error(s)
1	illegal hyphen between IDENTIFICATIØN and DIVISIØN
2	hyphen omitted between PRØGRAM
3	AUTHØR paragraph misspelled
4	no period following INSTALLATIØN
5	no period after 1976
6	hyphen omitted between DATE and CØMPILED
7[†]	no period after sentence

ANSWERS TO CHAPTER 4 QUESTIONS AND EXERCISE

QUESTIONS

1. When a program is written, both the source and object computers must be specified in the ENVIRØNMENT DIVISIØN. Thus, if there is any change, say from one installation to another where the computing machinery is different, then the contents of the SØURCE-COMPUTER and ØBJECT-CØMPUTER paragraphs must be modified to reflect the change.

2. The two requirements of both the SØURCE-CØMPUTER and ØBJECT-CØMPUTER

[†] Even though the alphabetic character O is not slashed in this sentence, it does not constitute an error.

paragraphs are that (a) the computer manufacturer (IBM, NCR, CDC, etc.) must be given followed by (b) the model number (360, 6400, etc.).

3. The FILE-CØNTRØL paragraph is responsible for assigning input and output file names and input and output device types.

4. Within the FILE-CØNTRØL both the SELECT clauses and the ASSIGN TØ clauses must be fully specified. The SELECT clauses specify the input and output file names. The ASSIGN TØ clauses specify the input and output device declarations.

5. a. DA—direct access—magnetic disk and drum

   b. UR—unit record—card reader, card punch, and printer

   c. UT—utility—magnetic tape

EXCERCISE

Line	Error(s)
1	ENVIRØNMENT misspelled
1-2	CØNFIGURATIØN SECTIØN missing
2	none
3	computer model missing
4	hyphen omitted between INPUT and ØUTPUT
5	FILE-CØNTRØL misspelled
	period missing
6	unnecessary hyphen between ASSIGN and TØ
7	ASSIGN TØ clause omitted

ANSWERS TO CHAPTER 5 QUESTIONS AND EXERCISES

QUESTIONS

1. The function of the FILE SECTIØN is to provide a detailed description of the input record(s). The output record(s) may also be described in this section, but it is not a mandatory requirement for all output files.

2. The only clause required in the file description paragraph is the LABEL RECØRD(S) IS (ARE) ØMITTED clause.

3. In the FILE SECTIØN all recrods will be labeled by the 01 level. Only records may be labeled with this number. All group items can be determined if there are any elements with a lower level (higher level number) immediately following the item in question. Elementary items are those items at the lowest level (highest level number) not immediately followed by a subordinate level. They are always described by a PICTURE clause.

4. Elementary items can be differentiated from independent elementary items by the fact that the former will always be labeled with a level number between 02 and 49, while the latter are normally labeled with the level number 77. The use of elemen-

tary items is normally for input or output records. Independent elementary items may represent a figurative constant or the intermediate result of some operation, but it cannot be used in an output record without being manipulated into some usable form.

5. In a PICTURE clause, an X represents alphanumeric data, A represents alphabetic data, and 9 represents numeric data. The X specification can contain alphabetic, numeric, and special characters. The A specification can contain only alphabetic characters and spaces. The 9 specification can contain numeric characters only.

6. The reserved word FILLER is used in the input and output records to provide for spaces or blanks in the input record and spacing in the output record.

7. The VALUE clause is a means of storing an initial value under an elementary item. It can be used in conjunction with numeric literals, nonnumeric literals, and figurative constants. The VALUE clause is primarily used in the WØRKING-STØRAGE SECTIØN, and thus it is applicable to independent elementary items and output records, which are defined in this section. It can also be used in the FILE SECTIØN to define a condition-name.

EXERCISES

1. a. 012345
    b. 012^340
    c. 7^8
    d. 78^90
    e. 56
    f. 5bb
    g. ABb
    h. COD
    i. error
    j. ABC
    k. ABCbb

2. a. 0293.65
    b. $293.65
    c. 293.65
    d. $0293.65
    e. 2 93.65
    f. $*293.65
    g.   3.65   †
    h. 293.650
    i. ***293   †

3. | Line | Error(s) |
    |------|----------|
    | 1 | hyphen between FILE and SECTIØN |
    | 2 | FD omitted |

---

†This PICTURE clause will result in a warning and truncation will occur.

Line	Error(s)
2-3	LABEL RECØRD clause omitted
3	RECØRD-1 begins in area A
	no period following RECØRD-1
4	02 begins in area A
5	VALUE clause illegal in FILE SECTIØN as used
6	none
7	incorrect level number (01), should be 03; hyphen omitted between ITEM and 1
8	period omitted after PICTURE clause
9‡	none

4.

Line	Error(s)
1	hyphen between STØRAGE and SECTIØN
2	edited PICTURE clause 99.99 should be 99V99
3	PICTURE misspelled; PICTURE clause and figurative constant do not match
4	none
5	none
6	FILLER misspelled
7	none
8	missing quotation mark (the quotation mark should be placed in Column 12 with the other information immediately following it); continuation (hyphen) missing in Column 7
9	PICTURE misspelled
10	PICTURE clause too small [should be X(11)]; quotation marks omitted. This should read '1ST PRØDUCT'
11	period omitted at end of statement
12	PICTURE clause too small [should be A(24)]
13	Continuation (hyphen) missing in Column 7
14‡	space (or blank) should be placed between VALUE and SPACE

ANSWERS TO CHAPTER 6 QUESTIONS AND EXERCISES

QUESTIONS

1. The PRØCEDURE DIVISIØN is the last division in the make-up of a COBOL

---

‡In this FILLER statement, in which the level number 03 is used, the level number 02 could have been applied. Also, in the PICTURE clause 9(65), the 9 is usually an X specification. Finally, it should be noted that this record is defined to have 90 card columns. This should be corrected by replacing the 65 in the FILLER PICTURE clause with 55.

‡The total number of print positions specified amounts to 146, which does not match the size of any existing printer.

program. It contains the source statements that instruct the computer during execution of the program. It is this division that causes data to be read, manipulated, or processed, and the resultant information to be written. It is the most flexible division, and its contents are left almost entirely to the discretion of the programmer.

2. The appearance of the ∅PEN statement is a COBOL signal to the computer that an input data set exists, which is to be read into the computer memory, and/or that an output report is to be written during the execution of the program.

   The CL∅SE statement will appear in a COBOL program to "release" the input or output device, which is allocated to every file name appearing in an ∅PEN statement. Thus, if a file is opened during execution of the program, it must be closed before execution is terminated. Also, if a file is closed, it must be reopened before any input or output procedure (depending on the file name associated with the device type) can be initiated.

3. The function of the READ statement is to cause a data record to be read from a file (containing one or more records) allocated an input device, such as a card reader, magnetic tape, magnetic disk, etc., and to be stored in the computer's memory. The principle of destructive reading explains the fact that when a record is read into the computer's memory it replaces the data of any previous records. Thus, the contents of the storage positions allocated to the record are destroyed and replaced with the data on a new record.

4. The ADVANCING option allows the programmer to govern the vertical positioning of output information on the printer page (if a printer is the output device). The LINES clause gives the programmer the choice of selecting the number of lines on the printer page that are to be skipped. The number of lines that can be skipped can vary from 1 to 100. The number of lines to be skipped is specified by stating the corresponding integer number. In addition, the programmer can specify a name (elementary item) to determine the number of lines to be skipped, in which case the number is a variable. Finally, the programmer can specify BEF∅RE or AFTER. In the case of the former, the line of print will be generated before lines are skipped. The AFTER clause reverses this operation.

5. The M∅VE statement is a basic data manipulation statement that causes the contents of one storage address to be duplicated in one or more other locations. When the sending field of a M∅VE statement is alphabetic, the receiving field may be either alphabetic or alphanumeric. When it is alphanumeric, the receiving field can be alphanumeric and possibly alphabetic if the sending field contains only alphabetic characters. When it is numeric computational, the receiving field can be numeric computational, numeric report, or alphanumeric if the sending field contains only integer numbers. When it is numeric report, the receiving field can only be alphanumeric.

6. An *operand* is a name or numeric literal involved in a computation. An arithmetic *operator* is an arithmetic operational word or symbol that represents one of the computer's basic arithmetic capabilities.

7. The receiving area for a COBOL arithmetic statement must be either a numeric

computational or numeric report field. Also, to eliminate errors that occur from truncating higher-order or lower-order digits, the PICTURE clause of the receiving area should be large enough to store the data transferred to them.

8. The principal difference in arithmetic statements without the GIVING clause, as distinguished from those with the GIVING clause, is that in the former the last principal operand serves as the receiving area, whereas in the latter the name following the reserved word GIVING is the receiving area. For example, in the statement

    ADD NAME-A TØ NAME-B

    the storage location NAME-A remains unchanged, while NAME-B is modified to include the result of NAME-A + NAME-B. To illustrate the GIVING clause, in the statement

    ADD NAME-A TO NAME-B GIVING NAME-C

    the storage locations NAME-A and NAME-B would remain unchanged, while NAME-C would be altered to represent the sum of NAME-A and NAME-B, and any previous contents of NAME-C would be destroyed.

9. The basic difference between the CØMPUTE statement and other arithmetic statements is that the reserved words (ADD, SUBTRACT, etc.) which represent arithmetic operations are replaced with symbolic operators (+, -, *, /, **). Thus, the CØMPUTE statement gives the same result as any arithmetic statement with a GIVING clause. However, the CØMPUTE statement is much more flexible, in that any combination of arithmetic operations can be performed, whereas other arithmetic statements are restricted to one operation per statement. Furthermore, the programmer can control the evaluation of the arithmetic statement by using parentheses.

10. The relational operations that can be employed in relational IF tests are

    a. GREATER THAN[†]
    b. NØT GREATER
    c. EQUAL[†]
    d. NØT EQUAL
    e. LESS THAN[†]
    f. NØT LESS

11. Using the class test, the programmer can determine whether or not the contents of a storage location are alphabetic or numeric. The relational test can be used to determine the relationship between two numbers expressed as numeric literals, names, arithmetic expressions and/or figurative constants. The sign test can be employed to determine whether a name or arithmetic expression is positive, zero, or negative.

[†]This relational operator can be expressed by an appropriate symbol.

12. The evaluation of any compund conditional statement is governed by the following hierarchy of execution:

   a.   All compound conditionals within parentheses.
   b.   All conditionals connected by AND.
   c.   All conditionals connected by ØR.
   d.   Left to right through the statement.

EXERCISES

1. The file named in the READ or WRITE statement has been assigned to a particular input or output device in an ASSIGN TØ clause in the ENVIRØNMENT DIVISIØN.

2. Contents of storage locations

   a.   A = 50; B = 40
   b.   A = 50; B = -10; C = - 60
   c.   A = 50; B = 75
   d.   A = -5; B = -10
   e.   A = 50; B = -10; C = 20; F = 10
   f.   D = Z; statement following IF statement will be executed
   g.   A = 50; B = -10; statement following IF statement will be executed
   h.   A = 50; C = 20; the transfer GØ TØ FINISH-RUN will be executed

3. a.   NAME-2 = 0390 [Since the PICTURE clause is only 9999, the higher-order digit (1) is truncated.]
   b.   NAME-1 = 234.56; NAME-2 = 1235
   c.   NAME-1 = 734.56
   d.   NAME-1 = 654.32; NAME-3 = 65.432
   e.   NAME-1 = 234.56; NAME-2 = 7890; NAME-3 = 65.432; transfer to ERRØR-RØUTINE will be executed
   f.   NAME-3 = 80.984; statement following CØMPUTE statement will be executed
   g.   NAME-1 = 565.43; NAME-2 = 7890; NAME-3 = 65.432

4. a.   ABC
   b.   the contents of ABC
   c.   100.00
   d.   SPACES
   e.   spaces

5. a.   010ʌ350
   b.   037
   c.   234
   d.   ʌ1
   e.   2ʌ3
   f.   ʌ99

6. a.   012ʌ35
   b.   012ʌ3
   c.   012ʌ350
   d.   2ʌ3

e. ∧350

f. 999∧9

7. a. AB12bb

   b. AB1

   c. XX

ANSWERS TO CHAPTER 7 QUESTIONS AND EXERCISES

QUESTIONS

1. The PERFØRM statement is used to branch to a series of statements in order to execute them a specified number of times or until a predetermined condition is satisfied. After the statement or statements are executed, the computer always branches back to the statement immediately following the PERFØRM statement.

2. A transfer can be made outside a PERFØRM's range during execution of the statements within that range. For example, an IF statement within the range could have as either its true or false branch a statement that transfers the computer to statements located outside the PERFØRM's range. If desirable, reentry to the PERFØRM's range is possible.

The value of any index maintained in the PERFØRM's range is available for use outside the range, whether the range was left either because of branching or because execution of the PERFØRM's range was completed. For example, if a certain condition is to be attained before the PERFØRM's range can be left, an index can be established within the range to indicate the iteration on which the condition is attained.

The range of a PERFØRM statement ends with the last statement in either the section or paragraph name specified as section-name-1 or paragraph-name-1 or, if present, section-name-2 or paragraph-name-2. The PERFØRM statement controls execution of the statements within its range. Thus, the last statement should not be a GØ TØ statement unless it is desired to break the PERFØRM's control of execution of the program, as control would be transferred to a statement outside the PERFØRM's range.

If a PERFØRM's range contains several branches, they must be rejoined prior to the last statement in the range being executed. However, in certain instances the logical execution of the program prevents the recombining of several branches. For example, the program may proceed along two mutually exclusive paths. In such a situation, a separation paragraph can be created that contains only the statement EXIT, and each branch is transferred to this paragraph. The general format of this paragraph is

PARAGRAPH-name. *EXIT*

This paragraph is mentioned as paragraph-name-2 in the PERFØRM statement and thus is the last statement in the PERFØRM's range.

Several PERFØRM statements can be used in a program. If appropriate, several of them can refer to the same section(s) and/or paragraph(s). In each instance, the particular PERFØRM referencing the range will control execution of the statements, and when execution of them is completed, control will be returned to the statement immediately following the referencing PERFØRM statement.

A PERFØRM statement can include in its range one or more PERFØRM statements. When this occurs, each inner PERFØRM statement is said to be "nested" in the next outer PERFØRM statement.

The following three rules must be observed when one is using nested PERFØRM statement:

a. The range of each PERFØRM statement must terminate with a different section or paragraph name.

b. An embedded PERFØRM statement must have its range either totally inside or totally outside the range of each of its outer PERFØRM statement. That is, the statement in the range of a PERFØRM statement cannot be continued within the range of the next embedded PERFØRM statement.

c. The ranges of two PERFØRM statements can overlap, provided that the second PERFØRM statement is not located within the range of the first PERFØRM statement.

While the ability to nest PERFØRM statements provides the programmer with great execution capability and flexibility, it is complicated and thus should be carefully used.

3. A table is an ordered set of computer memory storage spaces identified by a table name. All of the storage locations or a specific location within the table can be referenced. Its function is to store a set of related data so that manipulation of the set can be more easily handled.

4. A single dimensional table is referenced by a single subscript, which can be a name containing an integer number or an integer number. The single dimensional table is composed of a single column and represents a list of data. The two-dimensional table is referenced by two subscripts. The table is composed of rows and columns, and it is sometimes called a matrix. A three-dimensional table is referenced by three subscripts. It is composed of rows, columns, and ranks.

5. The ØCCURS clause appears in the DATA DIVISIØN and is used to define elementary items as tables. Thus, if a name is referred to by one ØCCURS clause, it is a single dimensional table; with two clauses, it is a two-dimensional table; with three clauses, it is a three-dimensional table. The integer number associated with the first clause represents the maximum size of the first subscript. The second integer represents the size of the second subscript, etc. The PICTURE clause associated with the lowest level (the highest level number) will determine the maximum size field for each location within the table.

EXERCISES

1. a. This statement will cause the statements within FIRST-PARAGRAPH to be executed one time.

b. This statement will cause the statements in FIRST-PARAGRAPH through the statements in SECØND-PARAGRAPH to be executed one time.

c. This statement will cause the statements in FIRST-PARAGRAPH to be executed VARIABLE-NUMBER times. Thus, if VARIABLE-NUMBER is equal to 20, the statements will be executed 20 times.

d. This statement will cause the statements in FIRST-PARAGRAPH to be executed until ACCUMULATØR is greater than 50. Thus, if the initial value of ACCUMULATØR is one and one is added to ACCUMULATØR everytime FIRST-PARAGRAPH is executed, the statements in FIRST-PARAGRAPH will be executed 50 times.

e. This statement will cause the statements in FIRST-PARAGRAPH to be executed 10 times. The value of QUANTITY will start at 2 and will be incremented by 4 (2, 6, 10, ..., 38, 42) for each time the statements in FIRST-PARAGRAPH are executed. The terminal value of QUANTITY will be 42; however, the statements in FIRST-PARAGRAPH will not be executed for this value.

f. This statement will cause the statements in FIRST-PARAGRAPH to be executed. For example, if FINAL-AMØUNT is equal to 11, the statements will be executed 60 times. AMØUNT will vary from 1 to 11 by 2, (1, 3, 5, 7, 9, 11) for every time QUANTITY is incremented by 1. Thus, there are six values AMØUNT can hold and 10 for QUANTITY, and, therefore, there will be 60 iterations (6 x 10).

2. a. TABLE-ELEMENT (30); a single dimensional table with 30 locations (numeric computational)

b. FIRST-ELEMENT (6); a single dimensional table with six locations (numeric computational)

SECØND-ELEMENT (6); a single dimensional table with six locations (alpha-numeric)

THIRD-ELEMENT (6); a single dimensional table with six locations (numeric computational)

FØURTH-ELEMENT (6); a single dimensional table with six locations (alpha-numeric)

This describes a pseudo-two-dimensional table with 24 locations.

c. SECØND-ELEMENT (7,10); a two-dimensional table with seven rows, 10 columns, and 70 locations (numeric report)

d. FIRST-SUB-ELEMENT (3,5); a two-dimensional table with three rows, five columns, and 15 locations (numeric computational)

SECØND-SUB-ELEMENT (3,5); a two-dimensional table with three rows, five columns, and 15 locations (alphanumeric)

THIRD-SUB-ELEMENT (3,5); a two-dimensional table with three rows, five columns, and 15 locations (numeric computational)

This describes a pseudo-three-dimensional table with three rows, five columns, and three ranks, and 45 locations.

e. THIRD-ELEMENT (4,6,10); a three-dimensional table with four rows, six columns, 10 ranks and 240 locations (alphabetic)

ANSWERS TO CHAPTER 8 QUESTIONS

1. The REDEFINES clause allows the programmer to assign different names to the same storage area. In a sense, it is the opposite of a MØVE statement, which creates a new storage area when it is assigned to another name. The basic rules governing the REDEFINES clause are (a) the name to be redefined and the statement containing the REDEFINES clause must be the same level numbers, and (b) there must be no level number between the name and the REDEFINES clause which is either equal to or higher than (lower level number) the level number of the name.

2. If an elementary item in the FILE SECTIØN is labeled a level number 88, it is a condition name. Then, the condition name can be used in conditional (IF) statements in the place of a numerical quantity; however, the condition name must have a VALUE clause to assign its value. This is the only circumstance in which a VALUE clause may be used in the FILE SECTIØN.

3. The JUSTIFIED RIGHT clause can be used in any statement describing a nonnumeric elementary item receiving field in the DATA DIVISIØN. It is placed after the PICTURE clause or the VALUE clause if present. Normally, nonnumeric data are left justified, but by using the JUSTIFIED RIGHT clause, the programmer forces the data to fill the rightmost positions of a field.

4. The SPECIAL-NAMES paragraph is located in the CØNFIGURATIØN SECTIØN. The options available to the programmer are (1) function-name IS, (2) CURRENCY SIGN IS, and (3) DECIMAL PØINT IS CØMMA clauses. The function names the programmer can choose from are (1) SYSIN, (2) SYSØUT, (3) SYSPUNCH, and (4) CØNSØLE.

5. The INTØ option of the READ statement is used to create an additional record in an area-name. This area name must be described in either the WØRKING-STØRAGE SECTIØN or FILE SECTIØN, and only one type of record image can be described. The function of the INTØ option is generally the same as the MØVE statement, in that a duplicate is made of every item on the record and either the original or its image can be used interchangably.

6. The FRØM option of the WRITE statement functions in a similar manner to the INTØ option of the READ statement. Normally, information is written from a record named in the WRITE statement. However, it is possible to write a secondary record from the record name defined in the FILE SECTIØN. The secondary record can be described in either the FILE SECTIØN or WØRKING-STØRAGE SECTIØN. Thus, the function of the FRØM option is similar to a MØVE statement and a WRITE statement in conjunction.

7. The MØVE statement is used to move the contents of one elementary item to another. The MØVE CØRRESPØNDING is used to move multiple elementary items from either a group or record to corresponding elementary items in another group or record. However, if the elementary items do not have corresponding names, the contents of the initial group or record will not be moved.

8. The INSPECT statement is used to determine when a specified character appears in a data field. The TALLYING option is used to count the number of times the character occurs in the data field. The REPLACING option is used to replace the specified character with another selected character.

ANSWERS TO CHAPTER 9 EXERCISE

The following program is a solution to the exercise problem:

COBOL Coding Form

SYSTEM	IBM 370-148		GX28-1464-5 U/M 050° Printed in U.S.A.
PROGRAM	THE CREATION OF A RANDOM ACCESS MODE FILE		PAGE C010F006
PROGRAMMER	V. THOMAS DUCK	DATE	CARD FORM # *

PUNCHING INSTRUCTIONS — GRAPHIC / PUNCH

```
SEQUENCE
(PAGE) (SERIAL)  A   B        COBOL STATEMENT
01      IDENTIFICATION DIVISION.
02      PROGRAM-ID. DISKFILE.
03    * ILLUSTRATION OF THE CREATION OF A RANDOM ACCESS FILE.
04      ENVIRONMENT DIVISION.
05      CONFIGURATION SECTION.
06      SOURCE-COMPUTER. IBM-370-148.
07      OBJECT-COMPUTER. IBM-370-148.
08      INPUT-OUTPUT SECTION.
09      FILE-CONTROL.
10          SELECT CARD-FILE ASSIGN TO UR-2540R-S-CARDIN.
11          SELECT DETAIL-FILE ASSIGN TO UT-3400-S-DETAIL.
12          SELECT MASTER-FILE ASSIGN TO DA-3330-D-MASTER.
13          IS RELATIVE. ACCESS IS RANDOM. ACTUAL KEY IS FILE-KEY. ORGANIZATION
14      DATA DIVISION.
15      FILE SECTION.
16      FD  CARD-FILE
17          LABEL RECORDS ARE OMITTED.
18      01  CARD-RECORD.
19          02 TRAN-NO-CARD
20          02 AMT
21      FD  DETAIL-FILE
22          LABEL RECORDS ARE STANDARD
23          BLOCK CONTAINS 20 RECORDS
24          RECORD CONTAINS 18 CHARACTERS.
```

PICTURE 9(5).
PICTURE 999V99.

°A standard card form, IBM Electro C61897, is available for punching source statements from this form. Instructions for using this form are given in any IBM COBOL reference manual. Address comments concerning this form to IBM Corporation, LDS Publishing, Dept. J04, 1501 California Ave., Palo Alto, Ca. 94304

*No. of forms per pad may vary slightly

IBM

GX28-1464-5 U/M 050*
Printed in U.S.A.

COBOL Coding Form

SYSTEM	IBM 370-148
PROGRAM	THE CREATION OF A DIRECT-ACCESS FILE
PROGRAMMER	V. THOMAS DOCK

PAGE 002 OF 006

PUNCHING INSTRUCTIONS — GRAPHIC / PUNCH — CARD FORM #   *

```
SEQUENCE
(PAGE) (SERIAL)  CONT  B
 0 1      0 1      TAPE-REC.
 0 2      0 2      TRAN-NO-TAPE      PICTURE 9(5).
 0 3      0 2      AMT               PICTURE 999V99.
 0 4      0 2      FILLER            PICTURE X(8).
 0 5
 0 6   FD   MASTER-FILE
 0 7           LABEL RECORDS ARE STANDARD
 0 8           RECORD CONTAINS 10 CHARACTERS.
 0 9      0 1      DISK-REC.
 1 0      0 2      TRAN-NO-DISK      PICTURE 9(5).
 1 1      0 2      AMT               PICTURE 999V99.
 1 2   WORKING-STORAGE SECTION.
 1 3   7 7   COUNTER               PICTURE 99  VALUE ZERO.
 1 4   7 7   MORE-DATA-CARDS       PICTURE AAA VALUE SPACES.
 1 5   7 7   MORE-TAPE-RECORDS     PICTURE AAA VALUE SPACES.
 1 6      0 1      FILE-KEY.
 1 7      0 2      TRACK-ID          PICTURE S9(5) USAGE IS
 1 8                SYNCHRONIZED.
 1 9      0 2      RECORD-ID         PICTURE 9(5).
 2 0   PROCEDURE DIVISION.
 2 1 * CONTROL-MODULE.
 2 2      PERFORM OPEN-FILES-1.
 2 3      PERFORM READ-RECORD-1 THRU FINISH-READING-1
 2 4      UNTIL MORE-DATA-CARDS EQUAL-1
```

*A standard card form, IBM Electro C61897, is available for punching source statements from this form. Instructions for using this form are given in any IBM COBOL reference manual. Address comments concerning this form to IBM Corporation, LDS Publishing, Dept. J04, 1501 California Ave., Palo Alto, Ca. 94304

*No. of forms per pad may vary slightly

COBOL Coding Form

SYSTEM	IBM-370-148
PROGRAM	THE CREATION OF A DIRECT-ACCESS FILE
PROGRAMMER	V. THOMAS DOCK

PAGE 0030F 006

GX28-1464-5 U/M 050
Printed in U.S.A.

PUNCHING INSTRUCTIONS — GRAPHIC / PUNCH — CARD FORM #

```
PERFORM READ-RECORD-2 THRU FINISH-READING-2
    UNTIL MORE-DATA-CARDS EQUAL 'NO'.
PERFORM CLOSE-FILES.
PERFORM OPEN-FILES-2.
PERFORM READ-RECORD-3 THRU FINISH-READING-3
    UNTIL MORE-TAPE-RECORDS EQUAL 'NO'.
PERFORM CLOSE-FILES-2.
STOP RUN.
OPEN-FILES-1.
    OPEN INPUT CARD-FILE
        OUTPUT DETAIL-FILE, MASTER-FILE.
READ-RECORD-2.
    READ CARD-FILE AT END
        STOP RUN.
PROCESS-RECORD-1.
    DIVIDE 265 INTO TRAN-NO-CARD GIVING TRACK-ID.
    MOVE TRAN-NO-CARD TO RECORD-ID.
WRITE-RECORD-1.
    WRITE DISK-REC FROM CARD-RECORD.
```

*A standard card form, IBM Electro C61897, is available for punching source statements from this form. Instructions for using this form are given in any IBM COBOL reference manual. Address comments concerning this form to IBM Corporation, LDS Publishing, Dept. J04, 1501 California Ave., Palo Alto, Ca. 94304

*No. of forms per pad may vary slightly

COBOL Coding Form

IBM

GX28-1464-5 U/M 050*
Printed in U.S.A.

PAGE 004 OF 006

SYSTEM	IBM-370-148		
PROGRAM	THE CREATION OF A DIRECT-ACCESS FILE	PUNCHING INSTRUCTIONS	CARD FORM #
PROGRAMMER	V. THOMAS DOCK	GRAPHIC / PUNCH	
	DATE		

COBOL STATEMENT · IDENTIFICATION

```
01   TEST-COUNTER-1.
02       ADD 1 TO COUNTER.
03       IF COUNTER EQUAL TO 12
04           MOVE 'NO' TO MORE-DATA-CARDS, MOVE 0 TO COUNTER
05           GO TO READ-RECORD-1.
06       ELSE
07   FINISH-READING-1.
08       EXIT.
09 *
10   READ-RECORD-2.
11       MOVE SPACES TO DATA-CARDS.
12       READ CARD-FILE AT END
13           MOVE 'NO' TO MORE-DATA-CARDS, GO TO FINISH-READING-2.
14 *
15   WRITE-RECORD-2.
16       WRITE TAPE-RECORD FROM CARD-RECORD.
17 *
18   TEST-COUNTER-2.
19       ADD 1 TO COUNTER.
20       IF COUNTER EQUAL TO 20 MOVE 'NO' TO MORE-DATA-CARDS,
21           GO TO FINISH-READING-2.
22   FINISH-READING-2.
23       EXIT.
24
```

*A standard card form, IBM Electro C61897, is available for punching source statements from this form. Instructions for using this form are given in any IBM COBOL reference manual. Address comments concerning this form to IBM Corporation, LDS Publishing, Dept. J04, 1501 California Ave., Palo Alto, Ca. 94304

*No. of forms per pad may vary slightly

IBM

COBOL Coding Form

GX28-1464-5 U/M 050*
Printed in U.S.A.

SYSTEM	IBM-370-148		PAGE 005 OF 006
PROGRAM	THE CREATION OF A DIRECT-ACCESS FILE		
PROGRAMMER	V. THOMAS DOCK	DATE	CARD FORM #

PUNCHING INSTRUCTIONS — GRAPHIC — PUNCH — IDENTIFICATION

```
01   CLOSE-FILES-1.
02 *
03       CLOSE CARD-FILE, DETAIL-FILE, MASTER-FILE.
04 *
05   OPEN-FILES-2.
06       OPEN INPUT DETAIL-FILE
07            I-O MASTER-FILE.
08 *
09   READ-RECORD-3.
10       READ DETAIL AT END
11            MOVE "NO" TO MORE-TAPE-RECORDS FINISH-READING-3.
12 *
13   PROCESS-RECORD-2.
14       DIVIDE 265 INTO TRAN-NO GIVING TRACK-ID.
15       MOVE TRAN-NO-TAPE-RECORD-ID.
16 *
17   READ-RECORD-4.
18       READ MASTER-FILE INVALID KEY DISPLAY 'INVALID TAPE RECORD'
19            FINISH-READING-3.
20       TAPE-REC, GO TO FINISH-READING-3.
21   PROCESS-RECORD-3.
22       MOVE AMT OF TAPE-REC TO AMT OF DISK-REC.
23   WRITE-RECORD-3.
24       WRITE-RECORD-3.
```

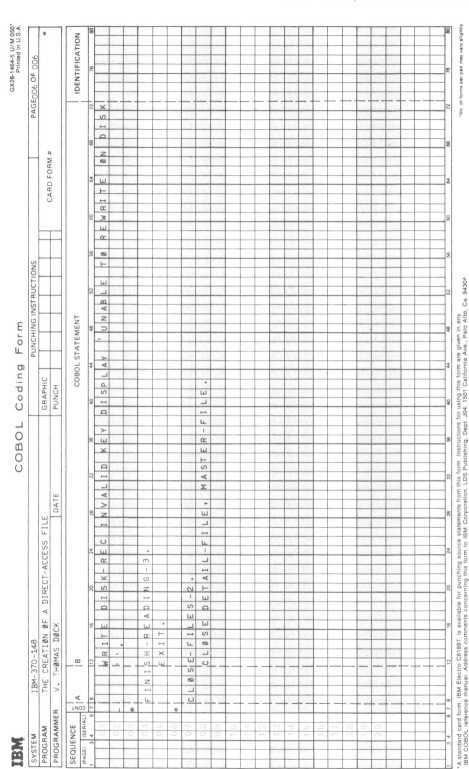

INDEX